THE ASSASSIN LEGENDS

To my mother
and
to the memory of my father

This painting is one of the very few known mediaeval European illustrations of a legend which depicted Nizari Isma'ilis as a sinister order of 'Assassins' led by a mysterious 'Old Man of the Mountain'. European myths and fantasies relating to Isma'ili Muslims originated in the time of the Crusaders and centred on the Isma'ili leadership represented by the 'Old Man of the Mountain'. These fantastic tales culminated in bizarre legends of drug-crazed violence which have survived into modern times when the word 'assassin' from *hashishin* – hashish-users – has entered European languages to mean murderer.

The above illustration showing the 'Old Man of the Mountain and his paradise' is taken from a manuscript describing the travels of Odoric of Pordenone (d. 1331) contained in the *Livre des Merveilles*, now part of the collection of the Bibliothèque Nationale, Paris [Ms. fr. 2810]. This manuscript was produced early in the fifteenth century for John the Fearless, Duke of Burgundy.

THE
ASSASSIN
LEGENDS
Myths of the Isma'ilis

Farhad Daftary

I.B. Tauris & Co Ltd
Publishers
London · New York

Published in 1994 by
I.B. Tauris & Co Ltd
45 Bloomsbury Square
London WC1A 2HY

175 Fifth Avenue
New York
NY 10010

In the United States of America
and Canada distributed by
St Martin's Press
175 Fifth Avenue
New York
NY 10010

A full CIP record for this book is available from the British Library

A full CIP record for this book is available from the Library of Congress

ISBN 1–85043–705–X

Typeset by Photoprint, Torquay, Devon
Printed and bound in Great Britain by
WBC Ltd, Bridgend, Mid Glamorgan

Contents

Note on Transliteration and Abbreviations

The system of transliteration used in this book for the Arabic and Persian scripts is essentially the same as that adopted in the new edition of *The Encyclopaedia of Islam*, with three modifications, namely, *j* for *dj*, *q* for *ḳ*, and *ch* for *č*. Also, ligatures and diacritical marks are dispensed with, except those for *ayn* and *hamza* when they occur in the middle of a word; as in Isma'ili and *fida'i*.

Christian era dates are generally used throughout the text. In the case of some of the dates appearing in de Sacy's *Memoir* and the publication dates of some of the books published in the Muslim world, however, the Islamic date, lunar or solar according to the Islamic calendar, is followed by the corresponding Christian date.

A few standardized abbreviations are used in this book, notably, b. for *ibn* (son of); d. for died; ed. for editor or edited; edn for edition; and tr. or trans. for translator or translation.

The following abbreviations are used for a few periodicals and encyclopaedias cited frequently in the Notes and Bibliography:

BSO(A)S   *Bulletin of the School of Oriental (and African) Studies*
EI2   *The Encyclopaedia of Islam*, new edition
EIR   *Encyclopaedia Iranica*
JRAS   *Journal of the Royal Asiatic Society*

Preface

The Nizari Isma'ilis, an important Shi'i Muslim community, became famous in mediaeval Europe as the Assassins. This misnomer, rooted in a term of abuse derived from hashish, had been given wide currency by the Crusaders and their occidental chroniclers, who had first come into contact with the members of this enigmatic oriental sect in the Near East during the early decades of the twelfth century. Mediaeval Europeans, who remained ignorant of Muslim beliefs and practices, also transmitted a number of inter-connected tales about the secret practices of the Assassins and their leader, a mysterious Old Man of the Mountain. In time, these Assassin legends, which found their culmination in Marco Polo's narrative, acquired an independent life; and the word 'assassin', with a forgotten etymology, entered European languages as a common noun meaning 'murderer'.

The Assassin legends transmitted by Europeans and the hostile accounts of mediaeval Muslim writers provided the primary sources on the basis of which the Nizaris were studied and evaluated by Silvestre de Sacy and other leading orientalists of the nineteenth century. This highly misinformed and distorted image of the Nizaris was essentially retained by the academic circles of the West until more recent times. But modern progress in Isma'ili studies, initiated by access to authentic Isma'ili sources, has at long last made it possible to distinguish myth from reality in the mediaeval history of the Nizari community. This book, drawing on the findings of modern scholarship in Isma'ili studies, aims to trace the origins and early development of the seminal Assassin legends, also investigating the historical context in which these legends were fabricated and transmitted.

I am deeply indebted to Azizeh Azodi for her masterful English translation of Silvestre de Sacy's famous *Memoir* on the Assassins and the etymology of their name, which appears in the Appendix to this book. Iradj Bagherzade and Anna Enayat facilitated in different ways the publication of this work; I am most grateful to them. I owe a special debt of gratitude to Farhad Hakimzadeh who meticulously searched the mediaeval collections of the British Library and other European libraries for a suitable cover illustration and finally found, at the Bibliothèque Nationale, Paris, what may perhaps be the only curious depiction of the Old Man of the Mountain and his paradise in a mediaeval European manuscript. I would also like to express my appreciation to Caroline Keane who typed the various drafts of the book.

F.D.

1

Introduction

Western readers of Edward FitzGerald's introduction to his English rendition of Umar Khayyam's quatrains will be familiar with the 'Tale of the Three Schoolfellows'. In this, the Persian poet-astronomer Umar Khayyam is linked with the Saljuq vizier Nizam al-Mulk and Hasan Sabbah, the founder of the so-called 'Order of Assassins'. The three famous Persian protagonists of this tale were, allegedly, classmates in their youth under the same master in Nishapur. They made a vow that whichever of them first achieved success in life would help the other two in their careers. Nizam al-Mulk attained rank and power first, becoming the vizier to the Saljuq sultan, and he kept his vow, offering Khayyam a regular stipend and giving Hasan a high post in the Saljuq government. However, Hasan soon became a rival to Nizam al-Mulk, who eventually succeeded through trickery in disgracing Hasan before the sultan. Hasan vowed to take revenge. He left for Egypt, where he learned the secrets of the Isma'ili faith, and later returned to Persia to found a sect that terrorized the Saljuqs through its assassins. Nizam al-Mulk became the first victim of Hasan's assassins. This is one of the eastern legends connected with the Nizari Isma'ilis, known to mediaeval Europe as 'Assassins'.

In the West, too, the Nizaris have been the subjects of several legends since the twelfth century. The first contact between the Europeans, or the Latin Franks, then engaged in the Crusading movement to liberate the Holy Land, and the members of this Shi'i Muslim community occurred in Syria during the earliest years of the twelfth century. At the time, the Nizari Isma'ilis had just founded, under the leadership of the redoubtable Hasan Sabbah, a special territorial state of their own, challenging the hegemony of the Saljuq Turks in the Muslim lands. Subsequently, the Nizari Isma'ilis of Syria became involved in a web of intricate alliances and rivalries with various Muslim rulers and with the

Christian Franks, who were not interested in acquiring accurate information about their Isma'ili neighbours, or indeed about any other Muslim community, in the Latin Orient. None the less, the Crusaders and their occidental observers began to transmit a multitude of imaginative tales about the so-called 'Assassins', the devoted followers of a mysterious 'Vetus de Montanis' or 'Old Man of the Mountain'. These Assassin legends soon found wide currency in Europe, where the knowledge of all things Islamic verged on complete ignorance and the romantic and fascinating tales told by the returning Crusaders could achieve ready popularity.

The Assassin legends, rooted in the general hostility of the Muslims towards the Isma'ilis and the Europeans' own fanciful impressions of the Orient, evolved persistently and systematically during the Middle Ages. In time, these legends were taken, even by serious western chroniclers, to represent accurate descriptions of the practices of an enigmatic eastern community.

The Assassin legends thus acquired an independent currency, which persistently defied re-examination in later centuries when more reliable information on Islam and its internal divisions became available in Europe. However, progress in Islamic studies, and a remarkable modern breakthrough in the study of the history and doctrines of the Isma'ilis, have finally made it possible to dispel once and for all some of the seminal legends of the 'Assassins', which reached their height in the popular version attributed to Marco Polo, the famous thirteenth-century Venetian traveller. It is the primary object of this study to trace the origins of the most famous of the mediaeval legends surrounding the Nizari Isma'ilis, at the same time investigating the historical circumstances under which these legends acquired such widespread currency.

The Nizari Isma'ilis, numbering several millions and accounting for the bulk of the Isma'ili population of the world, are now scattered over more than 25 countries in Asia, Africa, Europe and North America. They currently acknowledge Prince Karim Aga Khan as their 49th imam or spiritual leader. The Isma'ilis represent an important minority community of Shi'i Muslims, who themselves today account for about 10 per cent of the entire Muslim society of around one billion persons.

The Isma'ilis have had a long and eventful history, stretching over more than 12 centuries, during which they became subdivided into a number of major branches and minor groupings. They came into existence, as a separate Shi'i community, around the middle of the eighth century; and, in mediaeval times, they twice founded states of their own, the Fatimid caliphate and the Nizari state. At the same time, the Isma'ilis played an important part in the religio-political and intellectual history of the Muslim world. The celebrated Isma'ili *da'is* or propagandists, who were at once theologians, philosophers and political emissaries, produced numerous treatises in diverse fields of learning, making their own contributions to the Islamic thought of mediaeval times.

In 1094, the Isma'ili movement, which had enjoyed unity during the earlier Fatimid period, split into its two main branches, the Nizaris and the Musta'lians. The Nizaris, who are the main object of this investigation, succeeded in founding a state in Persia, with a subsidiary in Syria. This territorially scattered state, centred on the mountain fortress of Alamut in northern Persia, maintained its cohesiveness in the midst of a hostile environment controlled by the overwhelmingly more powerful and anti-Shi'i Saljuq Turks, who championed the cause of Sunni Islam and its nominal spokesman, the Abbasid caliph at Baghdad. It was under such circumstances that the Syrian Nizaris were forced to confront a new adversary in the Christian Crusaders who, from 1096, had set out in successive waves to liberate the Holy Land of Christendom from the domination of the Muslims (or the Saracens as they were commonly but incorrectly called). The Nizari Isma'ili state, which controlled numerous mountain strongholds and their surrounding villages as well as a few towns, finally collapsed in 1256 under the onslaught of the Mongols. Thereafter, the Nizaris of Persia, Syria and other lands survived merely as Shi'i minority communities without any political prominence.

The western tradition of calling the Nizari Isma'ilis by the name of Assassins can be traced to the Crusaders and their Latin chroniclers as well as other occidental observers who had originally heard about these sectarians in the Levant. The name, or more appropriately misnomer, Assassin, which was originally derived under obscure circumstances from variants of the word hashish, the Arabic name for a narcotic product, and which later became the common occidental term for designating the Nizari Isma'ilis, soon acquired a new meaning in European languages; it was adopted as a common noun meaning murderer. However, the doubly pejorative appellation of Assassins continued to be utilized as the name of the Nizari Isma'ilis in western languages; and this habit was reinforced by Silvestre de Sacy and other prominent orientalists of the nineteenth century who had begun to produce the first scientific studies about the Isma'ilis.

In more recent times, too, many western Islamists have continued to apply the ill-conceived term 'Assassins' to the Nizari Isma'ilis, perhaps without being consciously aware of its etymology or dubious origins.

Bernard Lewis, the foremost modern authority on the history of the Syrian Nizaris and a scholar who has also concerned himself with the etymological aspects of the term Assassin, has consistently used it in his work, even adopting it for the title of his well-known monograph on the Nizari Isma'ilis.[1] Marshall Hodgson also used it in the title of his standard scholarly treatment of the subject.[2] It is, therefore, not surprising that a non-specialist such as the famous English explorer Freya Stark (1893–1993), who visited Alamut in 1930, should have decided to use this term in the title of her romantic and still highly popular travelogue which, in fact, relates mainly to sites in Persia other than Alamut.[3] A similar choice was made by an Oxford expeditionary group of scholars who went to Persia in 1960 to conduct the most extensive archaeological investigation yet of the mediaeval Nizari strongholds of northern Persia, even though they had the renowned Isma'ili specialist Samuel Stern (1920–69) as their historical adviser.[4] Indeed, despite the long-standing correct identification of the people in question as Nizari Isma'ilis, the appellation of Assassins has by and large been retained in the West. Doubtless, the term Assassins, with its aura of mystery and sensation, has acquired an independent currency.

The myths and legends of the Nizari Isma'ilis, encouraged throughout the centuries by the retention of the name Assassins, seem to have had a similar history. Starting in the latter decades of the twelfth century, a number of inter-related legends began to circulate in the Latin Orient and Europe about this mysterious eastern sect, whose members had attracted attention because of their seemingly blind obedience to their leader, the 'Old Man of the Mountain'. Their self-sacrificing behaviour, carrying out dangerous missions at the behest of the 'Old Man', was soon attributed by their occidental observers to the influence of an intoxicating drug like hashish. This provided a rational explanation for behaviour that otherwise seemed irrational. The observers, however, had at best heard only fictitious details and distorted half-truths about the Nizaris from their numerous Muslim and Christian enemies in the Levant. Once the hashish connection was firmly established, it provided ample source material for yet more imaginative tales. The 'Old Man' was held to control the behaviour of his would-be assassins through regulated and systematic administration of some intoxicating potion like hashish, in conjunction with a secret 'garden of paradise' in which his drugged devotees would temporarily enjoy the delights of an earthly paradise; hence, they would carry out the dangerous commands of their chief in order to experience such bliss in perpetuity.

It did not take long for these legends to become fully elaborated and accepted as authentic descriptions of the secret practices of the Nizaris, who were now generally depicted in European sources as a sinister order of drugged and murderous Assassins. These popular legends were handed down from generation to generation, providing important source materials even for the more scholarly Isma'ili studies of the nineteenth-century orientalists, starting with Silvestre de Sacy who himself solved an important etymological mystery in this field, the connection between the words Assassin and hashish. Joseph von Hammer-Purgstall (1774–1856), the Austrian orientalist-diplomat who produced the first monograph in a European language on the Nizari Isma'ilis, had indeed accepted the authenticity of the Assassin legends wholeheartedly.[5] His book was treated as the standard account of the Nizaris of the Alamut period, at least until the 1930s.

In the meantime, Muslim authors from early in the ninth century had generated their own myths of the Isma'ilis, especially regarding the origins and aims of the Isma'ili movement. In particular, Sunni Muslims, who were generally ill-informed about the internal divisions of Shi'ism and could not distinguish between the Isma'ilis and the dissident Qarmatis, wrote more polemical tracts against the Isma'ilis than any other Muslim group, also blaming the Isma'ili movement for the atrocities of the Qarmatis of Bahrayn. In time, the anti-Isma'ili polemicists themselves contributed significantly to shaping the hostility of Muslim society at large towards the Isma'ilis.

By spreading their disparaging accounts widely from Transoxania to North Africa, aiming to discredit the entire Isma'ili movement, the Muslim polemicists gave rise to their own particular 'black legend' of Isma'ilism, which they portrayed as a sect with dubious founders and secret, graded initiation rites leading to irreligiosity and nihilism. Indeed, the most common feature of such anti-Isma'ili polemics, which greatly influenced all Islamic writings on the Isma'ilis until modern times, was the portrayal of Isma'ilism as an arch-heresy or *ilhad*, carefully designed to destroy Islam from within. It was further alleged that the Isma'ili imams, including especially the Fatimid caliphs, had falsely claimed Fatimid Alid descent from the Prophet's daughter Fatima and her husband Ali, the first Shi'i imam. Needless to say, the anti-Isma'ili sentiments of the polemicists also found expression in the writings of very many Muslim historians, theologians, jurists and heresiographers of mediaeval times, who rarely missed an opportunity to denounce the Isma'ilis and their doctrines. The anti-Isma'ili 'black legend' of the Muslim polemicists, and the general hostility of Muslim society towards the Isma'ilis, in time contributed to the westerners' imaginative tales about the Nizari Isma'ilis.

The Isma'ilis themselves did not help matters by guarding their literature and refusing to divulge their doctrines to outsiders. They were, though, essentially justified in maintaining their secretiveness; in the Middle Ages the Isma'ilis were perhaps the most severely persecuted community within the Muslim world, subjected to massacres in many localities. The Isma'ilis were, therefore, obliged from the beginning of their history to adhere closely to the Shi'i principle of *taqiyya*, precautionary dissimulation of one's true religious belief in the face of danger. In fact, with the major exception of the Fatimid period, when Isma'ili doctrines were preached openly in the Fatimid dominions, Isma'ilism developed in utmost secrecy and the Isma'ilis were coerced into what may be termed an underground or clandestine existence. In addition, the *da'i*s who produced the bulk of the Isma'ili writings were mainly theologians and, as such, were not keen on historiography. All this, of course, provided ideal opportunities for the Isma'ilis' numerous adversaries to falsify and misrepresent their actual beliefs and practices.

It was against this background that the orientalists of the nineteenth century, who had for the first time gained access to important collections of Islamic manuscripts held at major European libraries in Paris and elsewhere, began what promised to be a scientific study of the Isma'ilis. Unfortunately, they too achieved few results, mainly because they had no access to genuine Isma'ili texts and were therefore obliged to approach the subject from the narrow and fanciful viewpoint of the mediaeval Crusaders and the travesties of hostile Muslim authors. It is only against this literary background that one can read any sense into some of the conjectures and dubious inferences of Silvestre de Sacy (1758–1838), the greatest orientalist of the time, who summarized his main ideas on the Nizari Isma'ilis in his *Mémoire sur la dynastie des Assassins* (translated for the first time into English in the Appendix to this book). The distorted image of the Isma'ilis in general and the Nizari Isma'ilis in particular was maintained in orientalist circles until the opening decades of the twentieth century. A truly scholarly assessment of the Isma'ilis had to await the recovery and study of a large number of Isma'ili texts, a process that did not start until almost a century after de Sacy's death. It is due to the findings of modern scholarship that we are now finally in a position to distinguish fantasy or legend from reality in things Isma'ili, especially in connection with the Nizaris of the Alamut period who were the objects of the seminal Assassin legends.

In the light of these findings, this study contends that the Assassin legends, especially those based on the hashish connection and the secret 'garden of paradise', were actually fabricated and put into circulation by Europeans. It seems that the occidental observers of the Nizari Isma'ilis, especially those who were least informed about Islam and the Near East, generated these legends (initially in reference to the Syrian Nizaris) gradually and systematically, adding further components or embellishments in successive stages during the twelfth and thirteenth centuries. In this process, the westerners, who in the Crusaders' times had a high disposition towards imaginative and romantic eastern tales, were greatly influenced by the biases and the general hostility of the non-Isma'ili Muslims towards the Isma'ilis, hostility which had earlier given rise to the anti-Isma'ili 'black legend' of the Sunni polemicists as well as some popular misconceptions about the Isma'ilis. In all probability, such popular misconceptions also circulated about the Nizaris in the non-literary local circles of the Latin East during the Crusaders' times; they would have been picked up by the Crusaders through their contact with rural Muslims working on their estates and the lesser educated Muslims of the towns, in addition to whatever information they could gather indirectly through the oriental Christians. In this connection, it is significant to note that similar legends have not been found in any of the mediaeval Islamic sources, including contemporary histories of Syria. Indeed, educated Muslims, including their historians, did not fantasize at all about the secret practices of the Nizaris, even though they were hostile towards them. Similarly, those few well-informed occidental observers of the Syrian Nizaris, such as William of Tyre, who lived in the Latin East for long periods, did not contribute to the formation of the Assassin legends.

In sum, it seems that the legends in question, though ultimately rooted in some popular lore and misinformation circulating locally, were actually formulated and transmitted rather widely due to their sensational appeal by the Crusaders and other western observers of the Nizaris; and they do, essentially, represent the 'imaginative constructions' of these uninformed observers.

Notes and References

1. B. Lewis, *The Assassins: A Radical Sect in Islam* (London, 1967).
2. Marshall G.S. Hodgson, *The Order of Assassins: The Struggle of the Early Nizari Isma'ilis against the Islamic World* (The Hague, 1955).
3. F. Stark, *The Valleys of the Assassins and other Persian Travels* (London, 1934).
4. Peter R.E. Willey, *The Castles of the Assassins* (London, 1963).
5. See Joseph von Hammer-Purgstall, *Die Geschichte der Assassinen* (Stuttgart-Tübingen, 1818), pp 211–14. English trans., *The History of the Assassins*, tr. O.C. Wood (London, 1835; reprinted, New York, 1968), pp 136–8.

2

The Isma'ilis in History and in Mediaeval Muslim Writings

The Isma'ilis represent an important sect of Shi'i Islam; and, like other Shi'i communities, they trace their history to the time of the Prophet Muhammad. The origins of Shi'ism and Sunnism, the two main divisions of Islam, lie in the crisis of succession in the nascent Islamic community following the death of the Prophet Muhammad in Medina on 8 June 632. According to the message of Islam, Muhammad was the Seal of the Prophets, and, therefore, he could not be succeeded by another prophet. A successor was, nevertheless, needed to assume the Prophet's function as leader of the Islamic community and state, the foundations of which had essentially been laid during the last decade of Muhammad's prophetic mission. As the Prophet himself had not designated any successor, in the view of the majority, this important appointment now had to be made. After brief deliberations by the leading Muslim groups, the communal choice fell on Abu Bakr, who now became *khalifat rasul Allah*, Successor to the Messenger of God. The title for the head of the Muslim community was soon simplified to *khalifa*, hence the term 'caliph' in western languages.[1]

Abu Bakr led the Muslims for just over two years. The next three heads of the Muslim community, Umar (634–44), Uthman (644–56) and Ali (656–61), were also installed to office by various elective procedures. These four early caliphs all belonged to the influential Meccan tribe of Quraysh and they also ranked among those early converts to Islam and the Companions of the Prophet who had accompanied Muhammad on his historic emigration from Mecca to Medina in 622, which was to mark the initiation of the Islamic era. But only the fourth caliph, Ali, who occupies a unique position in the annals of Shi'ism, belonged to the Banu Hashim, the Prophet's own clan of Quraysh; he was also closely related to the Prophet, being his cousin and son-in-law, bound in matrimony to the Prophet's daughter Fatima.

Ali's caliphate was a period of strife and civil war, resulting in irreconcilable religio-political divisions within the Muslim community, later designated specifically as Sunni, Shi'i and Khariji.[2] In particular, Ali's authority was challenged by Mu'awiya, the powerful governor of Syria who belonged to the wealthy Meccan clan of the Banu Umayya. When Ali was murdered in 661, the caliphate was readily seized by the shrewd Mu'awiya who also succeeded in establishing the hereditary rule of the Umayyads (661–750), the first dynasty in Islam.

The Umayyads, under whom the Islamic empire acquired its full extent, were supplanted in a well-designed revolution by the Abbasids, who were from the Hashimite Banu Abbas family of the Prophet's uncle Abbas. The Abbasids ruled for almost five centuries over different parts of the Muslim world and with various degrees of independent caliphal authority, from their capital at Baghdad, until they were overthrown in 1258 by the Mongols, soon after the Mongol destruction of the Nizari Isma'ili state in Persia.

The doctrinal basis of Sunnism, representing a particular interpretation of the Islamic message by the Muslim majority who had also supported the historical caliphate, developed gradually, like that of Shi'ism. By the early Abbasid centuries, the Sunni Muslims, representing the central body of the community and designated in Arabic as the *Ahl al-Sunna wa'l-Jama'a* (People of the *Sunna* and of the Community), and the various Shi'i communities had already begun to possess their distinctive theological doctrines and schools of religious law, based primarily on the holy Quran and the *Sunna* (actions and sayings of the Prophet) and certain other foundations.

Immediately on the death of the Prophet, there had appeared a small group in Medina who believed that the succession was the legitimate right of his cousin and son-in-law, Ali b. Abi Talib. In time, this minority group expanded and came to be generally designated as the *Shi'at Ali* (Party of Ali), or simply as the Shi'a. Due to the lack of contemporary sources on the first century of Islam, the history of the formative period of Shi'ism is shrouded in obscurity, and later sources on the subject are unreliable due to their Sunni biases, Shi'i sympathies, or retrospective stances. Be that as it may, it is the fundamental belief of the Shi'a, including the Isma'ilis, that the Prophet had, in fact, designated Ali as his legatee (*wasi*) and successor; a designation or *nass* that had been instituted by divine command.[3]

The Shi'a further held that after Ali, the leadership of the Muslim community was the exclusive right of Ali's descendants, the Alids, who belonged to the Prophet's family or the *ahl al-bayt*. Thus, the rules of the first three caliphs as well as those of the Umayyads and the

Abbasids, constituted an arbitrary usurpation of the rights of Ali and his descendants, the dispossessed legitimate imams, as the Shi'a have always preferred to call the leaders of the Muslim community. This explains why most Shi'i groups accused the majority of the early Companions of the Prophet of apostasy, which also led to the Shi'i vilification of the first three caliphs. Thus, the intense desire to see justice restored by installing the Alids to the leadership of the community became the moving force behind numerous Shi'i revolts of the Umayyad and early Abbasid times. Meanwhile, the Sunnis had adopted their own anti-Shi'i measures, such as the cursing of Ali from the pulpits of mosques after Friday prayers, a policy instituted by Mu'awiya. Many of the Alids and their supporters from different Shi'i communities were also persecuted on the orders of the Sunni rulers.

The Shi'i viewpoint outlined here was rooted also in a particular conception of religious authority, which has continued to occupy a central position in Shi'i spirituality and thought. According to this conception, the most important question facing the Muslim community after the Prophet was the elucidation of Islamic teachings and tenets, since the Islamic message emanated from sources beyond the comprehension of ordinary men. From the very beginning the Shi'a had recognized the need for a religiously authoritative teacher and spiritual guide, or imam, after the Prophet. Hence, the Shi'a saw in this leadership a vital spiritual function connected with the explanation and interpretation of the true meaning of the Islamic revelation. Now, a person with a thorough knowledge of both the apparent and the hidden meanings of the Quran and the teachings of Islam had to be in possession of a special religious knowledge or *ilm*, not available to ordinary men; and such authoritative guides could belong only to the *ahl al-bayt* who, beginning with Ali himself, were inheritors of the Prophet's undivulged teachings and *ilm*.

The Shi'a were numerically small, but their zeal and unwavering loyalty to Ali and his descendants explain how Shi'ism managed to survive Ali himself and numerous subsequent defeats during its formative period. Soon, Shi'ism acquired lasting roots among the heterogeneous population of Kufa in Southern Iraq. It was also in or around Kufa that the main events in the early history of Shi'ism unfolded, events that in various ways contributed to the formation of the Shi'i ethos and the eventual consolidation of Shi'ism as a dynamic movement with a distinct ideology.

On Ali's death, the Shi'a recognized his eldest son Hasan as their new imam. Meanwhile, Hasan had also been acclaimed as caliph, in succession to Ali, in Kufa. However, Mu'awiya speedily succeeded in inducing Hasan's abdication from the caliphate. On Hasan's death in 669, the Shi'a revived their hope for challenging Umayyad rule through their next imam, Husayn, the second son of Ali and Fatima and Hasan's full brother. Husayn eventually responded to the Kufan summons and set off on his fateful journey from the Hijaz to Iraq. The tragic martyrdom of the Prophet's grandson Husayn and his small band of relatives and companions at Karbala, near Kufa, where they were massacred by an Umayyad army on 10 October 680, marked the establishment of the all-important Shi'i martyrology. This event infused an entirely new religious fervour into the Shi'a and led to the formation of radical trends among the partisans of Ali and the *ahl al-bayt*. The earliest of such radical trends, which left lasting marks on Shi'ism, became openly manifest a few years later in the movement of al-Mukhtar.

Al-Mukhtar b. Abi Ubayd organized his own anti-regime, Shi'i movement, with a general call for avenging Husayn's murder. In 685, al-Mukhtar successfully revolted in Kufa and proclaimed Muhammad, a third son of Ali, as the imam. However, Muhammad, who was not the son of Fatima, and was known after his own mother as Ibn al-Hanafiyya, remained a figurehead in al-Mukhtar's movement. Al-Mukhtar also proclaimed Ibn al-Hanafiyya as the Mahdi, 'the divinely guided one', the messianic restorer of Islam and the saviour imam who would establish justice on earth and deliver the oppressed from tyranny. This new eschatological concept of the imam-Mahdi proved particularly appealing to the *mawali* or clients, the non-Arab converts to Islam, who now swarmed to al-Mukhtar's side, calling themselves the *Shi'at al-Mahdi* (Party of the Mahdi). The success of al-Mukhtar, who speedily won control of Kufa, however, proved short-lived, although his movement survived under the name of Mukhtariyya, later commonly designated as Kaysaniyya.

By contrast to the first half-century in the history of Shi'ism, when the Shi'a represented a unified Arab party and accorded general recognition to a single succession of imams (namely, Ali, Hasan and Husayn), henceforth different Shi'i groups consisting of Arabs and *mawali* came to co-exist. Furthermore, the Shi'i imams now issued not only primarily from among the three major branches of the extended Alid family, namely, the Hanafids (descendants of Muhammad b. al-Hanafiyya who died in 700), the Husaynids (descendants of Husayn b. Ali) and, later, the Hasanids (descendants of Hasan b. Ali), but also from among other branches of the Prophet's clan of Banu Hashim; because the Prophet's family, whose sanctity was supreme for the Shi'is, was then still defined broadly in its old tribal sense. It was after the accession of the Abbasids that the Shi'is began to define the *ahl al-bayt* more restrictively to include only the direct descendants of the Prophet through Fatima (and Ali), known as the Fatimids (covering both the Hasanid and the Husaynid Alids), and the bulk of the Shi'a, including the Isma'ilis, came to acknowledge a particular Husaynid line of imams.

In this divided and fluid setting, Shi'ism developed in terms of two main branches or trends; and later another Alid movement led to the formation of a Shi'i sect known as the Zaydiyya. A radical branch, in terms of both doctrine and policy, evolved out of al-Mukhtar's movement and accounted for the allegiance of the Shi'i majority until shortly after the Abbasid revolution. This branch, breaking away from the religiously moderate attitude prevailing among the early Kufan Shi'a and generally designated as the Kaysaniyya by the heresiographers, was comprised of a number of inter-connected groups following various Hanafid Alids and other Hashimites as their imams. By the end of the Umayyad period, the majority body of the Kaysaniyya, notably the Hashimiyya, transferred their allegiance to the Abbasid family. With this transference, the Abbasids also inherited the party and the propaganda organization which became the main instruments for the eventual overthrow of the Umayyads.[4]

The Kaysaniyya drew mainly on the support of the superficially Islamicized *mawali*, non-Arab clients in southern Iraq and elsewhere who were treated as second-class Muslims under the Umayyads. The *mawali* played a significant part in transforming Shi'ism from an Arab party of limited size and doctrinal basis to a dynamic sectarian movement. The Kaysani Shi'is elaborated some of the beliefs and doctrines which came to characterize the radical branch of Shi'ism. Many of the Kaysani ideas were propounded by the so-called *ghulat*, 'exaggerators', who were accused by the more moderate Shi'is of later times of exaggeration in religious matters. The early Shi'i *ghulat* speculated rather freely on a host of issues and they were responsible for many doctrinal innovations, including the spiritual interpretations of the Day of Judgement, Resurrection, Paradise and Hell; they also held a cyclical view of the religious history of mankind in terms of eras initiated by different prophets. Much of the intellectual heritage of the Kaysaniyya was subsequently absorbed into the doctrines of the main Shi'i communities.

Meanwhile, there had appeared a second major branch or wing of Shi'ism, later designated as the Imamiyya. This branch, with its limited original following, remained completely removed from any anti-regime political activity. The Imami Shi'is, who were centred in Kufa, recognized a line of Husaynid imams after Ali, Hasan and Husayn, tracing the imamate through Husayn's sole surviving son Ali b. Husayn, who received the honorific epithet of Zayn al-Abidin, 'the Ornament of the Pious'.

It was with Zayn al-Abidin's son, Muhammad al-Baqir, that the Husaynid imams and the Imamiyya began to acquire their particular identity and prominence within the Shi'a. During the final Umayyad decades, with the rise of different theological and legal schools upholding conflicting views, many Shi'is sought the guidance of their imam as an authoritative teacher. Al-Baqir was the first imam of the Husaynid line fully to perform this role, and he acquired an increasing group of followers who regarded him as the sole legitimate religious authority of the time. In line with his quiescent policy, al-Baqir is also credited with introducing the important Shi'i principle of *taqiyya*, precautionary dissimulation of one's true religious beliefs in the face of danger. This principle was adopted by the Ithna'ashari or Twelver and Isma'ili Shi'is, and it particularly served to save the Isma'ilis from much persecution throughout the centuries. Having laid the founda- tions of Imami Shi'ism, the common heritage of the great Shi'i communities of Ithna'ashariyya and Isma'iliyya, Muhammad al-Baqir died around 732, almost a century after the death of the Prophet.

The Imamiyya expanded significantly and became an important religious community under al-Baqir's son and successor Ja'far al-Sadiq, who was the foremost scholar and teacher among the imams of the Husaynid line. Early in al-Sadiq's long and eventful imamate of some 30 or more years, his uncle Zayd b. Ali's movement unfolded. Zayd, too, was persuaded by the Kufans to lead them in an anti-Umayyad revolt. Zayd's revolt, launched in Kufa in 740, proved abortive, as the Kufans once again manifested their unreliability. However, Zayd's movement led to the formation of another major Shi'i sect, the Zaydiyya, who, unlike the Imamiyya, did not recognize a hereditary line of imams. The Zaydis retained the religiously moderate and politically militant stances of the early Kufan Shi'a. They were conservative in defining the religious status of their imams, who could be any descendants of Hasan or Husayn, and they also refrained from condemning the early caliphs before Ali and the rest of the Muslim community for having failed to acknowledge the legitimate rights of Ali and his descendants. Politically, the Zaydis adopted a militant position, advocating armed uprising against the illegitimate rulers of the time. By the second half of the ninth century, the Zaydis had succeeded in establishing two states, one in Tabaristan and adjacent regions on the southern coast of the Caspian Sea in northern Persia, and another one in Yaman. In both regions there were, subsequently, extended rivalries and numerous military encounters between the Zaydis and their neighbouring Isma'ili communities.

Meanwhile, the Abbasids had learned important lessons from the abortive revolts of the Umayyad period. Paying particular attention to the organizational aspects of their own secret revolutionary movement, the Abbasid religio-political mission or *da'wa* was preached in the name of the *ahl al-bayt* and on a largely Shi'i basis. At any rate, in 750, the Abbasids installed their own dynasty to the caliphate to the great disappointment of the Shi'is who had all along expected the Alids to succeed the Umayyads as the new rulers of the Muslim community. Shi'i disillusionment was further aggravated when the Abbasids, soon after their victory, became staunch supporters of Sunni Islam, adopting repressive measures against the Alids and their Shi'i supporters.

It was under these circumstances that Ja'far al-Sadiq emerged as the main rallying point for the allegiance of the Shi'is. Maintaining the Imami tradition of remaining aloof from any revolutionary activity, Ja'far al-Sadiq had gradually acquired a widespread reputation as a religious scholar and teacher, and, besides his own partisans, large numbers of Muslims studied or consulted with him. In time, he also acquired a circle of Imami associates which included some of the most learned scholars and theologians of the time. As a result of the intensive intellectual efforts of this circle, led by al-Sadiq himself, the Imamiyya now came to possess a distinctive legal school, as well as a body of ritual and theological thought.

The fundamental doctrine of Imami thought, however, has been the doctrine of the imamate which was formulated in al-Sadiq's time. It was based on the belief in the permanent need of mankind for a divinely guided, sinless and infallible (*ma'sum*) leader or imam who, after the Prophet Muhammad, would act as the authoritative teacher and guide of men in all their religious and spiritual affairs. This imam is also endowed with special knowledge or *ilm*, and has perfect understanding of all the exoteric and esoteric aspects of the Quran and the message of Islam. Indeed, the world could not exist for a moment without such an imam after the age of the prophets, which was sealed by Muhammad. Recognition of the true imam and obedience to him were made the absolute duty of every believer; and the ignorance or rejection of such an imam would be equal to infidelity. The Prophet himself had designated Ali as his successor, under divine command. After Ali, Hasan and Husayn, the imamate had remained vested in the Husaynid line; and after Ja'far al-Sadiq, it would be transmitted through his progeny until the end of time.

Imam Ja'far al-Sadiq, the last imam recognized by both the Twelvers and the Isma'ilis, died in 765. The dispute over his succession led to permanent divisions within Imami Shi'ism, also marking the appearance of Isma'ilism as an independent religio-political movement, which was initially comprised of a number of small Kufan groups.

Early or pre-Fatimid Isma'ilism, extending from the proto-Isma'ili origins of the movement in the middle of the eighth century to the establishment of the Fatimid caliphate in 909, is the most obscure major phase in the entire history of Isma'ilism.[5] Little reliable information is available on the history and doctrines of the pre-Fatimid Isma'ilis, who laid the intellectual foundations of Isma'ilism and successfully disseminated their religio-political preaching or *da'wa* in many Islamic lands, while their survival was continuously threatened by the persecutions of the Abbasids. The early Isma'ilis themselves seem to have produced very few treatises, preferring instead to propagate their doctrines by word of mouth. Research difficulties are further aggravated by the general dearth of information on Shi'ism during the early Abbasid period, when the major Twelver and Isma'ili communities were being formed.

As a result, despite the modern recovery of mediaeval Isma'ili literature, the early Isma'ilis still have to be studied mainly on the basis of non-Isma'ili sources, which are generally very hostile. Among these, heresiographies provide an important category, especially the accounts of the Imami (Twelver) scholars al-Nawbakhti and al-Qummi, who were rather well-informed about the internal divisions of Shi'ism and were basically interested in proving the legitimacy of their own line of imams while refuting the claims of those imams recognized by the Isma'ilis and other non-Twelver Shi'i groups.[6]

Imam Ja'far al-Sadiq had designated his eldest son, Isma'il, as his successor to the imamate. But, according to the majority of non-Isma'ili sources, Isma'il predeceased his father; subsequently, al-Sadiq does not seem to have made a clear second designation or *nass* in favour of another son. This explains why, on al-Sadiq's death, three of his sons, including Musa (later recognized as the seventh imam of the Twelver Shi'a), as well as his eldest grandson Muhammad b. Isma'il, simultaneously claimed his heritage. At any rate, in 765 the Imami Shi'i community, centred in Kufa, split into six groups, two of which constituted the nascent Isma'iliyya.

The two earliest Isma'ili groups acknowledging the imamate of Isma'il b. Ja'far al-Sadiq or that of his son Muhammad b. Isma'il, now issued from the Imamiyya. One group, denying the death of Isma'il during the lifetime of his father, maintained that Isma'il was al-

Sadiq's rightful successor, and that he remained alive and would return as the Mahdi. The Imami heresiographers, who are actually responsible for coining the designation of 'Isma'iliyya', refer to this group as *al-Isma'iliyya al-khalisa*, or the 'Pure Isma'iliyya'. There was a second group of the earliest Isma'ilis who, affirming Isma'il's death during his father's lifetime, now acknowledged Isma'il's eldest son Muhammad as their new imam. This group was known as the Mubarakiyya, originally named after Mubarak, one of Isma'il's epithets. The exact nature of the relationship between these two splinter groups, which were based in Kufa and were numerically rather insignificant, remains obscure. On the death of Muhammad b. Isma'il, not too long after 795, the Mubarakiyya themselves split into two groups. The bulk of the Mubarakiyya, refusing to accept Muhammad b. Isma'il's death, now began to await his return as the Mahdi. For these sectarians, comprising the largest of the three earliest Isma'ili groups, Muhammad b. Isma'il was their seventh and final imam. This also explains why the Isma'iliyya later acquired the denomination of the Sab'iyya or Seveners. Meanwhile, a small and obscure subgroup of the Mubarak-iyya had accepted Muhammad b. Isma'il's death and had traced the imamate in his progeny.

The Imami (Twelver) authorities, who aimed to discredit the Isma'ilis, generally identify the nascent Isma'iliyya with the extremist Shi'i *ghulat*, notably the Khattabiyya. However, later Fatimid Isma'ili sources actually repudiated Abu'l-Khattab, the founder of the Khatta-biyya, as a heretic, also denouncing his group. Indeed, fundamental differences existed in the doctrinal field between the views of the early Isma'ilis, who retained the Imami doctrine of the imamate as expounded by Ja'far al-Sadiq, and the Khattabis who believed in the divinity of the imams in addition to upholding other extremist views. In the political field, however, the earliest Isma'ilis did share the revolutionary ideals of the Khattabis and some other radical groups on the fringe of the Imamiyya. All these groups, belonging to a politically activist wing in the Imami milieu of Kufa, worked for the collapse of Abbasid rule; and, as such, they departed from the quiescent policy espoused by the teachings of the Imamiyya.

Muhammad b. Isma'il, unlike his father, was not personally involved in any revolutionary activity. Nevertheless, in order to escape from the Abbasid persecution of the Shi'i leaders and the Alids, he, too, was obliged to leave the seat of the Alid family in the Hijaz and go into hiding soon after al-Sadiq's death. This, in effect, initiated the long period of concealment (*dawr al-satr*) in the history of the early Isma'ilis, lasting until the establishment of the Fatimid caliphate; a period which provided the anti-Isma'ili Muslim authors of mediaeval times with an ideal opportunity to invent hostile tales about the origins of Isma'ilism.

Not much is known about the subsequent fate of the earliest Isma'ili groups until the sudden emergence of a unified Isma'ili movement shortly after the middle of the ninth century. Isma'ilism now appeared as a well organized and centrally led revolutionary movement with an elaborate doctrinal system; and its message was rapidly and secretly disseminated by a network of missionaries called *da'is* (summoners) throughout much of the Islamic world. The movement was now preached in the name of the absent Muhammad b. Isma'il, recognized as the expected Mahdi, or *qa'im* (Riser). It was held that Muhammad b. Isma'il had gone into hiding and that on his imminent reappearance he would establish justice in the world and initiate the final, seventh era of human history. The early Isma'ilis had also developed a cyclical view of religious history and a particular cosmological system.[7] It is to be noted that the pre-Fatimid Isma'ilis evidently never referred to themselves as Isma'ilis; they designated their movement simply as *al-da'wa*, 'the mission', or *al-da'wa al-hadiya*, 'the rightly guiding mission', reflecting the elitist attitude of the sectarians and their divine duty to invite other Muslims into their midst. They were soon generally designated by their contemporaries with the abusive term *malahida* (heretics).

It is certain that during this early period of Isma'ili history, from Muhammad b. Isma'il's death until the middle of the ninth century, a group of central leaders worked patiently and secretly for the creation of a unified and expanded Isma'ili movement. These leaders, members of the same family who succeeded to the leadership of the movement on a hereditary basis, had been originally attached to one of the earliest Isma'ili groups, and were in all probability the imams of one of the two subgroups into which the Mubarakiyya had split on the death of Muhammad b. Isma'il. At any rate, these leaders, observing *taqiyya* to safeguard themselves, did not at the time openly claim the imamate; instead, they adopted the guise of the *hujjas* or representatives of Muhammad b. Isma'il, on whose behalf the movement was organized. They also adopted cover names, such as Maymun (the Blessed) to protect further their true identities, which were actually known only by a few trusted associates. These points are clearly explained by Abd Allah (Ubayd Allah) al-Mahdi, the last of these early leaders and the future founder of the Fatimid caliphate, in a letter to the Isma'ili community of Yaman.[8]

The efforts of these leaders finally bore fruit around the year 873, when the Abbasid caliphate had already begun to disintegrate. Around that time numerous *daʿi*s appeared in Iraq, Yaman, eastern Arabia and in many localities in Persia, rapidly winning an increasing number of converts. The successful propagation of the Ismaʿili *daʿwa* aroused the enmity of the caliphs at Baghdad and their Sunni supporters; it also aroused the envy of the Imami Shiʿis, who were soon to become designated as the Ithnaʿashariyya or Twelvers.[9] This was not only because these two Shiʿi communities acknowledged different lines of imams after al-Sadiq, but also because as upholders of the same doctrine of the imamate each community regarded its own imams as the sole legitimate leaders of the Muslim community. The revolutionary, messianic movement of the early Ismaʿilis achieved special success among those Imami Shiʿis who had become increasingly disenchanted with the quietism and political inactivity of their own imams. All this may also explain why al-Fadl b. Shadhan, the great Imami scholar of Nishapur who died in 873, wrote the earliest known refutation of the Ismaʿilis.

It was under such circumstances that the Ismaʿili *daʿwa* in Iraq was initiated and placed under the local leadership of Hamdan Qarmat and his chief assistant Abdan. Hamdan won many converts in Iraq, who became known as the Qaramita (singular, Qarmati), named after their first local leader. Soon, the same term came to be applied to other sections of the Ismaʿili movement which were not organized or led by Hamdan Qarmat. The Ismaʿili *daʿwa* was extended to many other regions outside Iraq during the 870s. After his initial career in southern Persia, the *daʿi* Abu Saʿid al-Jannabi was sent by Hamdan to Bahrayn where he eventually founded a state in 899. In 879, the central leadership of the Ismaʿili movement sent two *daʿi*s to Yaman, where they achieved lasting success based on strong tribal support. It was also from Yaman that the *daʿi* Abu Abd Allah al-Shiʿi was sent to the Maghrib, where Ismaʿilism was preached successfully among the Kutama Berbers and the ground was prepared for the establishment there of the Fatimid caliphate. Around 873, the Ismaʿili *daʿwa* also appeared in many parts of central and north-western Persia, the region of the Jibal, where the *daʿi*s established their local headquarters at Rayy; and about three decades later, around 903, the *daʿwa* was officially taken to Khurasan and Transoxania, where for a while it penetrated the inner circles of the Samanid court at Bukhara.[10]

Between the middle of the ninth century and the year 899, Ismaʿilism represented a unified movement, preaching the Mahdiship of Muhammad b. Ismaʿil. Hamdan Qarmat and other local chief *daʿi*s had maintained correspondence with the central leaders of Isma'ilism, who then resided at Salamiyya, in Syria, and whose identity remained a closely guarded secret. In 899 the Isma'ili movement was rent by a major schism shortly after Abd Allah (Ubayd Allah), the future Fatimid caliph al-Mahdi, had succeeded to its central leadership.[11] Abd Allah felt secure enough openly to claim the imamate for himself and his predecessors, who had actually organized and led the Isma'ili movement during the ninth century. He soon instructed Hamdan and other chief *da'is* of different lands to start preaching the *da'wa* in his own name, instead of recognizing the Mahdiship of Muhammad b. Isma'il.

Abd Allah (Ubayd Allah) al-Mahdi's declarations split the unified Isma'ili movement into two rival branches in 899. One branch, consisting mainly of the Isma'ili communities of Yaman, Egypt and North Africa, remained loyal to Abd Allah and accepted his claim that the imamate had been uninterruptedly handed down among his ancestors. This loyalist branch now recognized a series of 'hidden imams', between Ja'far al-Sadiq and Abd Allah al-Mahdi, identified with the central leaders who had actually led the movement; and, subsequently, they traced the imamate among the descendants of Abd Allah who ruled as Fatimid caliphs. Indeed, it was the loyalist branch, designated as the Fatimid Isma'ilis, that soon prepared the ground for the rule of the Isma'ili imams as Fatimid caliphs. On the other hand, some of the chief *da'is* of the eastern communities, led by Hamdan and Abdan, refused to accept Abd Allah's claims; they either suspended their *da'wa* activities or continued to retain their original belief in the Mahdiship of Muhammad b. Isma'il. Abu Sa'id al-Jannabi, who established his rule over Bahrayn in the same eventful year of 899, sided with Hamdan Qarmat and severed his relations with Abd Allah. This dissident branch eventually encompassed the Isma'ili communities of Iraq and Bahrayn, as well as most of those situated in the Jibal, Khurasan and Transoxania. Henceforth, the term Qaramita came to be applied more specifically to the dissident Isma'ilis of Bahrayn and elsewhere who did not acknowledge Abd Allah al-Mahdi and his predecessors, as well as his successors in the Fatimid dynasty, as imams. However, with the devastating and antinomian activities of the Qarmatis of Bahrayn, who for a long time led the dissident wing, Muslim authors came to apply the term Qaramita in a derogatory sense to the entire Isma'ili movement, which they aimed to discredit.

Soon, the dissident Qarmatis began to manifest their hostility openly towards the Fatimid Isma'ilis and their imam, obliging Abd Allah al-Mahdi to flee from Salamiyya in 902 and embark on his long and historic journey to North Africa. There, through the extended efforts of the *da'i* Abu Abd Allah al-Shi'i and his Kutama Berber converts to Isma'ilism, Abd Allah al-Mahdi eventually made his triumphant entry into Raqqada, the former capital of the Aghlabids in Ifriqiya (Tunisia), where he was publicly proclaimed as caliph in January 910. The new caliphate was named al-Fatimiyyun, after the Prophet's daughter Fatima, whom Abd Allah al-Mahdi and his successors claimed as ancestress.

The Fatimid period (910–1171) was the 'golden age' of the Isma'ili movement. During this period the classical works of Isma'ili literature were composed by the renowned Isma'ili *da'i*-authors. At the same time, the Isma'ilis had for the first time acquired an important *dawla* or state of their own. At its peak, the Fatimid caliphate included all of North Africa, Sicily, Egypt, the Red Sea coast of Africa, Yaman, the Hijaz with the holy cities of Mecca and Medina, Syria and Palestine. Isma'ili doctrines were now preached openly throughout the Fatimid dominions, where the Isma'ilis no longer had to resort to *taqiyya* or dissimulation. After transferring the seat of their state from Ifriqiya to Egypt in 973, the Isma'ilis also paid considerable attention to Islamic sciences as well as economic and cultural activities in general, while maintaining a flourishing trade with India and many other lands. The newly founded Fatimid capital, Cairo, rivalled Abbasid Baghdad as the international metropolis of the Islamic world. The Isma'ilis had now truly emerged triumphant from their clandestine existence in pre-Fatimid times.[12]

The Fatimids, unlike the Abbasids, did not discontinue their *da'wa* activities in the aftermath of their victory. On the contrary, their *da'wa* was intensified because they never abandoned their aspiration to rule the entire Muslim world. This explains why the Fatimids continued to refer to their missionary activities as *al-da'wa al-hadiya*, the rightly guiding summons to mankind to follow the Fatimid Isma'ili imam. It should be pointed out, however, that the Fatimids, in line with a general Isma'ili position, were never interested in mass or forced conversions.

The organization and evolution of the Fatimid *da'wa*, as well as the scope and functions of the various ranks (*hudud*) within that complex organization, are among the most obscure aspects of Fatimid Isma'ilism. Organized hierarchically, the Fatimid *da'wa* evolved over time, attaining a definite shape during the reign of the Fatimid caliph-imam al-Hakim (996–1021) who established several institutions in Egypt for the training of *da'i*s and propagation of Isma'ili doctrines. The Fatimid *da'i*s were in general highly educated theologians who also produced the bulk of Isma'ili literature of the Fatimid period.

Although nothing is known about the procedures they used for winning and educating new converts, it is certain that different methods were adopted for peoples of different religious and socio-cultural back-grounds. The *da'is* seem to have treated each case individually, also observing a certain degree of gradualism in the initiation and education of converts. But there is no evidence to suggest, as claimed by anti-Isma'ili sources, that there ever existed at any time a fixed graded system of seven or nine degrees of initiation into Isma'ilism.[13]

Meanwhile, the Qarmatis of Bahrayn, like the Qarmati communities of Iraq, Persia and Transoxania, had continued to await the reappearance of Muhammad b. Isma'il as their expected Mahdi. Starting in 923, when Abu Tahir al-Jannabi had already succeeded to the leadership in Bahrayn, the Qarmatis of eastern Arabia began their prolonged career of raiding southern Iraq and pillaging the *hajj* caravans returning from Mecca. In one of their military campaigns against the Abbasids in 927, the Qarmatis of Bahrayn came close to seizing Baghdad itself. The ravaging activities of Abu Tahir culminated in his sack of Mecca, where he arrived at the head of a Qarmati army in 930, during the pilgrimage season. For several days the Qarmatis massacred the pilgrims and committed numerous acts of desecration. They finally dislodged and carried off the Black Stone of the Ka'ba to their new capital, al-Ahsa, presumably to symbolize the end of the era of Islam. The sacrilege of the Qarmatis at Mecca shocked the entire Muslim world.

In 931, Abu Tahir turned over the reins of the state in Bahrayn to a young Persian in whom he had recognized the expected Mahdi. However, this proved to be a disastrous decision for the Qarmati movement. Manifesting strong anti-Arab and antinomian sentiments, he cursed Muhammad and other prophets in addition to instituting a number of strange ceremonies that further shocked the Muslims. At any rate, after some 80 days, when the Persian Mahdi had begun to execute the notables of Bahrayn, Abu Tahir was obliged to admit that the Mahdi had been an imposter, and had him killed. The episode of the Persian Mahdi further damaged the image of the Qarmatis of Bahrayn and weakened their influence over the Qarmati communities in the East.

In Bahrayn itself, in the aftermath of the episode of the Persian Mahdi, the Qarmatis had reverted to their former beliefs and Abu Tahir once again claimed to be acting on the orders of the hidden Mahdi. Soon he also resumed his devastating activities, plundering the pilgrim caravans and conducting military raids for booty into Iraq and southern Persia. He died in 944. The Qarmatis finally returned the

Black Stone in 951 for a large sum paid by the Abbasids, not, as stated in some anti-Ismaʿili sources, in response to the request of the Fatimid caliph-imam al-Mansur (946–53). Hostilities between the Qarmatis of Bahrayn and the Fatimids broke into open warfare during the reign of the Fatimid caliph-imam al-Muʿizz (953–75), in the aftermath of the Fatimid conquest of Egypt in 969.

The Qarmatis of Bahrayn, indeed, frustrated a quick Fatimid victory in Syria, also providing serious impediments to the extension of Fatimid rule over the eastern Abbasid lands beyond Syria. By the end of the tenth century, the Qarmatis of Bahrayn had been reduced to a local power, and little is known about their subsequent history. By the middle of the eleventh century, the Qarmati communities of Iraq, Persia and Transoxania had been largely won over to the side of the Fatimid *daʿwa*, or they had disintegrated. In 1077, a local tribal chief put a definite end to the Qarmati state of Bahrayn, founding the Uyunid dynasty of eastern Arabia.[14]

Much has been written in modern times about the relations between the Qarmatis and the Fatimids. Michael Jan de Goeje (1836–1909) was the earliest orientalist who, on the basis of the anti-Ismaʿili Muslim sources available in nineteenth-century Europe, arrived at the conclusion that very close relations had existed between them. Subsequently, similar views were expressed by other scholars. More recent scholarship, however, based on a much better understanding of early Ismaʿilism, Fatimid Ismaʿilism and Qarmatism, does not lend support to such views. It has now become clear that essential differences existed between the beliefs of the Qarmatis and the Fatimid Ismaʿilis, differences that dated back at least to the schism of 899. The Qarmatis of Bahrayn and elsewhere, who continued to await the emergence of their hidden Mahdi, never acknowledged the Fatimids as their imams or caliphs, nor did they ever recognize their expected Mahdi in any of the Fatimids. This is why the Qarmatis of Bahrayn were so readily drawn into the catastrophic episode of the Persian Mahdi. But, as the Qarmatis and the Fatimids shared a common hostility towards the Abbasids, it may have appeared that at times they acted according to a joint strategy.

However, Sunni Muslim authors of the Fatimid and later times, who were bent on discrediting the entire Ismaʿili movement and who were generally ill-informed about the internal divisions of Shiʿism and Ismaʿilism, readily attributed the atrocities of the Qarmatis of Bahrayn to the machinations of the Fatimids, their alleged secret masters. Similarly, they found it convenient to blame the Fatimids for the anti-Islamic and libertine practices of the Qarmatis of Bahrayn, which culminated in their desecrating acts in Mecca and the fiasco of the Persian Mahdi. The unfounded accusations of the Muslim authors contributed significantly to shaping anti-Isma'ili opinion in mediaeval Muslim society; they also provided source materials for many of the erroneous conclusions reached by later Muslim writers as well as the orientalists of the nineteenth century.

Indeed, the establishment of the Fatimid caliphate, marking the peak of the Isma'ili challenge to Sunni Islam, called forth a systematic and often organized anti-Isma'ili intellectual reaction on the part of the Sunni majority, while the hostilities of the Twelver and Zaydi Shi'is had become further accentuated by the new success of the Isma'ili Shi'is. As a result, the Isma'ilis now began to be widely condemned by the majority of Muslim theologians, heresiographers and historians as *malahida* or *mulhids* (heretics or deviators in religious beliefs); and the Sunni polemicists in particular began to fabricate evidence that would lend support to that condemnation on specific doctrinal grounds. This general anti-Isma'ili campaign was encouraged and supported by most of the ruling dynasties of the mediaeval Muslim world.

The Sunni polemicists who wrote anti-Isma'ili tracts and pamphlets had a particular goal in mind; they aimed to discredit the Isma'ili movement from its origins. Consequently, they began to produce varied fictitious accounts of the sinister objectives, immoral doctrines and libertine practices of the Isma'ilis, while utilizing every opportunity to refute the Alid descent of the Isma'ili imams. By spreading these accounts, the polemicists gradually created a 'black legend' of Isma'ilism, which was cleverly portrayed as the arch-heresy (*ilhad*) in Islam, carefully designed by some non-Alid imposters, or even Jewish magicians disguised as Muslims, to destroy Islam from within. Soon, these polemical writings came to be accepted as accurate descriptions of Isma'ili motives, beliefs and practices, leading to further anti-Isma'ili polemics and mobilizing the opinion of the Muslim society at large against the Isma'ilis.

Numerous Sunni polemicists, as well as Muslim authors of other genres of writings, contributed to the slanderous literary campaign. In particular, the Abbasids, whose legitimacy had been directly challenged rather successfully by the Fatimids, encouraged and commissioned the systematic composition of polemical treatises against the Isma'iliyya, or the *malahida* as they were now commonly called. The Isma'ilis were designated sometimes also as the Batiniyya, referring essentially to the Isma'ili distinction in the doctrinal domain between the apparent or exoteric (*zahir*) and the hidden or esoteric (*batin*) meanings of the religious scriptures and commandments. This appellation was often taken to imply antinomianism and irreligiosity, because it could easily be misinterpreted to mean that the Isma'ilis laid excessive or even exclusive emphasis on the significance of the *batin* at the expense of the *zahir*, or the letter of the law and the religious duties as specified by the Quran and the sacred law of Islam (*shari'a*).

As a part of the same official anti-Isma'ili campaign, the Abbasid caliph al-Qadir (991–1031) assembled a number of Sunni and Twelver Shi'i scholars at his court in Baghdad and commanded them to declare in a written statement that the contemporary Fatimid caliph al-Hakim and his predecessors lacked genuine Fatimid Alid ancestry. This manifesto, issued in 1011, was read in mosques throughout the Abbasid dominions. In addition, al-Qadir commissioned several theologians to write treatises condemning the Isma'ilis and their doctrines. Starting in 1017, the dissident Druze movement, which propagated the divinity of al-Hakim along with other extremist ideas, split off from Isma'ilism. This movement provided further grounds for confusion and anti-Isma'ili defamation, even though the headquarters of the Fatimid *da'wa* organization at Cairo had officially rejected Druze teachings and the Druzes themselves were suppressed in Fatimid Egypt. In 1052, the Abbasid caliph al-Qa'im (1031–75) sponsored yet another anti-Fatimid manifesto at Baghdad, which again aimed at discrediting the Alid genealogy of the Fatimid dynasty.

Nevertheless, the Fatimid Isma'ili *da'wa* continued to be preached secretly in the Abbasid lands; and its success was briefly crowned in the East during 1058–9 when, due to the pro-Fatimid activities of the Turkish general al-Basasiri in Iraq, Fatimid suzerainty was briefly acknowledged in Baghdad itself, where the Abbasid al-Qa'im was now temporarily held captive. As Isma'ilism continued to spread successfully in Iraq and Persia during the long reign of the Fatimid caliph-imam al-Mustansir (1036–94), the Isma'ilis found a formidable enemy in the Saljuq Turks, the new overlords of the Abbasids who, as the zealous champions of Sunni Islam, intended to rid the Muslim world of the Isma'ilis and the Fatimids. Nizam al-Mulk, the learned vizier of the early Saljuqs and the virtual ruler of the Saljuq dominions for more than two decades, devoted a long section in his *Siyasat-nama* to the denunciation of the Isma'ilis whose object, according to him, was 'to abolish Islam, to mislead mankind and cast them into perdition'.[15] Nizam al-Mulk was certainly echoing an official anti-Isma'ili attitude when he categorically declared that

> never has there been a more sinister, more perverted or more iniquitous crowd than these people, who behind walls are plotting

harm to this country and seeking to destroy the religion . . . and as far as they can they will leave nothing undone in the pursuit of vice, mischief, murder and heresy.[16]

Meanwhile, the Abbasids themselves had continued to encourage the writing of polemical works against the Isma'ilis. The most famous of such works was written by Abu Hamid Muhammad al-Ghazali (d. 1111), the celebrated Sunni theologian, jurist, philosopher and mystic. Al-Ghazali was appointed in 1091 by Nizam al-Mulk to a teaching position at the famous Nizamiyya Madrasa in Baghdad, where he was commissioned by the Abbasid caliph al-Mustazhir (1094–1118) to write a treatise in refutation of the Batinis (Isma'ilis). This work, which became commonly known as *al-Mustazhiri*, was written shortly before al-Ghazali left Baghdad in 1095. Subsequently, al-Ghazali produced several shorter works against the Isma'ilis and the legitimacy of their imam while upholding the rights of the Abbasid caliph to the leadership of the Muslim community.

It was, however, the treatise of a Sunni polemicist which had the greatest and the most enduring impact on the anti-Isma'ili writings of mediaeval Muslim authors. This major protagonist of the anti-Isma'ili 'black legend' was a certain Abu Abd Allah Muhammad b. Rizam al-Ta'i al-Kufi, who flourished in the first half of the tenth century and headed the *mazalim* court for the investigation of public grievances in Baghdad. Ibn Rizam wrote an elaborate treatise in refutation of Isma'ilism shortly after the foundation of the Fatimid caliphate. This treatise, which has not been recovered, was utilized extensively in another anti-Isma'ili book written around 980 by an Alid genealogist and polemicist who lived in Damascus; Abu'l-Husayn Muhammad b. Ali, better known by his nickname of Akhu Muhsin or 'Brother of Muhsin'. Akhu Muhsin's book, too, which contained separate histori-cal and doctrinal parts, has been lost, though substantial portions of it have been preserved by some later Muslim historians, notably al-Nuwayri, Ibn al-Dawadari and al-Maqrizi.

The Ibn Rizam–Akhu Muhsin account, which acquired wide popu-larity, basically portrayed Isma'ilism as a secret conspiracy for the abolition of Islam founded by a non-Alid (Abd Allah b. Maymun al-Qaddah) who was also depicted as the progenitor of the Fatimid caliphs. According to this account, Maymun al-Qaddah was a Bardesanian who became a follower of Abu'l-Khattab and founded a sect called Maymuniyya. His son Abd Allah, who desired to destroy Islam from within, founded the Isma'ili movement with its seven (or nine) grades of initiation culminating in unbelief and atheism. But in order to hide his sinister intentions, Abd Allah pretended to be a Shi'i working on behalf of Muhammad b. Isma'il as the expected Mahdi. Eventually, one of Abd Allah's Qaddahid successors went to North Africa and founded the Fatimid dynasty, claiming to be a descendant of Muhammad b. Isma'il.

Modern scholarship, in clarifying the true biographies of Maymun al-Qaddah and his son Abd Allah, who were loyal companions of the imams al-Baqir and al-Sadiq and lived long before the appearance of the Isma'ili movement, has finally dispelled this most derogatory aspect of the Ibn Rizam–Akhu Muhsin account, designated by W. Ivanow as the myth of Ibn al-Qaddah. At the same time, progress in the study of early Isma'ilism has provided some plausible explanations for the basis of this myth which was originally put into circulation by Ibn Rizam, probably under the influence of anti-Isma'ili ideas propagated by the early Qarmatis.[17] But the majority of later Muslim authors treated this myth as reality and contributed their own interpolations to the catalogue of Ibn al-Qaddah's intellectual ancestry and heresies.[18]

The Ibn Rizam–Akhu Muhsin account was utilized by numerous famous heresiographers, such as al-Baghdadi (d. 1037) who included one of the most hostile descriptions of the Isma'ilis in his *al-Farq bayn al-firaq*. Al-Baghdadi excludes the Isma'ilis (Batinis) from the Islamic community and categorically states that

> the damage caused by the Batiniyya to the Muslim sects is greater than the damage caused them by the Jews, Christians and Magians; nay, graver than the injury inflicted on them by the Materialists and other non-believing sects; nay, graver than the injury resulting to them from the Antichrist who will appear at the end of time.[19]

The same account influenced the anti-Fatimid manifesto of Baghdad, issued in 1011, as well as Nizam al-Mulk's section on the Isma'ilis in his *Siyasat-nama*. It was also drawn upon in the polemics of the Zaydis, including the theological views of al-Haruni al-Husayni (d. 1020), an imam of the Caspian Zaydis who refuted the claims of the Fatimid al-Hakim to the imamate and acknowledged Ibn al-Qaddah as the progenitor of the Fatimids. Al-Kirmani, the most learned Fatimid *da'i* of al-Hakim's time and one of the greatest Isma'ili philosophers who also developed a new Isma'ili Neoplatonic cosmology, wrote a special treatise in response to such Zaydi attacks;[20] it was the same al-Kirmani who was called to Cairo to produce several works in refutation of Druze ideas during the early years of that movement.

The defamatory inventions of Ibn Rizam and Akhu Muhsin also

provided ample material for a number of maliciously travestied accounts of Isma'ili teachings and practices, which for centuries circulated as genuine Isma'ili texts and proved extremely effective in further portraying the Isma'ilis as a community of 'heretics' to other Muslims.[21]

In sum, the 'black legend' invented by the chief anti-Isma'ili polemicists of the tenth century came to be accepted as an accurate description by successive generations of the mediaeval Muslim writers and by Muslim society at large; Muslims were now prepared to apply any term of abuse to the Isma'ilis, even before Nizari Isma'ilis themselves became targets for particular defamations. It was within such a hostile milieu that the Europeans of the Crusader and later times began their superficial investigation of the Nizari Isma'ilis, adding their own legends to the catalogue of heresies and absurd practices attributed to the Isma'ilis. In time, these hostile and fanciful eastern and western sources provided the basis of the Isma'ili studies of the orientalists of the nineteenth century.

In a sense, the Isma'ilis almost seem to have been destined to be misrepresented and misjudged. This is rather ironic in view of the extensive literature they themselves produced throughout their history, especially during the Fatimid period.[22] Indeed, while Ibn Rizam, Akhu Muhsin, al-Baghdadi and many other anti-Isma'ili writers were busy inventing their elaborate and imaginative myths, a vast volume of literature was being produced in Persia and elsewhere by celebrated Isma'ili theologians and philosophers such as al-Sijistani, al-Kirmani and Nasir-i Khusraw, who were at the same time functioning as capable *da'i*s spreading the cause of the Fatimid caliph-imams and their religio-political *da'wa*. Meanwhile, starting with the work of the Qadi al-Nu'man (d. 974), the foremost Fatimid jurist, the Isma'ili Shi'i system of law was elaborated under the Fatimids, who placed equal emphasis on the literal meaning as well as the hidden significance and inner spirituality of the Quran and the religious commandments of Islam.

As a rare instance of its kind in the history of Isma'ilism, the Isma'ili imams, who ruled over the Fatimid state and desired the events of their dynasty and *dawla* to be recorded by trustworthy chroniclers, also concerned themselves with historical writings. They commissioned or encouraged the compilation of chronicles of the Fatimid dynasty and histories of the Fatimid state, especially after transferring the seat of their caliphate to Egypt in 973. Many chroniclers contributed to this temporary tradition of Isma'ili historiography.[23] These Fatimid chronicles, a few of which have survived in fragmentary form or in

quotations by later historians, were readily available to all contemporary Muslim authors living within and outside the Fatimid
dominions.

With the fall of the Fatimid dynasty in 1171, however, their
renowned libraries were effectively destroyed, while the Isma'ilis and
their religious literature were severely suppressed in Egypt during the
subsequent Ayyubid and Mamluk periods. But a few decades earlier, a
good portion of the Isma'ili literature of the Fatimid period found its
way to Yaman, from where it was subsequently transmitted to India.
This explains why many Fatimid Isma'ili texts of a philosophical or
theological nature remain extant while the Fatimid chronicles, compiled
at different times, have not survived.

There have also always been available valuable archival documents
for the Fatimid state, as well as various non-literary sources of
information on the Fatimids. Nevertheless, historians, like other
Muslim writers of mediaeval times, preferred to retain their own hostile
approaches rooted mainly in the misconceptions and defamations of
anti-Isma'ili polemics.

The Isma'ili movement was rent by a major schism in 1094, which
had drastic consequences for its future. During the long reign of the
Fatimid caliph-imam al-Mustansir (1036–94), the caliphate had already
begun its general decline, especially after the 1050s. The dispute over
al-Mustansir's succession in 1094 split the Isma'ili movement itself into
two rival branches, the Nizaris and the Musta'lians.

Al-Mustansir had designated his eldest son Abu Mansur Nizar as his
successor. However, al-Afdal, who a few months before al-Mustansir's
death had succeeded his own father, Badr al-Jamali, as the all-powerful
vizier and military dictator of the Fatimid state, had different plans.
Aiming to retain the reins of the state, al-Afdal favoured the succession
of al-Mustansir's youngest son Abu'l-Qasim Ahmad, who would be
entirely dependent upon him. At the time, the youthful Ahmad was
married to al-Afdal's sister. At any rate, in what amounted to a palace
coup d'état, al-Afdal placed Ahmad on the Fatimid throne with the title
of al-Musta'li billah, speedily obtaining the endorsement of this act
from the notables of the Fatimid state and the leaders of the Isma'ili
da'wa organization in Cairo.

The dispossessed Nizar, whose succession rights were never revoked
by his father, hurriedly fled to Alexandria, where he received strong
local support and rose in revolt. After some initial success, however, his
revolt was crushed in 1095. Nizar himself was captured and taken to
Cairo where he was executed on al-Musta'li's orders. As a result of
these developments, the unified Isma'ili movement of the latter decades

of al-Mustansir's rule was now split into two rival factions, which were to remain bitter enemies. The imamate of al-Musta'li, who had been firmly installed to the Fatimid caliphate, was recognized by the bulk of the Isma'ilis in Egypt, by many in Syria, and by the whole Isma'ili community in Yaman and its subsidiary Indian community in Gujarat. These Isma'ilis, known as the Musta'liyya, maintained their relations with the central headquarters of the *da'wa* in Cairo. On the other hand, almost all the Isma'ili communities of the Muslim East, headed by the Persian Isma'ilis who were already under the leadership of Hasan Sabbah, as well as a large number in Syria, upheld Nizar's succession rights, recognizing him as their nineteenth imam in succession to his father. These Isma'ilis, known as the Nizariyya, permanently severed their relations with the Fatimids and Cairo, which had now become the seat of the Musta'lian *da'wa*.

Al-Musta'li remained a puppet in the hands of al-Afdal throughout his short reign (1094–1101), during which the Crusaders first appeared (in 1097) in the Levant to liberate the Holy Land of Christendom. The Crusaders easily defeated a local Fatimid garrison and then seized their main target, Jerusalem, in 1099. By 1100, the Crusaders had firmly established themselves in Palestine, and had founded several principalities based on Jerusalem and other localities in Palestine and Syria. In the midst of the Fatimids' continued attempts to repel the Crusaders, al-Musta'li died in 1101. Al-Afdal now proclaimed al-Musta'li's five-year-old son as the new Fatimid caliph with the title of al-Amir bi-Ahkam Allah, and himself retained the reins of the state for another 20 years until his assassination in 1121.

During the reign of al-Amir, when the Nizaris were successfully consolidating their power in Persia and Syria, an assembly was convened in 1122 in the Fatimid palace in Cairo to publicize the rights of al-Musta'li and al-Amir to the Isma'ili imamate and to refute the competing claims of Nizar and his descendants. The proceedings of this assembly were subsequently committed to writing in the form of an epistle which has survived under the title of *al-Hidaya al-Amiriyya*, or the 'Guidance according to al-Amir'. This epistle, which was read from pulpits throughout Fatimid Egypt, represents the earliest official Musta'lian refutation of the Nizari claims to the imamate.[24] The *Hidaya* was also sent to Syria, where it caused uproar among the Nizaris of Damascus. One of the Syrian Nizaris forwarded al-Amir's epistle to his chief, who wrote a refutation of it. Soon afterwards, al-Amir issued an additional epistle, refuting the Nizari refutation of *al-Hidaya*.[25] The Isma'ilis were now embarked on their own internal polemics, to the joy of the rest of Muslim society. It is interesting to note that in al-Amir's second anti-Nizari epistle, issued early in 1123 and sent to Syria, the Nizari Isma'ilis were for the first time designated as the 'Hashishiyya', without any explanation.[26]

With the assassination of al-Amir in 1130, at the hands of a group of Nizari *fida'i*s or devotees, the internal situation of Fatimid Egypt deteriorated rapidly, and soon afterwards the Musta'lian Isma'ilis themselves were rent by an important schism, which split their community into Hafizi and Tayyibi factions. Al-Amir's successor al-Hafiz (1130–49) and the later Fatimid caliphs were acknowledged as imams by the official *da'wa* organization in Cairo and by the majority of the Musta'lian Isma'ilis of Egypt and Syria, as well as by some of the Musta'lians of Yaman. However, Hafizi Isma'ilism did not survive long after the collapse of the Fatimid dynasty.

During the final decade of Fatimid rule, Egypt was invaded several times by Crusader armies under the command of King Amalric I of Jerusalem, while Nur al-Din, the Sunni Zangid ruler of Aleppo, pursued plans of his own for annexing Egypt to his dominions and uprooting the Shi'i Fatimids. Eventually, Nur al-Din gained the upper hand in Egypt; in 1169, Shirkuh entered Cairo at the head of the third Zangid expedition dispatched from Syria and appointed himself vizier of the last Fatimid caliph al-Adid. When Shirkuh died suddenly shortly afterwards, his nephew Salah al-Din Yusuf b. Ayyub, or Saladin of the European sources, succeeded to that post.

Saladin, the last Fatimid vizier and the founder of the Ayyubid dynasty, put an end to Fatimid rule in September 1171 when he deposed al-Adid and proclaimed the suzerainty of the Abbasids. In the immediate aftermath of the collapse of the Fatimid dynasty, the Isma'ilis of Egypt, belonging mainly to the Hafizi branch, were persecuted severely and the claimants to the Hafizi imamate along with other surviving members of the Fatimid family were detained in captivity. By the time the Fatimid prisoners were finally released a century later in 1272, Isma'ilism had disappeared almost completely from Egypt.

Tayyibi Isma'ilism fared better, however, and Tayyibis have survived to the present time as the sole representatives of the Musta'lian branch of Isma'ilism. With the establishment of an independent Tayyibi *da'wa* in Yaman, headed by an absolute *da'i*, or *da'i mutlaq*, soon after al-Amir's death, Yaman remained for several centuries the chief strong-hold of the Tayyibi Isma'ilis, whose imams have remained hidden and inaccessible since the disappearance of al-Amir's infant son, al-Tayyib, in 1130. In time, the Tayyibi *da'wa* succeeded in winning numerous converts from among the members of a trading community in western

India, where the Tayyibi converts became locally designated as Bohras. In 1591, the Tayyibi community, then represented mainly by the Bohras of Gujarat, was split into two factions, the Da'udis and the Sulaymanis, who henceforth followed different lines of *da'is*. The Indian Tayyibis, belonging mainly to the Da'udi branch, have experienced a few minor schisms in the course of their history. By contrast, the minority Sulaymani community, centred in Yaman, has maintained its unity.

In the meantime, the Nizaris, now representing the politically active branch of Isma'ilism, were successfully extending their movement in the East, throughout the Saljuq lands. As noted, by the final decades of al-Mustansir's imamate, the Isma'ilis of Persia and other parts of the Muslim East had largely rallied to the side of the Fatimid *da'wa*, while the ardently Sunni Saljuqids had replaced various local dynasties in those regions. At least by the early 1070s, the Isma'ilis of Persia owned the authority of a chief local *da'i*, Ibn Attash, who had his headquarters at Isfahan in central Persia. Ibn Attash was also responsible for launching the career of Hasan Sabbah, the first leader of the Nizari Isma'ilis.

Hasan Sabbah, born into a Twelver Shi'i family in Qumm, in central Persia, converted to Isma'ilism in his youth, and by 1072 he had been appointed to a post in Rayy in the service of the Isma'ili *da'wa*. Later, in 1076, he set off for Egypt, where he spent three years furthering his training. Returning to Isfahan in 1081, Hasan spent the next nine years travelling to different localities in Persia as a secret Isma'ili *da'i*. He was now, in fact, reinvigorating the Isma'ili cause in Persia while planning to launch an open revolt there against the alien rule of the Saljuq Turks; an objective that also reflected the general Persian sentiments of the time. At any rate, in his travels Hasan carefully searched for a suitable site which could be utilized as the headquarters of his revolutionary movement, while simultaneously assessing the political and military power of the Saljuqs in different localities. Eventually Hasan's attention came to be concentrated on the Caspian provinces in northern Persia, the mediaeval region of Daylam, which had traditionally been a safe haven for the Alids and a stronghold of Zaydi Shi'ism. There he selected the castle of Alamut, situated on a high rock in the central Alburz mountains, to the north-east of the city of Qazwin; and it did not take him long to gain possession of that mountain fortress. The seizure of Alamut in 1090 by Hasan Sabbah initiated the open anti-Saljuq activities of the Persian Isma'ilis, also marking the effective foundation of what was to become the Nizari Isma'ili state.[27]

Once established at Alamut, which was to remain the central headquarters of the Nizari movement until its surrender to the Mongols in 1256, Hasan Sabbah systematically renovated the old fortress, making it truly impregnable. He also improved and extended the systems of irrigation and cultivation in the Alamut valley, where he dug water canals and planted numerous trees. It was in this same locality that, according to the legendary account of Marco Polo, a secret 'garden of paradise' had been built by the leader of the Isma'ilis.[28]

Hasan seized or constructed many other mountain strongholds in northern Persia and in a few other regions, notably in southern Khurasan, known then as Kuhistan (Arabicized, Quhistan), where the Isma'ilis came to control a number of towns as well. By 1092, Hasan Sabbah's activities had already attracted so much attention that the Saljuq sultan Malikshah (1072–92) decided, probably on the advice of his vizier Nizam al-Mulk, to send armies against the Isma'ilis of northern Persia and Khurasan, initiating the first of numerous military encounters between the Persian Isma'ilis and the Saljuqs.

As Hasan Sabbah was consolidating his position in Persia, Isma'ilism came to be confronted with its greatest internal conflict, the Nizari–Musta'li schism. As noted, Hasan Sabbah acknowledged the rights of Nizar to the imamate, and his decision was endorsed without any dissent by the entire Isma'ili community of Persia and also by the Isma'ilis of Iraq and by many Syrian Isma'ilis who, like their Persian co-religionists, were then under Saljuq rule.

Soon afterwards, from the beginning of the twelfth century, Hasan Sabbah began to dispatch da'is to Syria to organize and lead the Nizaris there. The political and religious fragmentation of Syria at the time as well as the religious traditions of the region, where almost all types of Shi'i and Sunni communities had existed, also favoured the spread of the Nizari da'wa. The appearance of the Crusaders in the Levant, which accentuated the local rivalries in Syria, and the rapid collapse of Fatimid rule under al-Mustansir's successors, further contributed to the eventual success there of the Nizaris.[29]

From early on, the Persian emissaries who were dispatched from Alamut for organizing and leading the Syrian Nizaris used the same methods of struggle as devised by Hasan Sabbah for the Persian community. Accordingly, they attempted to seize strategic strongholds for use as bases of military operations, and resorted to political assassination, in addition to allying themselves with various local rulers when such temporary alliances seemed expedient. However, the Nizaris found their task in Syria much more difficult than it had been in Persia. In fact, the Nizaris had to struggle for almost half a century, first from

Aleppo and then from Damascus, before they finally succeeded during a third phase of their operations (1130–51) in acquiring a number of fortresses in a mountainous area of central Syria known as the Jabal Bahra. These fortresses, including Qadmus, Kahf and Masyaf, which often served as the headquarters of the chief Nizari leader in Syria, became collectively designated as the *qila al-da'wa*, 'fortresses of the da'wa'.[30]

Meanwhile, in the absence of the Nizari imams, who remained hidden from their followers for several decades after Nizar's death in 1095, Hasan Sabbah, and then his next two successors at Alamut, were acknowledged as the supreme central leaders of the Nizari community and *da'wa*; they were the *hujjas* or chief representatives of the absent imams (similarly, the central leaders of the early Isma'ili movement had originally acted as the *hujjas* of the hidden Mahdi, Muhammad b. Isma'il). The early Nizari Isma'ilis had also retrieved, with much greater militancy, the revolutionary and millenarian zeal of the pre-Fatimid Isma'ili movement. In both cases, the Isma'ilis represented the politically most active wing of Shi'ism and, as such, they dedicated themselves to the overthrow of the leading established dynasties of the time, notably the Abbasids and their later overlords, the Saljuqids.

Hasan Sabbah had now founded an independent religio-political Isma'ili mission, designated as the 'new preaching' (*al-da'wa al-jadida*) by outsiders. From early on, the revolutionary ardour and psychological self-assessment of the Nizari Isma'ilis also found expression in the doctrinal domain. Hasan Sabbah reiterated the permanent need of mankind for a divinely guided and authoritative teacher, which had constituted the central belief of the Shi'a at least from the time of the imam Ja'far al-Sadiq. In a series of propositions, Hasan reformulated this old Shi'i doctrine of *ta'lim*, and concluded that only the Isma'ili imam was such an authoritative teacher and the sole legitimate leader of mankind; this doctrine also served to refute, in a new theological and philosophical manner, the similar claims of the Abbasid caliph of Baghdad as well as those of the non-Isma'ili Shi'i imams. It was due to the centrality of this doctrine in early Nizari thought that the Nizari Isma'ilis now became generally designated also as the Ta'limiyya.

In the political field, as noted, Hasan Sabbah initiated a policy of armed revolt against the Saljuqs, who were backed by the Sunni establishment under the titular leadership of the Abbasid caliph. The Nizari revolt and methods of struggle had their distinctive features and patterns, which were dictated by the vastly superior military power of the Saljuqs and the decentralized nature of their power. Under such conditions, the Nizari revolt came to be conducted from a multiplicity of mountain strongholds, each stronghold at once serving as a defensible abode or refuge (*dar al-hijra*) for the Nizaris and as headquarters for the local operations of their armed groups. At the same time, the local activities of all such Isma'ili groups were well coordinated by the central leadership of the movement at Alamut. The decentralized pattern of Saljuq power suggested to Hasan Sabbah an important auxiliary technique for achieving military and political aims, that of assassination. It was in connection with the self-sacrificing behaviour of the Nizari *fida'is*, who killed prominent opponents of their community in particular localities, that the main myths of the Nizaris, the Assassin legends, were developed during the Middle Ages. The Nizaris of the Alamut period were not the inventors of the policy of assassinating religio-political adversaries in Muslim society; nor were they the last group to resort to such a policy; but they did assign a major political role to the policy of assassination, which they utilized rather openly in a spectacular and intimidating fashion. As a result, almost any assassination of any religious, political or military significance during the Alamut period was attributed to them. This provided a most convenient pretext for other individuals or groups to remove their own enemies, resting assured that the Nizaris would be blamed.

The Nizari assassinations were carried out by their *fida'is*, also called *fidawis*, the young self-sacrificing devotees who offered themselves for such suicidal missions. The assassinations of famous military or civilian personalities, who were normally surrounded by guards, were more often than not carried out in mosques and other public places, since part of this policy was to intimidate other enemies. Few details are known about the selection and training of the Nizari *fida'is*, who were glorified by their co-religionists as heroes for their bravery and devotion.[31] Rolls of honour of their names and assassination missions were compiled and retained at Alamut and other Nizari fortresses. It is doubtful whether the *fida'is* formed a special corps in Persia, while in Syria the Nizari *fida'is* were organized, at least for a time, into a special corps. The *fida'is* do not seem to have received any training in languages and other subjects, as suggested by the elaborate accounts of some occidental chroniclers of the Crusaders and later European writers. But at some point during the Alamut period, the practice evidently arose of sending some would-be assassins, under different guises, into the households of a number of the more notorious enemies of the sect. Such undercover agents were placed in an ideal position of readiness for possible assassination missions, and rumours about their existence would prove rather intimidating.

As we shall see, designations such as *hashishiyya*, *hashishiyyin*, or *hashishin* (singular, *hashishi*), meaning supposedly hashish users, which were originally applied as terms of abuse to the Nizari Isma'ilis by their Muslim opponents, in time found particular application to the Nizari *fida'is* whose conduct seemed extraordinary to westerners. However, despite the existence of such terms of abuse and the related mediaeval legends fabricated by uninformed observers and writers, there is no evidence suggesting that hashish or any other narcotic product was ever administered to motivate the *fida'is* or condition them to perform their dangerous tasks. On the contrary, the *fida'is*, who displayed an intensive group sentiment and sense of devotion in both Persia and Syria, were highly alert and sober individuals who often had to wait patiently and for extended periods in order to find a suitable opportunity to accomplish their missions. Indeed, the available evidence indicates that the Nizari *fida'is* were young devotees who personally volunteered to sacrifice their lives, as a matter of conviction, in the service of their religion and community.

The armed revolt of the Nizaris, with the spectacular assassinations attributed to them, posed a mounting threat to the Sunni establishment and speedily qualified the Nizaris as a new Isma'ili target for persecution and refutation by the Muslim majority. The vizier Nizam al-Mulk, who was assassinated in 1092, possibly by a Nizari *fida'i*,[32] had already alarmed his Saljuqid master of the imminent danger of the rising power of the Persian Isma'ilis. At any rate, by condemning the Isma'ilis in the strongest possible terms in his *Siyasat-nama (The Book of Government)*, Nizam al-Mulk had in fact signalled the beginning of a new era in the persecution of the Isma'ilis and the literary campaign against them within Muslim society. From the earliest years of the Nizari state, the Saljuqs sent military expeditions against their territories in northern Persia and in Khurasan. Despite their overwhelming military power, however, the Saljuqs failed to defeat the Nizaris on the battlefield, mainly due to the astonishing solidarity of the Nizaris and the impregnability of their scattered mountain strongholds. As a result, the Saljuqs and their Sunni judges adopted an auxiliary policy of their own: large-scale massacres of the Nizari Isma'ilis. It became an established practice in many urban localities to round up all those accused of being Isma'ili and to consign them to fire or put them to the sword, especially in the aftermath of a Nizari-suspected assassination. Large numbers of Nizaris were thus massacred, and their properties confiscated, in great cities like Aleppo, Damascus, Qazwin and Isfahan, the main Saljuq capital in Persia, as well as in the towns of southern Khurasan and elsewhere. New records were eventually set in such massacres by the Mongols, who practically exterminated the

entire Persian Nizari community. Meanwhile, the Nizaris had continued to consolidate their position and expand their network of
strongholds under Hasan Sabbah (d. 1124) and his next two successors, Kiya Buzurg-Ummid (1124–38) and Muhammad b. Buzurg-
Ummid (1138–62).

The Muslim opponents of the Nizaris, whose hostility towards the
Isma'ilis in general had now been rekindled at a higher level, were
much more successful in their anti-Nizari literary campaign. This vast
and semi-official campaign, involving polemicists, heresiographers,
theologians, jurists and historians, which was rooted in the earlier anti-
Isma'ili 'black legend', went a long way towards shaping the anti-
Nizari opinion of mediaeval Muslims. It succeeded in making the
Nizaris perhaps the most feared community in the mediaeval Islamic
world.

The Abbasids now began, as they had done in the case of the
Fatimids, to sponsor polemical treatises in refutation of the Nizari
Isma'ilis and their doctrines. Highly imaginative accounts of Nizari
heresies and libertine practices began to pour forth, essentially
depicting the sectarians as a group of immoral assassins who were
capable of any sort of crime or mischievous act desired by their cunning
leaders. In this category, the earliest and one of the most widely
circulated anti-Isma'ili books, was al-Ghazali's *al-Mustazhiri* which
was in fact mainly directed against the Nizaris and their doctrine of
ta'lim, or authoritative teaching in religion. Al-Ghazali concocted his
own elaborate 'Nizari system' of graded teaching and indoctrination,
which would allow for any conceivable heresy before leading the
initiate to an ultimate stage of unbelief and atheism.[33] Al-Ghazali's
anti-Isma'ili defamations were adopted and reformulated during the
Alamut period by other Sunni writers, all of whom were also
acquainted to various degrees with the myths fabricated by Ibn Rizam
and Akhu Muhsin.

The Shi'is indulged in their own anti-Nizari polemics. The Imami or
Twelver Shi'i writers, constituting a quiescent minority in the predominantly Sunni Persia until the sixteenth century, produced several
treatises in refutation of the Nizaris and their competing claims to the
Shi'i imamate; while the Imami scholars living during the Alamut
period generally denounced the Nizaris as *malahida* par excellence. For
instance, Abd al-Jalil Qazwini Razi, a renowned Imami scholar of the
twelfth century, wrote a major treatise in refutation of the Nizaris
which is lost. He also attacks the Nizaris extensively throughout his
only extant work, *Kitab al-naqd*, which is a detailed refutation of a
polemical work written against Imami Shi'ism by a former member of

that community. Reiterating many of the anti-Ismaʻili stances of Ibn Rizam and Akhu Muhsin, Abd al-Jalil concluded that the Ismaʻilis were worse than unbelievers.[34] This damaging verdict was repeated in many other anti-Nizari polemics of the period.

The Zaydi Shiʻis, who were the closest rivals of the Nizaris in northern Persia and had prolonged military confrontations with them in the Caspian region, launched their own anti-Nizari literary campaign. It has recently come to light that the Caspian Zaydis, too, referred to the Persian Nizaris as 'Hashishis' in some of their early thirteenth-century writings.[35]

These generally hostile attitudes found expression to various degrees also in the works of Muslim historians. For the history of the Persian Nizaris of the Alamut period, the chief authorities are three Persian historians of the Ilkhanid period (1256–1353), namely Juwayni, Rashid al-Din Fadl Allah and Kashani, who had direct access to certain contemporary Nizari chronicles and other sources which are no longer extant. Of these three, Juwayni, who had accompanied his master Hulagu in his campaigns against Alamut and other Persian Nizari strongholds in 1256, was particularly hostile towards the Nizaris, doubtless desiring to please Hulagu who had aimed to extirpate the Nizari community. The Persian Nizaris are treated with equal vindictiveness in the chronicles of the Saljuqs, their arch-enemies. It is interesting to note that, in one of the few surviving written instances of its kind, the Syrian Nizaris are referred to as 'Hashishiyya' in the earliest known Saljuq chronicle, the *Nusrat al-fatra*, written in 1183 by Imad al-Din Muhammad al-Katib al-Isfahani (d. 1201), a work that is extant only in an abridgement completed in 1226 by al-Bundari.[36]

The Syrian Nizaris of the Alamut period, too, are treated with contempt in numerous contemporary or later regional histories of Syria.[37] In this category, Abu Shama (1203–67), who lived in the time of the Sunni Ayyubids and Mamluks, is evidently the only Syrian chronicler to refer to the Syrian Nizaris with the designation of 'Hashishiyya' (singular, 'Hashishi').[38] Abu Shama was used as a main source by Silvestre de Sacy for his etymological explanation of the word assassin. Ibn Muyassar (d. 1278), who produced an extensive history of Fatimid Egypt during the second half of the thirteenth century under the early Mamluks, is one of the few other Arab historians of that period to use the term *hashishiyya* in reference to the Syrian Nizaris.[39] The Syrian Nizaris, and to a lesser extent their Persian co-religionists, are also discussed with hostility in the general Arabic chronicles, including the celebrated *Taʼrikh* of Ibn al-Athir (d. 1233), representing the zenith of Muslim annalistic historiography. It is, therefore, not surprising that the Nizaris, the targets of so much animosity and abuse, came to be commonly designated by all sorts of derogatory terms such as *malahida* and *hashishiyya*. It was under such circumstances that imaginative tales and legends about them began to be circulated.

The Nizaris of the Alamut period themselves made no special efforts to dispel their distorted image within Muslim society. Modern scholarship has made it abundantly clear, however, that the Nizaris were definitely not an 'order of assassins' bent on destroying Islam. Their community was, and remained, a Shi'i Muslim community led initially by *da'is* and then, after 1164, by the Nizari imams themselves. This highly disciplined community, scattered in different territories stretching from Syria to eastern Persia, managed to establish and maintain a cohesive state, centrally directed from Alamut, despite formidable odds. In the doctrinal domain, the Nizaris adhered to Shi'i teachings, with a central role assigned to their imam. In the imam's absence, his chief representatives were followed with as much devotion and obedience. In addition, they encouraged and patronized the intellectual activities of numerous non-Isma'ili scholars who had found refuge among them.

Hasan Sabbah, the founder of this community and state, was at once a strategist, an administrator and a thinker who led a highly ascetic life and enforced the sacred law of Islam very strictly throughout his community. Possessing an unrivalled sense of purpose, he was highly revered by the Nizaris, who called him *sayyidna*, 'our lord'; and his grave at Alamut became a place of pilgrimage for the Nizaris until it, too, was destroyed by the Mongols in 1256. Hasan produced some doctrinal treatises in which he set down the religious guidelines of the Nizari Isma'ili community. However, the Nizaris, initially conducting an armed revolt and always extremely concerned with their survival in different hostile milieus, did not have time for complex theological or philosophical speculations. In a sense, the intellectual activities of the Nizaris were by and large geared to the more pressing and practical needs of their state and struggle; and the Nizari *da'is* often acted as military commanders of the various strongholds. As a result, the Nizaris never produced a voluminous religious literature.[40] The few Nizari texts which were actually composed during that turbulent period do not seem to have been readily accessible to outsiders, with whom the sectarians rarely discussed their doctrines. Thus, the Nizaris themselves unwittingly encouraged the fabrication of Nizari tales and the unfounded accusations levelled against them.

Like their predecessors on the Fatimid throne, the Persian lords of

Alamut, too, sponsored the compilation of official chronicles recording the detailed history of the Persian Nizari community and state. These chronicles, few in number and arranged in terms of the reigns of the successive lords of Alamut, starting with the *Sargudhasht-i Sayyidna* which covered the life and times of Hasan Sabbah, represented another rare and temporary tradition of Isma'ili historiography.[41] The official Nizari chronicles and other Nizari sources and documents, including the decrees and epistles (*fusul*) of the imams, were seen and utilized extensively by that group of Persian historians of the Ilkhanid period already mentioned, namely, Juwayni (d. 1283), Rashid al-Din Fadl Allah (d. 1318), and Kashani (d. ca. 1337). Juwayni was an eyewitness to the Mongol invasions of Persia and personally participated in the final negotiations between Hulagu and the Nizari leadership, leading to the downfall of the Nizari state there. He relates how, with Hulagu's permission, he examined the celebrated Isma'ili library at Alamut, from where he selected many 'choice books', before consigning to the flames those treatises which, in his view, related to the heresy and error of the Isma'ilis. Utilizing the Nizari sources at his disposal, Juwayni produced an account of the Nizari state at the end of his history of the Mongols and their conquests, soon after the fall of Alamut.[42] Interspersing his narrative with an arsenal of invectives and defamatory epithets, Juwayni missed no opportunity to express his contempt for the Nizaris and their leaders.

The Isma'ili histories of Rashid al-Din, the famous Sunni historian, vizier and physician, and Kashani, who was a Twelver Shi'i and participated in the compilation of Rashid al-Din's vast universal history (*Jami al-tawarikh*), are more detailed and less hostile than Juwayni's account.[43] Both these historians quote extensively from the Nizari chronicles of the Alamut period, often also naming their sources. All the Nizari sources utilized by these historians perished in Mongol Persia; and, thus, their histories of the Persian Nizari state and community during the Alamut period remain our chief sources for the subject.

The Nizari community of the Alamut period, comprised of high-landers and mountain dwellers, villagers, and urban groups in small towns, did nevertheless maintain a sophisticated outlook and literary tradition, also valuing intellectual and scientific activities in general. Hasan Sabbah himself founded a renowned library at Alamut, whose collections of Isma'ili and non-Isma'ili works had grown impressively by the time the Mongols destroyed it. In Khurasan and Syria, too, the Nizaris established libraries, containing not only religious and historical works of all sorts, but also archival documents, and scientific tracts and equipment. The Nizaris, thus, manifested genuine interest in different branches of learning and Islamic sciences, despite their long-drawn military entanglements with Saljuqs and other adversaries. This explains why many Muslim scholars, both Sunni and Twelver Shi'i, and even Jewish scientists, availed themselves of the Nizari libraries and patronage of learning. Some of these outside scholars, who played an active part in the intellectual life of the Nizari community, even converted to Isma'ilism, at least temporarily. The most prominent member of this special group was the celebrated philosopher, theologian and astronomer Nasir al-Din al-Tusi (1201–74), who was originally a Twelver Shi'i. He spent some three decades (1227–56) among the Nizaris of Khurasan and northern Persia, during which time he embraced Isma'ilism; and he was with the last lord of Alamut when the latter surrendered to the Mongols. It was during this period that al-Tusi produced some of his best known works, such as the *Akhlaq-i Nasiri* (*The Nasirean Ethics*), as well as several Isma'ili treatises, which remain our main sources of information on the Nizari teachings of the late Alamut period. On the fall of Alamut, al-Tusi entered the service of Hulagu, and later became a vizier to the Mongol Ilkhanids.

The Nizaris also developed their mountain enclaves, consisting of fortresses with their surrounding villages, into viable socio-economic and military entities, utilizing highly ingenious techniques in their water supply and fortification systems. Surely the Nizari heritage should not be based solely or even chiefly on their much publicized religio-political assassinations and the related Assassin legends.

In the meantime, the Nizaris had entered a period of stalemate in their relations with the Saljuqs; both the Nizari revolt initiated by Hasan Sabbah and the Saljuq offensive against them having proved ineffective. The Nizaris did not, however, abandon the ultimate objectives of their political struggle, and they managed to hold on to their strongholds in Persia and Syria. In the event, the Nizari community had now transformed itself into a permanent state, taking its precarious place among the small states and territorial principalities within the Saljuq realm. At the same time, the Nizaris had been waiting impatiently, since Nizar's death, for the appearance of their imam, who would personally take charge of their leadership and guide them in those troubled times.

It was under these circumstances that the fourth ruler of Alamut, Hasan II (1162–6), whom the Nizaris designated *ala dhikrihi'l-salam* (on his mention be peace), initiated a religious revolution in the community. On 8 August 1164, in a solemn ceremony held at Alamut in the presence of the representatives of different Nizari territories,

Hasan II proclaimed the *qiyama* or Resurrection which ushered a second phase in the life of the Nizari Isma'ilis of the Alamut period. The *qiyama*, the awaited 'last day' when mankind would be judged and committed for ever to either Paradise or Hell, was however interpreted spiritually on the basis of the well-known Isma'ili method of *ta'wil* (esoteric interpretation). Accordingly, the *qiyama* was essentially held to mean the manifestation of the unveiled truth in the person of the Nizari imam. Only the Nizaris were now capable of comprehending spiritual reality, the immutable truths hidden behind all the religious laws; and, as such, Paradise was made real for them in this world. By contrast, all others, non-Nizari Muslims as well as non-Muslims, who did not accord recognition to the Nizari imam, were henceforth cast into eternal Hell, which was in effect a state of spiritual non-existence. In sum, the Nizaris were now collectively introduced into Paradise on earth, while the rest of mankind was made non-existent and irrelevant. Soon, the Nizaris recognized Hasan II and his son and successor Nur al-Din Muhammad II (1166–1210), as their imams from the progeny of Nizar. Muhammad II devoted his long reign to the elaboration of the doctrine of the *qiyama* while the Nizaris were increasingly isolating themselves in their mountain strongholds from the rest of Muslim society. Juwayni and other Persian historians also relate that in line with the expectations regarding the time of Resurrection, the sacred law of Islam was abrogated in the Nizari community. The believers, as was fitting in Paradise, could henceforth dispense with the obligations specified by the letter of the law, since they had now found access to the meanings hidden behind those commandments. According to Rashid al-Din and Kashani, it was due to their alleged abolition of the law that the Nizaris qualified themselves more precisely for the term *malahida*.

In Syria, the *qiyama* phase in Nizari history coincided with the career of Rashid al-Din Sinan, the most famous Nizari leader there. Sinan, known to the Crusaders as the 'Old Man of the Mountain', reorganized the Syrian Nizari community, also fortifying their strongholds. He adopted suitable policies and shifting alliances in dealing with the various regional rulers and powers, including the Crusaders and Saladin who was then leading the Muslim holy war against the Crusaders.

Sinan established peaceful relations with the Crusaders, who had periodical entanglements with the Nizaris over the possession of various strongholds. Meanwhile, the Syrian Nizaris had acquired a more serious Frankish enemy in the Hospitallers, who in 1142 had received from the lord of Tripoli the celebrated fortress of Krak des Chevaliers at the southern end of the Jabal Bahra. The Nizaris

continued to have periodic confrontations with the Knights Hospitaller
and Knights Templar (Hospitallers and Templars), military orders
which acted rather independently in the Latin East. In 1173, Sinan sent
an embassy to Amalric I, evidently seeking formal rapprochement with
the Latin kingdom of Jerusalem. As Amalric died soon afterwards in
1174, however, negotiations between the Franks and the Old Man of
the Mountain proved fruitless.

A few years earlier, in 1171, the Zangids of Aleppo had succeeded
through Saladin in overthrowing the Fatimid dynasty. Subsequently,
Saladin became the champion of Sunnism and Muslim unification and,
as such, he posed a greater threat than the Crusaders to the
independence of the Syrian Nizaris. It was against this background that
Sinan now attempted to have Saladin assassinated. The *fida'is*, however, failed to carry out their missions on two separate occasions during
1174–6, when Saladin was conducting military campaigns in Syria.
Later, Saladin concluded a truce with Sinan, and the Ayyubids actually
extended vital assistance to the Syrian Nizaris in their hours of need.

It also fell upon Sinan to inaugurate the *qiyama* for the Nizari
community in Syria. As reported by Sunni historians, Sinan did
proclaim, some time after 1164, the spiritual Resurrection of the Syrian
Nizari community. There are indications, however, that the doctrine of
the *qiyama* was not fully understood by all the Syrian Nizaris,
particularly by those who lived in the Jabal al-Summaq and in towns to
the south of Aleppo. In 1176, a faction of the Nizaris of those districts
reportedly embarked on a programme of libertinism, attracting the
attention of outsiders and the Sunni historians of Syria such as Ibn al-
Adim (d. 1262).[44] Sinan personally dealt with the dissidents, who had
armed themselves in their mountain strongholds, and ended their
rebellious activities. The Persian Nizaris were not accused of similar
behaviour; and even Juwayni does not report any lawlessness there.
Sinan died in 1192, or 1193, soon after the Syrian *fida'is* had
assassinated their most famous Frankish personality, the marquis
Conrad of Montferrat, King of Jerusalem.

In the third and final phase of their history during the Alamut period,
the Nizaris, who had become increasingly weary of their isolation
within Muslim society, attempted a tactical rapprochement with the
Sunni world. Immediately upon his accession in 1210, Jalal al-Din
Hasan III (1210–21), the sixth lord of Alamut, publicly repudiated the
teachings associated with the declaration of the Resurrection and
proclaimed his adherence to Sunni Islam, ordering his followers to
observe the sacred law of Islam in its Sunni form. The Nizari
community, viewing the unprecedented proclamations of their infallible

imam as a reimposition of dissimulation (*taqiyya*), obeyed Hasan III's orders without dissent. The outside world, too, accepted Hasan III's proclamations; and the Abbasid caliph al-Nasir (1180–1225), who in the aftermath of the disintegration of Saljuq rule was reviving the power and prestige of the caliph at Baghdad, issued a decree confirming the Nizari leader's new policy. Hasan III's bold accommodation to the outside world accorded the Nizari community a valuable respite from the continued Sunni persecutions. During the reign of Hasan III's son and successor, Ala al-Din Muhammad III (1221–55), however, enforcement of Sunni law was gradually relaxed and the Nizari community openly reverted to its earlier traditions.

The long reign of Muhammad III coincided with a turbulent period in the mediaeval history of Persia and the Muslim East, which now experienced a foretaste of the Mongol devastations. Muhammad III attempted in vain for some time to establish friendly relations with the Mongols and to save his community from their wrath. The Mongols had already been turned against the Nizari Isma'ilis by the Sunni scholars at their court; and fresh complaints about them from the Sunni judges of Qazwin and other Persian cities flowed into the Great Khan's court in Mongolia. As a result, when the Great Khan Mongke (1251–9) decided to complete the Mongol conquest of western Asia, he assigned first priority to the destruction of the Nizari community in Persia. In 1252, Mongke entrusted this task to his brother Hulagu, who was to lead a major Mongol expedition against the Nizari strongholds and the Abbasid caliphate, the two powers that still held out in the Muslim lands.

The Mongols had already started to attack the Nizari strongholds in Persia, especially in Khurasan, when Ala al-Din Muhammad III was succeeded in 1255 by his son Rukn al-Din Khurshah, who reigned for just one year as the last ruler of Alamut. After some fierce fighting as well as extended negotiations between the Nizari leadership and Hulagu, who had arrived in Persia at the head of the main Mongol expedition, Khurshah finally surrendered to the Mongols in November 1256. The surrender of the castle of Alamut a month later marked the end of the Persian Nizari state and of the Alamut period in Nizari history. Soon after, the Mongols killed Khurshah, the twenty-seventh Nizari imam, and massacred the Nizari Isma'ilis of Persia wherever they were found. The Syrian Nizaris, demoralized by events in Persia, could not maintain their independence for much longer, even though they had been spared the Mongol catastrophe. In 1273, Kahf was the last of the Syrian strongholds to submit to Baybars I, the Mamluk sultan of Egypt and Syria. Unlike the Mongols in Persia, the Mamluks and their Ottoman successors permitted the Syrian Nizaris to live in their fortresses as a peaceful community.

In Persia, the Nizaris survived the Mongol massacres and many of them sought refuge in Afghanistan, India, Badakhshan and other regions of Central Asia. At the same time the Nizari imamate continued in the progeny of Rukh al-Din Khurshah. In the early post-Alamut centuries, however, the Nizari imams, like their followers in most regions, lived clandestinely, often disguising themselves under the mantle of Sufism, then flourishing in Persia. By the later decades of the fifteenth century, the imams who were by then settled at Anjudan, in central Persia, began to revive the Nizari *da'wa* activities. The imams soon succeeded in effectively re-establishing their central control over the various Nizari communities, which had developed independently under the leadership of their own local dynasties of *da'is*. The literary and proselytising activities of the Nizari *da'wa* were also revived now, leading to the appearance of new types of doctrinal works and an increasing number of converts, particularly on the Indian subcontinent. By the second half of the eighteenth century, the Nizari imams had also appeared on the political scene of Persia as regional governors, while the Indian Nizaris, generally known as Khojas, had come to account for a large proportion of the Nizari community.[45]

The seat of the Nizari imamate was transferred permanently from Persia when the forty-sixth Nizari imam, Hasan Ali Shah (1817–81), left his ancestral homeland in 1841 and sought refuge in British India, following his military entanglements with the Persian government; in 1848 he settled in Bombay among his Khoja followers. Hasan Ali Shah, who had acquired the epithet of Mahallati after his earlier place of residence in central Persia, also received the title of Agha Khan (simplified to Aga Khan) from one of the early Qajar monarchs of Persia. The title of Aga Khan has been borne on a hereditary basis by Hasan Ali Shah's descendants who have succeeded to the Nizari imamate. Under the leadership of the two most recent Nizari imams, namely, Sultan Muhammad Shah, Aga Khan III (1885–1957) and his grandson Shah Karim al-Husayni, Aga Khan IV, the forty-ninth and current imam of the community, the Nizari Isma'ilis have entered the modern world as a progressive and prosperous Shi'i Muslim community.

Notes and References

1. For interesting ideas on how the caliphal title may have evolved in early Islam, with concomitant changes in the caliph's religious authority, see P. Crone and

M. Hinds, *God's Caliph: Religious Authority in the First Centuries of Islam*
(Cambridge, 1986). See also H. Dabashi, *Authority in Islam: From the Rise of
Muhammad to the Establishment of the Umayyads* (New Brunswick, NJ,
1989).

2. The classical treatment of these divisions in early Islam and their underlying
causes is contained in J. Wellhausen, *The Religio-Political Factions in Early
Islam*, tr. R.C. Ostle and S.M. Walzer (Amsterdam, 1975).

3. The Shi'i view on the origins and early history of Shi'ism is propounded in
numerous works by Shi'i theologians and authors of mediaeval times. For
instance, see Abu Abd Allah Muhammad b. Muhammad al-Mufid, *Kitab al-
Irshad*, tr. I.K.A. Howard (London, 1981). The best modern exposition of this
view in the English language may be found in Sayyid Muhammad Husayn
Tabataba'i, *Shi'ite Islam*, ed. and tr. S.H. Nasr (London 1975), especially
pp 39–50, 173 ff. For general surveys of Shi'ism, see S. Husain M. Jafri,
Origins and Early Development of Shi'a Islam (London, 1979); M. Momen,
An Introduction to Shi'i Islam (New Haven, 1985), concentrating on Twelver
Shi'ism; and H. Halm, *Shiism*, tr. J. Watson (Edinburgh, 1991).

4. Claude Cahen, 'Points du vue sur la Révolution Abbaside', *Revue Historique*,
230 (1960), pp 295–338, reprinted in his *Les peuples Musulmans dans
l'histoire médiévale* (Damascus, 1977), pp 105–60; T. Nagel, *Untersuchungen
zur Entstehung des abbasidischen Kalifates* (Bonn, 1972), pp 45–92, 116–50;
and M. Sharon, *Black Banners from the East: The Establishment of the
Abbasid State – Incubation of a Revolt* (Jerusalem-Leiden, 1983), pp 73–151.

5. For some of the results of modern scholarship on early Isma'ilism, see S.M.
Stern, 'Isma'ilis and Qarmatians', in *L'Élaboration de l'Islam*, Colloque de
Strasbourg (Paris, 1961), pp 99–108, reprinted in S.M. Stern, *Studies in Early
Isma'ilism* (Jerusalem-Leiden, 1983), pp 289–98; and W. Madelung, 'Das
Imamat in der frühen ismailitischen Lehre', *Der Islam*, 37 (1961), especially
pp 43–86. See also F. Daftary, *The Isma'ilis: Their History and Doctrines*
(Cambridge, 1990), pp 91–143, 593–614.

6. See al-Hasan b. Musa al-Nawbakhti, *Kitab firaq al-Shi'a*, ed. H. Ritter
(Istanbul, 1931), pp 57–64; Sa'd b. Abd Allah al-Ash'ari al-Qummi, *Kitab al-
maqalat wa'l-firaq*, ed. M.J. Mashkur (Tehran, 1963), pp 79–87; English
trans. in S.M. Stern, 'The Account of the Isma'ilis in *Firaq al-Shi'a*', in Stern,
Studies, pp 47–55. See also F. Daftary, 'The Earliest Isma'ilis', *Arabica*, 38
(1991), pp 214–45.

7. For aspects of the gnostic doctrines of the early Isma'ilis, especially their cosmology, see S.M. Stern, 'The Earliest Cosmological Doctrines of Isma'ilism', in
his *Studies*, pp 3–29; H. Halm, *Kosmologie und Heilslehre der frühen Isma'iliya*
(Wiesbaden, 1978), and 'The Cosmology of Pre-Fatimid Isma'iliyya', in
F. Daftary (ed.), *Essays in Mediaeval Isma'ili History and Thought* (Cambridge, forthcoming).

8. For the Arabic text and English translations of this important letter, see
Husayn F. al-Hamdani, *On the Genealogy of Fatimid Caliphs* (Cairo, 1958),
and A. Hamdani and F. de Blois, 'A Re-examination of al-Mahdi's Letter
to the Yemenites on the Genealogy of the Fatimid Caliphs', JRAS (1983),

pp 173–207, also containing a new hypothesis on the Alid ancestry of the Fatimid caliphs.

9. The belief in a line of twelve imams, established firmly in the first half of the tenth century, distinguishes Twelver Shi'ism from the earlier Imamiyya. With the rising predominance of the Twelvers, the terms Imamiyya and Ithna'ashariyya became gradually synonymous, while the Isma'ilis, too, continued to refer to themselves often as Imami Shi'is. See E. Kohlberg, 'From Imamiyya to Ithna-'ashariyya', BSOAS, 39 (1976), pp 521–34, reprinted in his *Belief and Law in Imami Shi'ism* (London, 1991), article XIV.

10. See Nizam al-Mulk, *The Book of Government or Rules for Kings*, tr. H. Darke (2nd edn, London, 1978), pp 208–18, 220–6; and S.M. Stern, 'The Early Isma'ili Missionaries in North-West Persia and in Khurasan and Transoxania', BSOAS, 23 (1960), pp 56–90, reprinted in his *Studies*, pp 189–233.

11. See Madelung, 'Das Imamat', especially pp 65–86; and F. Daftary, 'A Major Schism in the Early Isma'ili Movement', *Studia Islamica*, 77 (1993), pp 123–39.

12. On the Fatimids, and the history of Isma'ilism during the Fatimid period in general, see F. Dachraoui, *Le califat Fatimide au Maghreb, 296–365H./909–975 Jc* (Tunis, 1981); T. Bianquis, *Damas et la Syrie sous la domination Fatimide, 359–468/969–1076*, 2 vols (Damascus, 1986–89); L.S. al-Imad, *The Fatimid Vizierate, 969–1172* (Berlin, 1990); Y. Lev, *State and Society in Fatimid Egypt* (Leiden, 1991); H. Halm, 'Die Fatimiden', in U. Haarmann (ed.), *Geschichte der arabischen Welt* (Munich, 1987), pp 166–99, 605–6; and *Das Reich des Mahdi, 875–973: Der Aufstieg der Fatimiden* (Munich, 1991); Daftary, *The Isma'ilis*, pp 144–255, 615–54; and M. Canard, 'Fatimids', EI2, Vol 2, pp. 850–62.

13. See S.M. Stern, 'Cairo as the Centre of the Isma'ili Movement', in *Colloque international sur l'histoire du Caire* (Cairo, 1972), pp 437–50, reprinted in his *Studies*, pp 234–56; and A. Hamdani, 'Evolution of the Organisational Structure of the Fatimi Da'wah', *Arabian Studies*, 3 (1976), pp 85–114.

14. The classical treatment of the history of the Qarmati state of Bahrayn, some of whose general conclusions and inferences are no longer valid, remains M. de Goeje, *Mémoire sur les Carmathes du Bahrain et les Fatimides* (2nd edn, Leiden, 1886). For the results of modern scholarship here, see W. Madelung, 'Fatimiden und Bahrainqarmaten', *Der Islam*, 34 (1959), pp 34–88, revised English version in Daftary (ed.), *Essays in Mediaeval Isma'ili History and Thought*; W. Madelung, 'Karmati', EI2, Vol 4, pp 660–5; and F. Daftary, 'Carmatians', EIR, Vol 4, pp 823–32.

15. Nizam al-Mulk, *The Book of Government*, p 231.

16. Ibid., p 188.

17. Daftary, *The Isma'ilis*, pp 106–15.

18. See W. Ivanow, *The Alleged Founder of Ismailism* (Bombay, 1946), especially pp 28–103; and *Ibn al-Qaddah* (2nd edn, Bombay, 1957); S.M. Stern, 'Heterodox Isma'ilism at the Time of al-Mu'izz', BSOAS, 17 (1955), pp 10–33, reprinted in his *Studies*, pp 257–88; and H. Halm, 'Abdallah b. Maymun al-Qaddah', EIR, Vol 1, pp 182–3.

19. Abu Mansur Abd al-Qahir b. Tahir al-Baghdadi, *Moslem Schisms and Sects*, Part II, tr. A.S. Halkin (Tel Aviv, 1935), p 107.

20. See Hamid al-Din al-Kirmani, *al-Risala al-kafiya*, in M. Ghalib (ed.), *Majmu'at rasa'il al-Kirmani* (Beirut, 1983), pp 148–82. See also S.M. Stern, 'Abu'l-Qasim al-Busti and his Refutation of Isma'ilism', JRAS (1961), pp 14–35, reprinted in his *Studies*, pp 299–320.

21. Stern partially reconstructed the Arabic text of one such work, entitled variously as the *Kitab al-balagh al-akbar* (*Book of the Highest Initiation*) or the *Kitab al-siyasa* (*Book of the Policy*), and which purported to explain the heretical doctrines taught at different stages of initiation into Isma'ilism, from quotations preserved by several anti-Isma'ili authors, including al-Baghdadi, al-Nuwayri and al-Daylami. See S.M. Stern, 'The Book of the Highest Initiation and other anti-Isma'ili Travesties', in his *Studies*, pp 56–83.

22. For further details, see Ismail K. Poonawala, *Biobibliography of Isma'ili Literature* (Malibu, CA, 1977), especially pp 47–132.

23. See A.F. Sayyid, 'Lumières nouvelles sur quelques sources de l'histoire Fatimide en Égypte', *Annales Islamologiques*, 13 (1977), pp 1–41; and A. Hamdani, 'Fatimid History and Historians', in M.J.L. Young et al. (eds), *The Cambridge History of Arabic Literature: Religion, Learning and Science in the Abbasid Period* (Cambridge, 1990), pp 234–47.

24. al-Amir, *al-Hidaya al-Amiriyya*, ed. Asaf A.A. Fyzee (Bombay, etc., 1938), pp 3–26, reprinted in Jamal al-Din al-Shayyal (ed.), *Majmu'at al-watha'iq al-Fatimiyya* (Cairo, 1958), pp 203–30. This epistle is fully analysed in S.M. Stern, 'The Epistle of the Fatimid Caliph al-Amir (al-Hidaya al-Amiriyya) – its Date and Purpose', JRAS (1950), pp 20–31, reprinted in S.M. Stern, *History and Culture in the Medieval World* (London, 1984), article X.

25. This additional epistle, entitled *Iqa' sawa'iq al-irgham*, is added as an appendix, pp 27–39, to the edition of *al-Hidaya*, reprinted in al-Shayyal (ed.), *Majmu'at al-watha'iq*, pp 231–47.

26. *Iqa'*, pp 27, 32; in al-Shayyal (ed.), *Majmu'at al-watha'iq*, pp 233, 239.

27. For the history of the Nizari state and the general situation of the Nizari community and *da'wa* during the Alamut period, see Hodgson, *Order of Assassins*, pp 37–278; and 'The Isma'ili State', in *The Cambridge History of Iran*: Vol 5, *The Saljuq and Mongol Periods*, ed. J. A. Boyle (Cambridge, 1968), pp 422–82: Lewis, *The Assassins*, pp 38–140, 145–60, and Daftary, *The Isma'ilis*, pp 324–434, 669–99.

28. For detailed descriptions of the castle of Alamut and its environs, see W. Ivanow, *Alamut and Lamasar: Two Mediaeval Ismaili Strongholds in Iran* (Tehran, 1960), pp 30–59; and Willey, *Castles of the Assassins*, pp 204–26.

29. Bernard Lewis is the foremost modern authority on the history of the Syrian Nizaris during the Alamut period; see his 'The Isma'ilites and the Assassins', in *A History of the Crusades*, ed. K.M. Setton: Vol I, *The First Hundred Years*, ed. M.W. Baldwin (2nd edn, Madison, WI, 1969), pp 99–132; and *The Assassins*, pp 97–114. See also Charles F. Defrémery, 'Nouvelles recherches sur les Ismaéliens ou Bathiniens de Syrie', *Journal Asiatique*, 5 série, 3 (1854), pp 373–421, and 5 (1855), pp 5–76, which is still valuable for its historical details.

30. On these Syrian Nizari fortresses and their valuable epigraphic inscriptions, which are non-existent in the case of the Nizari fortresses of Persia, see Max

van Berchem, 'Épigraphie des Assassins de Syrie', *Journal Asiatique*, 9 série, 9 (1897), pp 453–501, reprinted in his *Opera Minora* (Geneva, 1978), Vol 1, pp 453–501.

31. See W. Ivanow, 'An Ismaili Poem in Praise of Fidawis', *Journal of the Bombay Branch of the Royal Asiatic Society*, New Series, 14 (1938), pp 63–72.

32. See M. Th. Houtsma, 'The Death of Nizam al-Mulk and its Consequences', *Journal of Indian History*, 3 (1924), pp 147–60; and H. Bowen and C.E. Bosworth, 'Nizam al-Mulk', EI2, Vol 8, pp 69–73.

33. Selections from al-Ghazali's *al-Mustazhiri*, with commentaries of the cited fragments, were first published by Ignaz Goldziher in his *Streitschrift des Gazali gegen die Batinijja-Sekte* (Leiden, 1916); but the complete edition of the Arabic text of this book, entitled *Fada'ih al-Batiniyya*, was produced by Abd al-Rahman Badawi (Cairo, 1964).

34. Abd al-Jalil Qazwini Razi, *Kitab al-naqd*, ed. Mir Jalal al-Din Muhaddith (2nd edn, Tehran, 1980), especially pp 80 ff., 119 ff., 206 ff., 301–17, 411–30, 433–4, 448, 462, 469–70, 475–80, 586.

35. See W. Madelung (ed.), *Arabic Texts Concerning the History of the Zaydi Imams of Tabaristan, Daylaman and Gilan* (Beirut, 1987), pp 146, 329.

36. Al-Fath b. Ali al-Bundari, *Zubdat al-nusra*, ed. M. Th. Houtsma, in his *Recueil de textes relatifs à l'histoire des Seldjoucides* II (Leiden, 1889), pp 169, 195.

37. See B. Lewis, 'The Sources for the History of the Syrian Assassins', *Speculum*, 27 (1952), pp 475–89, reprinted in his *Studies in Classical and Ottoman Islam (7th–16th Centuries)* (London, 1976), article VIII.

38. Abu Shama, *Kitab al-rawdatayn fi akhbar al-dawlatayn* (Cairo, 1287–88/ 1870–71), Vol 1, pp 240, 258.

39. Ibn Muyassar, *Akhbar Misr*, ed. A.F. Sayyid (Cairo, 1981), p 102.

40. See Poonawala, *Biobibliography*, pp 251–63, 287 ff.

41. See F. Daftary, 'Persian Historiography of the Early Nizari Isma'ilis', *Iran, Journal of the British Institute of Persian Studies*, 30 (1992), pp 91–7.

42. Ala al-Din Ata-Malik Juwayni, *Ta'rikh-i jahan-gushay*, ed. M. Qazwini (Leiden-London, 1912–37), Vol 3, pp 186–278; English trans. *The History of the World-Conqueror*, tr. J.A. Boyle (Manchester, 1958), Vol 2, pp 666–725.

43. Rashid al-Din Fadl Allah Tabib, *Jami al-tawarikh; qismat-i Isma'iliyan va Fatimiyan va Nizariyan va da'iyan va rafiqan*, ed. M.T. Danishpazhuh and M. Mudarrisi Zanjani (Tehran, 1959), pp 97–195; and Abu'l-Qasim Abd Allah b. Ali Kashani, *Zubdat al-tawarikh; bakhsh-i Fatimiyan va Nizariyan*, ed. M.T. Danishpazhuh (2nd edn, Tehran, 1366/1987), pp 133–237.

44. See B. Lewis, 'Kamal al-Din's Biography of Rašid al-Din Sinan', *Arabica*, 13 (1966), pp 225–67, reprinted in his *Studies*, article X.

45. For the general history of the Nizari Isma'ilis during the post-Alamut period, see Daftary, *The Isma'ilis*, pp 435–548, 699–724.

3

Mediaeval European Perceptions
of Islam and the Isma'ilis

In order to acquire a proper perspective of the genesis of the Assassin legends, it is necessary first to take stock of the state of the mediaeval Europeans' knowledge and perceptions of Islam as a religion and its internal divisions, including especially the Isma'ili branch of Shi'i Islam. After all, the Europeans' possible perceptions of the Isma'ilis during the twelfth and thirteenth centuries, when the legends appeared and acquired currency, would have been greatly influenced by their overall knowledge of Islam and the religious beliefs and practices of the Muslims.

Soon after the Prophet Muhammad's death in 632, as the Muslim armies embarked on their wars of conquest outside the Arabian peninsula, and the boundaries of the nascent Islamic state were rapidly being extended both to the east and the west, Islam began to impress outsiders as a thunderous military might bent on territorial expansion. The subjects of the neighbouring Byzantine and Sasanid empires were among the first of the conquered peoples to be deeply shocked by the victories of the Muslims, though their conversion to Islam was never demanded forcibly by their new conquerors. However, Christendom suffered a humiliating defeat when Muslim soldier-tribesmen occupied parts of the Byzantine empire in Syria and elsewhere in the seventh century; and Christian Europeans were even more alarmed when the Muslims extended their hegemony from North Africa to Spain in the eighth century, and later, in the ninth century, to Sicily and other western Mediterranean islands.

Thus, the seeds of prolonged antagonism between the Christian and Muslim worlds were planted, and Islam, the 'Other' world, began to be perceived as a problem by western Christendom, a problem which in time acquired important religious and intellectual dimensions, in addition to its original political and military aspects. However, this

complex problem, which had aroused so much fear and apprehension
in Christian Europe, seemed to defy any easy solution, as subsequent
Christian–Muslim encounters during the Middle Ages were to confirm.
Indeed, Islam had now become a lasting trauma for Europe;[1] and this
basically negative perception of Islam was retained for almost a
thousand years, well into the seventeenth century when the Ottoman
Turks, who had rekindled the past aspirations and glories of the
Muslims in their own impressive empire, still represented a serious
military threat to the peace and stability of Christendom and western
Europe.

Alarmed by the expanding fortunes of the Muslims and their military
exploits, how did Christian Europe respond to the challenge of Islam?
Originally, Europeans were both unwilling and unable to take up arms
against this new enemy on their frontiers, although a military reaction
did materialize several centuries later in the Crusading movement.
Indeed, for almost four centuries, Europeans effectively chose to ignore
Islam, both as a military and an intellectual phenomenon, also denying
its status as a new monotheistic religion in the Judaeo-Christian
tradition. Under such circumstances, the Europeans' perceptions of
Islam were essentially rooted in fear and ignorance, resulting in a highly
distorted and absurd image of Islam in western minds. It is also
important to recall that this image was generally retained throughout
the Middle Ages and beyond, even though Europeans had gradually
found access to information about Islam from different sources.
Western ignorance of Islam and the resulting misconceptions had their
own evolutionary process in the Middle Ages; and there were also those
rare 'moments' when attempts were made by a few individuals to study
Islam in a more serious fashion, even though they, too, pursued
polemical goals. In recent decades, a number of scholars, notably
Norman Daniel (d. 1992) and Richard Southern, have investigated the
complex Christian–Muslim encounters of mediaeval times, attempting
to identify various stages in the development of the Europeans'
conception of Islam; this chapter owes much to their scholarship.[2]

During the first few centuries of contact between Christendom and
Islam, lasting until around the end of the eleventh century when the
Crusading movement began, knowledge about Islam was extremely
limited in Europe, as were the scattered sources of this knowledge;
these sources included the polemical works of St John of Damascus,
one of the great theologians of the Eastern Church who lived in
Umayyad Syria, and those of the Byzantine theologians, as well as the
occasional reports of the Mozarabs, Christians living in Spain under
Muslim domination. In the course of these early centuries of Christian–

Muslim encounters, designated by Southern as the 'age of ignorance', Europeans viewed Islam as one of their major enemies and they attempted to understand it and interpret its religious status solely in the light of the Bible. The distant origins of the Muslims, or the Saracens as they came to be called incorrectly in mediaeval Europe, were relentlessly sought in the Old Testament. It was Bede (d. 735), the Biblical master of the early Middle Ages in northern Europe, who lent currency to the identification of the Muslims with the Saracens, or the Ishmaelite descendants of Abraham by Hagar, even though the people in question could not be called Saracens (sons of Sarah) because they descended from Abraham through Hagar and not Sarah, Abraham's other wife. At any rate, Muslims were now placed in opposition to Christians even on the basis of Biblical history.[3] Bede, in fact, regarded the Muslims as unbelievers.

There were also those Europeans who turned from Biblical history to Biblical prophecy for their understanding of Islam. In this connection, around the middle of the ninth century, several Christian theologians living in Spain, including Eulogius (d. 859), Bishop of Toledo, saw in Islam a sinister conspiracy against Christianity; for them, Muhammad was the Anti-Christ and the rise of Islam heralded the imminent end of the world. This apocalyptic vision of Islam, too, was solidly rooted in ignorance, although its protagonists actually lived among Muslims and could obtain some information about their religion.

By the final decades of the eleventh century, Europeans had begun to respond militarily to the challenge of Islam by means of the Reconquista in Muslim Spain and the Crusading movement. The political fragmentation of Spain, in the aftermath of the collapse of Umayyad rule there in 1031, made it possible for the independent Christian kingdoms of the north to expand their territories southwards. This marked the beginning of the Christian Reconquista which culminated in the conquest of Toledo in 1085. The early success of the Reconquista was halted for more than a century by the intervention, from North Africa, of the Muslim Almoravids and their successors in the Almohad dynasty. But when they abandoned Spain, most of its Muslim cities, including Cordova, fell into Christian hands during the thirteenth century. However, Muslim rule under the Nasirids continued for another two and a half centuries in the province of Granada, which was transformed into a flourishing centre of Islamic culture. With the union of Castile and Aragon which brought about the unification of Spain, Granada, the last Muslim bastion in Spain, fell to the Christians in 1492.

In the meantime, the Crusading movement for fighting the enemies of

Christendom in the East had been launched in Europe in response to the appeal made, in November 1095, by Pope Urban II (1088–99) at the Council of Clermont in France. The original papal appeal stressed the need for providing military support for the eastern Christians who were allegedly subjected to the oppressive rule of the Muslims; the Europeans themselves had for some time deemed it undesirable that their Holy Places and pilgrimage routes in Palestine should be under Muslim control. In fact, a new era in Christian–Muslim encounters was about to commence in the form of numerous Crusades to the Holy Land, where the Crusaders acquired permanent bases for the next two centuries.[4]

Following the papal appeal of 1095, numerous Crusading contingents were quickly mobilized by different princes and knights in western Europe. The Christian pilgrim-soldiers of the mixed army of the First Crusade began to arrive in Constantinople, the Byzantine capital, in 1096; by 1097 they had already entered Syria. The Crusaders then marched towards their final destination, Jerusalem, which a year earlier had fallen once again into Fatimid hands. The Crusaders easily defeated the local Fatimid garrison and entered Jerusalem in July 1099; thereupon the Crusading pilgrims massacred practically the entire Muslim and Jewish populations of Jerusalem before giving thanks to God for their victory in the Church of the Holy Sepulchre. Jerusalem had now been recovered for Christendom.

The swift victory of the First Crusade (1096–9) was in no small measure due to political decline and disunity in the Muslim camp. The major Muslim powers had been engaged in prolonged rivalries of their own, to the detriment of their overall military strength, while the Levant had recently become the scene of factional fighting among the Saljuqs and other regional powers. Syria and Palestine had long been contested by the Isma'ili Fatimids and the Sunni Abbasids, the major caliphal powers in the Near East, with a number of local dynasties and tribal rulers contributing further to the region's political intricacies. By 1097, when the Crusaders appeared in Syria, the declining Fatimid dynasty had lost its earlier political prominence in the Levant; and the Nizari–Musta'li schism of 1094 had further devastated the fortunes of the Fatimids, affecting their control of the eastern Islamic lands beyond Egypt. On the other side, the Abbasid caliphs themselves had long been reduced to mere puppets at Baghdad in the hands of the Saljuq sultans, though they were retained as the official spokesmen of Sunni Islam. The Saljuq sultanate, too, had passed its apogee; and with the death of sultan Malikshah in 1092, the Saljuqs were experiencing their own succession problems and internal disputes. In Syria proper, which had been transformed into a somewhat independent Saljuq principality, the death in 1095 of its Saljuq overlord, Tutush, had led to a prolonged period of political instability, with Tutush's two sons ruling in rivalry with one another over different parts of Syria from Aleppo and Damascus. The situation was further complicated by the activities of various local dynasties which now aspired to assert their own independence.

All this explains why the potentially superior Muslim forces failed so helplessly to check the advance of the Crusaders into the Holy Land. It was left for Saladin, the founder of the Ayyubid dynasty, to unite the Muslims some eight decades later in a *jihad* or holy war of their own against the Crusaders. Having uprooted the Fatimids in 1171, Saladin succeeded in unifying Egypt and Syria under his own rule; he then led his unified army of Turks, Arabs and Kurds in common cause against the Crusaders, culminating in the Muslim recapture of Jerusalem in 1187. The Franks or al-Faranj, as the Crusaders and western Europeans in general had come to be designated by the Muslims, had now lost, at least temporarily, most of their important possessions in the Levant, except for a few coastal towns.

In the immediate aftermath of the First Crusade, its Frankish leaders established four small states in the conquered territories of the Near East, a region which became known to them as Outremer, or the 'land beyond the sea'. The Frankish states of Edessa and Antioch, established respectively by Baldwin of Boulogne and Bohemond, guarded the north-eastern and northern approaches to Syria. Jerusalem with a few towns along the coast and in the highlands formed another state, the Latin kingdom of Jerusalem, which enjoyed supremacy among the Frankish territories by the virtue of possessing the Holy Places. The first Frankish ruler in Jerusalem, elected by other leaders of the First Crusade, was Godfrey of Bouillon (1099–1100), who would be called *Advocatus Sancti Sepulchri*, 'the defender of the Holy Sepulchre'; he was soon succeeded by his younger brother, Baldwin I of Boulogne (1100–18), who had earlier established the state of Edessa. After capturing the port of Tortosa in 1102, a fourth Frankish principality, based later on Tripoli, was founded by Raymond of St Gilles (d. 1105), foremost among the early leaders of the Crusades.[5]

Soon, there also appeared two military monastic orders of knights, the Hospitallers and the Templars, founded in 1113 and 1119 respectively. Acting as autonomous powers accountable directly only to the papacy, they provided military assistance to the Crusaders in the Frankish states and also guarded the pilgrim routes of the Holy Land.

Growing steadily in numbers and in wealth, these military orders had large and well-organized fighting forces at their disposal and also possessed numerous castles in the region, in the vicinity of the fortresses later acquired in Syria by the Nizaris. During the twelfth century, the knights of these orders had extended encounters with the Syrian Nizari Isma'ilis.

The Frankish territories in Outremer had colourful histories of their own until their final collapse in the closing decades of the thirteenth century. Modelling themselves largely on the feudal structure then prevalent in western Europe, the leaders of the Frankish states entered into an endless series of local conflicts and alliances among themselves, also establishing shifting relations with the Muslim rulers of the region, including the leaders of the Nizari Isma'ili community in Syria. The political and diplomatic fabric of the region was further complicated by the independent activities of the rival Hospitallers and Templars, who also had their own hostile relations with the Isma'ilis and often successfully exacted tribute from them.

Of the four Latin states, Edessa had the shortest history; it was lost to the Zangids of Iraq and Syria in 1144, an event that led to the indecisive Second Crusade (1147–8). Meanwhile, Bohemond's nephew Tancred had effectively succeeded to the leadership of the principality of Antioch in 1101. Tancred (d. 1112) was the first Crusading prince who came into contact with the Nizari Isma'ilis, who were then securing a temporary foothold in northern Syria. Later, Antioch was ruled by the princes of the house of Hauteville until it was captured in 1268 by Baybars I, the same Mamluk sultan who finally subdued the Syrian Nizari Isma'ilis in the early 1270s. Tripoli was ruled by the descendants of Raymond of St Gilles until 1187, when it, too, passed to the house of Hauteville. Tripoli was eventually captured by the Mamluks in 1289, leaving only the Latin kingdom in Frankish hands.

The kingdom of Jerusalem was restored soon after the seizure of Jerusalem by Saladin in 1187, with Acre serving as its new capital. The leadership of the kingdom had then fallen intermittently into the hands of King Amalric I's daughters, Sibylla and Isabella, and some of their husbands, including Guy of Lusignan (1186–92), Conrad of Montferrat (1192) and Henry of Champagne (1192–7), some of whom had dealings with the most famous leader of the Syrian Nizari Isma'ili community, namely, Rashid al-Din Sinan. In 1291, the Mamluks conquered Acre and what remained of the Latin kingdom of Jerusalem, ending Frankish rule in Outremer.

The events of the Crusades and the four Frankish states in Outremer, especially those relating to the Latin kingdom, have been recorded by numerous contemporary occidental chroniclers who flourished during the twelfth and thirteenth centuries. Some of these chroniclers actually lived in the Latin East and were eyewitnesses to some of the events they describe. As such, they represent highly important primary sources for the Crusaders' knowledge of contemporary Muslims and Isma'ilis.

William, Archbishop of Tyre, was the greatest of the Crusader historians who lived and worked in the Latin East. He was also the earliest of the occidental chroniclers of the Crusades to have written about the Syrian Nizari Isma'ilis. His famous *Historia* contains a detailed account of the Crusades as well as the history of the lands conquered by the Crusaders, in particular the Latin kingdom of Jerusalem from 1095 to 1184.[6] He also makes numerous references to the relations between the Crusaders and the Fatimids. It is important to note that for the period 1120–84, William's *Historia* is the only contemporary or near-contemporary historical account of the Latin East written by a Christian resident in that region. In addition, being learned and a man of public affairs, he was very well informed about his subject, having had access to both literary and oral sources then existing in Outremer.

William of Tyre was born in Jerusalem in or about 1130. He spent almost 20 years (circa 1146–65) studying in France and Italy. He entered public service soon after returning to the Latin East in 1165. In 1170, he was recruited to the service of King Amalric I (1163–74), who in 1174 appointed him to the office of Chancellor of the Latin kingdom; he also acted as tutor to Amalric's son and successor Baldwin IV (1174–85). William was elected Archbishop of Tyre in 1175, and as such he ranked second only to the Patriarch of Jerusalem in the ecclesiastical hierarchy of the Latin kingdom. William spent many years compiling his annalistic history, writing its final sections in 1184 shortly before he died. William knew Arabic but, according to his own statements, he did not utilize any literary Arabic sources, although he did rely extensively on oral traditions.[7] Indeed, the oral traditions and memoirs of others, in addition to his own experiences, and the earlier Christian narratives of the First Crusade were the main primary sources of his *Historia*.[8] Among other early occidental chronicles, he particularly relied on the anonymously written *Gesta Francorum*,[9] which had been also used by Raymond of Aguilers and Fulcher of Chartres, authorities on the First Crusade, who in turn were used by William of Tyre. William evidently also wrote a history of the Muslim lands, which has not been recovered. Strangely enough, his *Historia* does not contain any important information on Islam as a religion; this was clearly not one of his concerns. In line with the tradition established by the earlier historians of the Crusading movement, William's main objective was to show that the Crusade was a holy war against the Saracen infidels, and that its triumphs were, therefore, *Gesta Dei per Francos*, divine deeds done through the Franks.

The Crusaders themselves were not interested in gathering accurate information about the Muslims and their religion, a lack of interest which becomes all the more significant when it is recalled that both they and some of their learned historians, such as William of Tyre and James of Vitry (d. 1240), lived for long periods in close proximity to the Muslims, with whom they had extensive military, diplomatic, social and commercial contacts. In the aftermath of the First Crusade, Crusaders who had come from northern France, Provence, Lorraine and other parts of western Europe, began to settle in the territories of the Latin states in Outremer. Their ranks were continuously swelled by waves of newcomers from the West. The Crusaders brought with them ideas and institutions from the feudal society of mediaeval Europe, which they put into practice with very little regard for the indigenous realities of the Latin East. As a result, a very complex social structure developed in the territories of the Latin states, which were now ruled by a class of Frankish nobility.[10] Besides the Crusading knights and higher nobility, the Frankish settlers also included burgesses who dwelled in the towns and engaged in small-scale domestic trade. The larger international trade was in the hands of Venetian and other European concerns in Acre, Tyre and other ports of Outremer. Native Christian, Muslim and Jewish communities occupied lower ranks in the social system of the Latin East. The more numerous oriental Christians, who spoke Arabic and belonged mainly to the Greek Orthodox Church, and on whose behalf the Crusading movement had been launched, became second-class citizens of the Frankish states; and the Muslim inhabitants of these territories, many of whom were engaged in the cultivation of land for the Crusader lords, occupied even a lower social status and paid a special poll-tax to the Franks.

In this complex social setting, the feudal superstructure of the Latin states was quite separate from the indigenous society, although there were extensive contacts between them. The Frankish rulers and the Crusader settlers were, in effect, sustained by an Arabic-speaking indigenous community, comprised mainly of Muslims. Many of the Frankish settlers themselves learned to speak Arabic, while they also utilized the services of Muslim scribes. Thus, the Crusaders had varied encounters with the Muslim inhabitants of the Latin states and the neighbouring Muslim states, but there was very little cultural contact between them, such as existed in Muslim Spain and Sicily. As a result, the Crusaders remained in ignorance of almost every aspect of Islam as a religion or civilization.

In sum, direct contact between the Franks and the Muslims, during the First Crusade and subsequently, did not result in improved western perceptions of Islam, either in the Latin East or in Europe. As a result of the Crusading movement, however, Europeans did become more aware of the reality of Islam; and in the aftermath of the military victories of the First Crusade, their earlier fears about Islam gave way, at least temporarily, to hopeful aspirations.

Thus, Islam and its founder became more familiar concepts in Europe from the early decades of the twelfth century, but these concepts were largely based on imagination. In the words of Southern, the authors of this picture had luxuriated in the ignorance of triumphant imagination.[11] Based on oral testimony and misinformation, and stimulated significantly by the fireside tales of the returning Crusaders, this picture of Islam was fabricated at a time of great imaginative development in western Europe, which was then also witnessing the appearance of a host of European tales such as the romances of Charlemagne, the legends of Virgil, and the legendary history of Britain. It is, therefore, not surprising that legends about Islam circulated so readily, purporting to be accurate descriptions of Muslims and their practices at least until the middle of the thirteenth century. According to these legends, which like the contemporary Assassin legends soon acquired a literary life of their own, the Saracens (Muslims) were idolators worshipping a false trinity, and Mahomet (Muhammad) was a magician; he was even a cardinal of the Roman Church who had rebelled and fled to Arabia where he founded a church of his own.[12]

In the meantime, some scattered but highly valuable attempts were made by a few individuals in Europe to study Islam on a more serious basis, supplementing fiction with observation and textual analysis, though their basic aim continued to remain refutation and condemnation. This new spirit of enquiry, which led to the first factual observations about Islam as a religion in Europe, appeared mainly in Spain; and its earliest protagonist was Moses Sefardi (d. ca. 1130), a Spanish Jew who in 1106 converted to Christianity, adopted the name of Pedro de Alfonso and later went to live in England where he became physician to King Henry I. Having lived among the Muslims in Spain, Pedro de Alfonso knew Arabic and was the first translator into Latin of some of the stories circulating in the Muslim East; he also seems to have acquired a good knowledge of the Quran in addition to some first-hand information about Muslim tenets and practices. At any rate, he produced the earliest written account of Islam and Muhammad in the fifth of his *Dialogi*, containing dialogues between a Christian and a Jew.[13] Pedro de Alfonso's polemical account of Islam, composed around 1108 on the basis of oral traditions as well as written sources which remain unknown, was the best informed statement on the subject throughout the twelfth century and, perhaps, the later Middle Ages. But his account did not have a widespread influence on the Europeans' perceptions of Islam.

A far more ambitious project to gather factual knowledge about Islam was launched through the efforts of Peter the Venerable, abbot of the important Benedictine monastery of Cluny in France from 1122 until his death in 1156. Peter the Venerable had a deep concern for guarding Christianity against heresies; for him, Islam represented the greatest of these. He was also convinced that instead of defeating them militarily, Muslims could more readily be won over through missionary activity. For both of these reasons, he was concerned to collect accurate information about Islam, in particular about its weaknesses, so that the false tenets of this religion could then be exposed. It was with these objectives in mind that, while on a journey to Spain in 1142, he conceived a grandiose project involving the translation of a number of Islamic texts, including the Quran, from Arabic into Latin. He entrusted this task to a team of translators in Toledo, which had recently become a centre for the translation of Arabic scientific works into Latin.

The Latin translation of the Quran, a landmark in western Islamic studies and now undertaken for the first time by Robert of Ketton, was completed in 1143 with the title of *Liber legis Saracenorum quem Alcoran vocant*; Peter the Venerable himself utilized his commissioned translations to produce a summary of Islamic teachings (*Summa totius haeresis Saracenorum*), and an anti-Islamic polemic (*Liber contra sectam sive haeresim Saracenorum*).[14] The results of this project, a dozen Latin texts known as the Culniac Corpus or the Toledo Collection,[15] constituted the first scholarly instruments for studying Islam in mediaeval Europe. The synthesizing tracts composed by Peter the Venerable himself were free from many of the crude and absurd misconceptions then current in Europe. But the Culniac Corpus, too, failed to have any immediate impact on Europeans' perceptions, despite its rather wide circulation. The serious study of Islam did not present itself as a generally attractive objective to Christian Europeans who were then, in the second half of the twelfth century, still hopeful of defeating the Muslims through the Crusades; consequently, legends about the Muslim East continued to be circulated in the Latin West as well as among the Crusading circles in Outremer. Legends about Islam, accepted as reliable accounts, had by now acquired a life of their own.

By the end of the twelfth century, another type of factual knowledge about the philosophical achievements of the Muslims was becoming accessible in Europe, at least to the learned Latins. This new knowledge of Muslim philosophy was obviously at great variance with the negative religio-political image of Islam still in circulation. Numerous treatises of the most renowed Muslim philosophers, including al-Kindi, al-Farabi and Ibn Sina (Latin, Avicenna), were now for the first time rendered from Arabic into Latin by Gerard of Cremona (d. 1187) and others belonging to that famous group of translators connected with Toledo, opening up new intellectual vistas to western thinkers.[16] Thus, not only did learned Europeans like Roger Bacon (d. 1292) now become aware of the impressive intellectual achievements of the Muslims, but they also began to adopt some of the ideas and methodologies of the Muslim philosophers in their own theological and philosophical discourses. Even recognition of the philosophical achievements of the Muslims failed to dispel the European legends about Islam as a religion.

Meanwhile, Christian Europeans had retained their hope of crushing the Muslims through military power; and this hope was temporarily reinvigorated by the appearance of the Mongols. The thunderous victories of Chingiz Khan during the early decades of the thirteenth century had brought to the notice of Europeans the existence of a pagan world beyond Islam in Asia. The appearance of the Mongols, generally known in the Latin West as Tartars (derived from *Tartarus*, the Latin term for the Hell of classical mythology), significantly broadened the geographical and religious horizons of western Christendom. It also had an important impact on Christian–Muslim relations. After some initial confusion, the Europeans recognized the Mongols as a suitable instrument for destroying the Muslims and, hence, made numerous diplomatic efforts to forge an alliance with them against the Muslims. At the same time, the Muslims, who had already experienced a foretaste of Mongol devastation, made peaceful overtures of their own, hoping to avert further catastrophes. It was in this spirit that the ambassadors of the Abbasid caliph at Baghdad and the Nizari Isma'ili ruler at Alamut went to Mongolia, in 1246, on the occasion of the enthronement of the Great Khan Guyuk. The Muslims had already failed in their attempts to win the support of the Christians against the Mongols. According to Matthew Paris (d. 1259), the English Benedictine monk and historian, in 1238 the Isma'ili ruler of Alamut and the Abbasid caliph had sent a joint mission to Europe to seek the assistance of King Louis IX of France and King Henry III of England against the Mongols. But the envoys had found no sympathy for their cause at the European courts.[17] At any rate, a most intricate series of embassies and messages were now exchanged between the European powers and the Mongols, and between the latter and the Muslim rulers, in addition to the less noteworthy Christian–Muslim diplomatic encounters of the time.

It was against this background that King Louis IX of France, better known as St Louis, led the Seventh Crusade (1248–54), the last major Crusader campaign, and also entered into diplomatic negotiations with the Mongols. After his early defeat in 1250 at Damietta, however, St Louis went to Acre and remained in Palestine for four years until 1254. During this period he exchanged embassies and gifts with the Old Man of the Mountain, the then local leader of the Nizari Isma'ilis in Syria. Encouraged by the news of the Mongols' inclination towards Nestorian Christianity, St Louis also sought to establish an alliance with the Mongols against the Muslims. In pursuit of this objective he dispatched a Flemish Franciscan friar, William of Rubruck, on a mission to the court of the Great Khan Mongke in Mongolia. In 1254, William reached the Mongol capital Karakorum, where he participated in a great theological debate before Mongke with representatives of the Nestorian Christians, Buddhists and Muslims. William of Rubruck has left a valuable account of this debate[18] and other events of his mission to Mongolia, in which he refers to the Persian Isma'ilis. He also related that a large group of Isma'ili *fida'i*s had entered Karakorum in 1254 under different guises for the purpose of killing Mongke, who had already sent a major expedition under the command of his brother Hulagu against the Isma'ili strongholds in Persia.[19]

Soon afterwards, the Mongols completed, on their own initiative, their conquest of western Asia, causing the destructions of the Nizari Isma'ili state of Persia in 1256 and that of the Abbasid caliphate in 1258. Their further advance was successfully checked in Syria by the Muslims. As a result, the Latin states of Outremer, too, survived for a few decades longer. Western hopes for a joint Christian–Mongol attack against Islam were once again temporarily revived when the Mongols sent their own embassies to Europe between 1285 and 1290. But these negotiations, too, proved fruitless, and the fall of Acre into Muslim hands in 1291 initiated yet another chapter in Christian–Muslim relations; it not only marked the collapse of Frankish rule and military presence in Outremer, but also dispelled any remaining Christian hopes for a lasting military victory over the Muslims. The Crusading movement had finally run its course after almost two centuries (1096–

1291) of pilgrimage and holy war; and the historical reality of Islam was now about to receive some recognition by the Europeans and Christendom.

In the meantime, individual attempts of a somewhat scholarly nature to study Islam for polemical purposes had continued in Europe, reaching their culmination in the works of Raymond Lull (d. 1315) and Ricoldo da Monte Croce (d. 1321). Expressing a Christian point of view, these men talked of replacing the Crusading movement by missionary endeavours among the Muslims, endeavours that would require serious studies of the Islamic tenets and languages.[20] Lull himself founded, in 1276, a school of Arabic for future Christian missionaries in Majorca; and in no small measure it was due to his ideas that the Council of Vienne in 1311 recommended that chairs of oriental languages be established at five European universities. These efforts, too, had few lasting results. By the end of the fourteenth century, the number of people who knew Arabic in Europe was probably less than 20; and missionary efforts, going back to the earlier activities of Franciscan and Dominican friars who were employed from 1234 as preachers of the Crusades, had all proved ineffective.

Indeed, during the fourteenth century and later Middle Ages, the impulse to know and understand Islam died out almost completely, and popular imagination was once again given a free rein. In particular, the colourful eastern tales of Marco Polo gave new impetus to European fantasies about Islam and the Muslim East. By the end of the fifteenth century, the standard Christian perception of Islam, sanctioned by the Roman Church, still represented a highly distorted image rooted in ignorance and fantasy. According to W.M. Watt, the four main features of this image, which essentially retained a central place in European thinking until the nineteenth century, were as follows: (1) the religion of Islam was falsehood and a deliberate perversion of truth: (2) it was a religion of violence and the sword: (3) it was a religion of self-indulgence; and (4) Muhammad was the Anti-Christ.[21]

With the fall of the Byzantine capital, Constantinople, in 1453 into the hands of the Ottoman Turks, now the major Muslim power, the interest of Christian theologians in Islam was reawakened for a brief period, designated by Southern as 'the moment of vision'.[22] None the less, by the end of the Middle Ages, the accumulated knowledge of Europeans about Islam was still extraordinarily negligible.

Considerations of the later developments in European perceptions of Islam and the early histories of Orientalism and Islamic studies in the West, are beyond the scope of this enquiry. It is sufficient to recall that the beginnings of systematic studies of Islamic theology and history in

Europe may be traced to the late sixteenth century, the century of the Reformation, when regular teaching of Arabic commenced at the Collège de France in Paris; and it was only after the establishment of chairs of Arabic at Leiden in 1613 and at Cambridge and Oxford in the 1630s that serious studies of Arabic sources really began in Europe. However, it was not until the end of the seventeenth century that scientific attitudes towards the study of Islam finally began to displace the narrow and strictly polemical frame of mind within which all the mediaeval Christian investigations of Islam had been conducted. The disappearance of the general tendency to prefer false and polemical statements to objective knowledge based on authentic textual evidence, together with an increased availability of rich collections of Islamic manuscripts in the Bibliothèque Royale and other libraries in Europe, finally prepared the ground for the scholarly study of Islam within the broader field of Orientalism in early modern times.

If the mediaeval Europeans, both in the West and in Outremer, were ignorant of the most basic aspects of the Islamic message, they surely knew even less about its internal divisions, including the broad Sunni–Shi'i division, and the intricacies of Islamic sects and tenets. Indeed, there is no evidence to suggest that even the most learned of the Crusader historians, who spent long periods in the Latin East where they had continuous contacts with the local Muslims, made any efforts to gather details on the Muslim communities of the region. Ironically, some of these occidental historians, such as William of Tyre and James of Vitry, were theologians who served as bishops and archbishops in the Crusader states and also aimed at converting members of the local Muslim communities. This is in marked contrast to the practices of the contemporary or even earlier Isma'ili *da'i*s who, as a matter of policy, familiarized themselves with the religions and languages of their prospective converts; while many of these *da'i*s received extensive training at the Dar al-Hikma and other special institutions of learning in Fatimid Cairo. Modern scholarship has revealed, for instance, that al-Kirmani, an eminent Isma'ili philosopher and the most learned *da'i*-theologian of the Fatimid period, was well acquainted with the Judaeo-Christian scriptures and the Hebrew and Syriac languages;[23] he died around 1021, when Christian theologians were still investigating Islam on the basis of the Bible and the name of Muhammad was practically unknown to Christians in Europe outside Spain and Sicily.

Perceiving Islam as a false religion or even as a Christian heresy, the Crusaders and their historians were not interested in acquiring facts and first-hand knowledge about Islam. On the contrary, they aimed to refute and condemn a phenomenon that represented something evil to them; and, under these circumstances, their purpose would be more readily served by fabricating or imagining the required evidence, in addition to believing in false reports or exaggerating half-truths about the tenets and practices of the Muslims or any segment of their community, including especially the 'Assassins' who had attracted the attention of the Crusaders.

Mediaeval Europeans remained almost completely ignorant of Shi'i Islam and its main doctrinal differences with the Sunni majority, even though the Crusaders had come into contact from the opening years of the twelfth century with Shi'i communities as represented by the Nizari Isma'ilis in Syria and the Fatimids in Egypt. The Crusaders obviously also failed to realize that the Syrian Nizaris and the Fatimids belonged to the rival wings of Isma'ilism, which itself represented a major branch of Shi'i Islam; nor were they aware that the Imami Twelver communities, then present in Syria and other regions of the Near East, constituted another major branch of Shi'ism.

Nevertheless, as a result of their contacts with Shi'i (Isma'ili) Muslims, the Crusaders had somehow become aware, though in a highly confused manner, of the differences that separated the Shi'a from the rest of the Muslim community. For instance, William of Tyre, the earliest Crusader historian who has something to say on the subject, summed up around 1180 his knowledge of Shi'ism by merely stating that, according to the Shi'a, God had intended to entrust the message of Islam to Hali (Ali), the only true prophet, but the angel Gabriel erred and handed the message to Mehemeth (Muhammad).[24] Later Crusader historians basically drew upon his statements. James of Vitry (Jacques de Vitri), another well-informed Crusader historian who was Bishop of Acre from 1216 to 1228, shows some awareness of the ritual differences between Sunnis and Shi'is, but he too misunderstands these differences and states that the followers of Ali observed a law different from that instituted by Muhammad who, according to him, was slandered by the Shi'a.[25] Even Ricoldo da Monte Croce, who later made a more serious study of Islam and journeyed to the Near East where he evidently talked to some Twelver Shi'is in Iraq, was way off the mark in believing that the majority of Muslims followed Muhammad, while fewer members followed Ali, holding that Ali's rights had been usurped by Muhammad.[26]

It was only after the adoption of Twelver Shi'ism as the state religion of Safavid Persia in 1501 that the Europeans travelling to that land began to collect more reliable information about Shi'ism. Even that proved to be a slow process as is shown by the available accounts produced by Portuguese, Spanish, Italian and other European emissaries, merchants, diplomats and travellers visiting Persia in Safavid and later times. Indeed, even in modern times Shiʿi studies have remained on the periphery of Islamic studies in the West, where Islamicists still continue to investigate Islam mainly from the viewpoint of the Sunnis and the Arabs. At any rate, in the light of the Crusaders' complete ignorance of Shiʿi Islam, including its main Twelver and Ismaʿili branches, it is reasonable to assume that they must have been equally ill-informed about the actual beliefs and practices of the Nizari Ismaʿilis. The remainder of this chapter reviews the available evidence on 'Crusader–Assassin' encounters and the extent of the Crusaders' factual knowledge about the Nizari Ismaʿilis during the twelfth and thirteenth centuries. It is only against this background that a proper understanding of how the Assassin legends were generated and transmitted in mediaeval times can be acquired.

A few years after the fall of Jerusalem into the Crusaders' hands, Persian emissaries of Hasan Sabbah began to arrive in northern Syria to organize and lead the Nizari Ismaʿili movement there. As already noted, these Nizari *daʿi*s found their task much more arduous in Syria, and almost half a century of continuous efforts were needed before they could finally realize their objective and gain control of a group of strongholds. From early on, the Nizari *daʿi*s in Syria came into contact and conflict with the Crusaders who had already started to extend their military presence in the region. During an initial period lasting until 1113, Nizari activities in Syria were centred on Aleppo, where the sectarians had found a temporary protector in the city's Saljuq ruler, Ridwan. It was perhaps due to a cooperative pact that the first local chief of the Syrian Nizaris, a Persian *daʿi* known as al-Hakim al-Munajjim (the Physician-Astrologer), dispatched a group of *fidaʾi*s to kill Janah al-Dawla, the ruler of Hims and one of Ridwan's main enemies. The assassins themselves were killed on the spot by Janah al-Dawla's guards. This event, taking place in May 1103 during a Friday prayer in the great mosque of Hims, was the first of the daring public assassinations committed by the Syrian Nizaris, self-sacrificing acts which were to attract so much attention in Crusader circles.

Operating from their base in Aleppo, the Nizaris next extended their influence to Apamea, a fortified outpost of Aleppo which fell easily into their hands in 1106, upon the assassination of its ruler at the hands of a group of *fidaʾi*s. But the attempt to make Apamea the first Nizari stronghold in Syria proved short-lived. A few months later, in September 1106, Tancred, the able regent of Antioch who had already occupied the surrounding districts, successfully besieged Apamea and forced its surrender. Abu Tahir, the new Nizari chief, and his close associates, who then stayed at Apamea, ransomed themselves from captivity and returned to Aleppo. These events at Apamea marked the first encounters between the Crusaders and the Nizari Isma'ilis of Syria. A few years later, in 1110, the Syrian Nizaris also lost Kafarlatha, a lesser locality in the Jabal al-Summaq, to Tancred.

By 1111, the position of the Nizaris had become rather untenable in Aleppo, where the local majority Imami Shi'i and Sunni populations had turned against them. Furthermore, a new Saljuq ruler in Persia, who was then pursuing a strong anti-Isma'ili policy, had begun to exert pressures on his Saljuq kin in Aleppo to adopt a similar stance against the local Nizaris. Nizari fortunes were irrevocably reversed in Aleppo when, in 1113, Ridwan's son and successor finally authorized a widespread anti-Nizari campaign in his domain. Abu Tahir and a group of some 200 leading Nizaris were arrested and executed; the popular outburst against the Nizaris in Aleppo culminated in a massacre. Nevertheless, many of the Aleppine Nizaris found refuge in the surrounding areas, including the Frankish territories, while smaller Nizari communities survived clandestinely in a few other towns and districts of northern Syria.

In the aftermath of their debacle in Aleppo, the Nizaris were reorganized in Syria by their new leader, another Persian *da'i* called Bahram. During this second period, they moved the base of their operations to Damascus in southern Syria, where they acquired a significant following. By 1125, when Damascus was threatened by the Crusaders, the Nizaris were strong enough to send an armed contingent to fight in the company of the troops of Tughtigin, the Turkish ruler of Damascus, against the encroaching Franks. In 1126, Bahram demanded and was given by Tughtigin the fortress of Baniyas, situated on the border of the Latin kingdom of Jerusalem. Bahram fortified Baniyas and used it as his headquarters. Henceforth, Bahram preached Nizari doctrines openly in Damascus to the annoyance of the city's Sunni inhabitants. The Nizari *da'i*s were now dispatched in all directions within Syria, where they won an increasing number of converts both in towns and rural areas.

The Nizari success in southern Syria was also short-lived. In 1128, Bahram lost his life in a battle fought near Baniyas against a local Arab tribe, and in the same year the Nizaris witnessed the death of Tughtigin, their protector in Damascus. In 1129, Tughtigin's son and successor, Buri, sanctioned a general massacre of the Nizaris; some 6000 perished at the hands of the town militia supported by the predominantly Sunni inhabitants of Damascus. It was shortly after these events that Bahram's successor, Isma'il al-Ajami, realizing the untenability of his position at Baniyas, wrote to King Baldwin II (1118–31), who was then planning to advance on Damascus, and offered to surrender Baniyas to the Franks in exchange for receiving asylum.[27] Accompanied by some of his associates, the *da'i* Isma'il found refuge in the Latin kingdom of Jerusalem where he died soon afterwards at the beginning of 1130. Buri himself was later killed in revenge by two Nizari *fida'is* who did not survive their act; but the Nizaris never recovered their position in Damascus and southern Syria. In the meantime, the rivalry between the Nizari and Musta'lian Isma'ilis had intensified, leading to the decisive victory of the Nizari cause in Syria.

During this period, the early 1120s, the Fatimid caliph al-Amir had issued his anti-Nizari epistle, in which the Nizaris were for the first time referred to with the abusive designation of 'Hashishiyya'. Al-Amir, as noted, was assassinated by a group of *fida'is* in 1130; and soon Musta'lian Isma'ilism disappeared almost completely from Syria.

During the first half of the twelfth century, there had also occurred numerous encounters between the Franks and the Fatimids. Al-Afdal, the all-powerful Fatimid vizier who had originally underestimated the threat of the Crusaders, had early entered in vain into negotiations with them. As has been noted, the Crusaders had easily seized Jerusalem from the Fatimids, also defeating a Fatimid army sent against them under the command of al-Afdal himself. Al-Afdal's subsequent attempts to deal more effectively with the Crusaders had all proved unsuccessful. By 1124, when Tyre was lost to the Crusaders, only Ascalon remained of the former Fatimid possessions in the Levant; and that last Fatimid coastal outpost, too, was lost in 1153. Meanwhile, in 1117, Egypt itself had been temporarily invaded by King Baldwin I. By 1121, when al-Afdal was murdered at the instigation of the caliph al-Amir, the reputation of the Nizari assassinations had already become so widespread that this one, too, was readily attributed to them, especially because al-Afdal who had deprived Nizar of his succession rights in 1094 had been generally considered as the arch-enemy of the Nizaris.

In the final decades of the collapsing Fatimid regime, there were further military entanglements between the Crusaders and the Fatimids. King Amalric I of Jerusalem, who had his own designs for annexing the Fatimid dominions to the Latin kingdom in rivalry with the Zangids of Aleppo, led three expeditions into Egypt during the 1160s, reducing Fatimid Egypt to a virtual Frankish protectorate.[28] It was also in these closing years of the Fatimid caliphate that Amalric sent in 1167 an embassy to the last Fatimid caliph al-Adid (1160–71) and successfully imposed a treaty on him to receive a substantial annual tribute from the Fatimid treasury. The Frankish knights of this delegation, headed by

Hugh of Caesarea, were greatly impressed by the splendour and ceremony of the Fatimid court.[29]

Meanwhile, the Syrian Nizari Isma'ilis during a third period of their early history, lasting some two decades after their debacle of 1129 in Damascus, had finally succeeded in acquiring a network of mountain fortresses in the southern part of the Jabal Bahra (modern-day Jabal Ansariyya). The Franks had earlier attempted unsuccessfully to establish themselves in the same area. In 1133, the Syrian Nizaris purchased their first fortress, Qadmus, from a Muslim lord who had recovered the place from the Franks in the previous year. In 1137, the Frankish garrison of the fortress of Khariba was dislodged by the local Nizaris. In 1140, the Nizaris captured Masyaf, their most important stronghold in Syria which then normally served as the headquarters of the chief *da'i* of the Syrian Nizaris. Around the same time, the Nizaris acquired Kahf and a few other fortresses in the Jabal Bahra, in proximity to the Frankish territories of Antioch and Tripoli. The Syrian Nizaris were to have numerous entanglements in this region with the Franks, especially with the Hospitallers who in 1142 received from the lord of Tripoli a large fortress situated at the southern end of the Jabal Bahra; it became known as the Krak des Chevaliers.

The history and external relations of the Syrian Nizaris during the period when they were consolidating their position in the Jabal Bahra remain obscure. However, it is known that a group of Nizaris led by a certain Ali b. Wafa cooperated with Raymond of Antioch in his campaign against the Zangid ruler of Aleppo, who had also aroused the enmity of the Isma'ilis by his anti-Shi'i persecutions. Both Raymond and Ali lost their lives on the battlefield at Inab in 1149.[30] A few years later, in 1152, a band of *fida'is* assassinated count Raymond II of Tripoli at the gates of his city; Ralph of Merle and another knight who were with the count and tried to save him, also perished.[31] The motives behind the assassination of Raymond II, the first Frankish victim of the Syrian Nizaris, were never revealed. King Baldwin III of Jerusalem, who was then in Tripoli, was greatly distressed by this event and ordered a majestic funeral for his relative. In a frenzy of retaliation, the Franks then turned on the Muslims and massacred a large number, and the Templars invaded the nearby territory of the Syrian Nizaris forcing the sectarians to start paying them an annual tribute of some 2000 gold pieces.

In the early 1160s, the Syrian Nizaris entered a new phase of their history under Rashid al-Din Sinan, their greatest leader and the original 'Old Man of the Mountain' of the Crusaders. Sinan fortified the Nizari castles, consolidated the position of the Syrian Nizari community, and also adopted suitable policies towards the Franks and the surrounding Muslim powers, always aiming to safeguard the security and independence of his community. He also reorganized the corps of the Nizari *fida'is*, who were utilized most effectively in the realization of his objectives.

By the time Sinan succeeded to the leadership of the Syrian Nizaris, the Franks of Tripoli and Antioch had had intermittent border clashes with the Nizaris for several decades. These entanglements began to be accentuated from the late 1160s, when King Amalric I of Jerusalem, who had increasingly come to rely on the services of the Templars and Hospitallers, ceded to them a large number of fortresses and their surrounding lands. Meanwhile, the Nizaris had continued to pay an annual tribute to the Templars, who now controlled Tortosa and almost all of its northern districts. This period also witnessed the rise of Saladin who, as the champion of Muslim unity, soon came to pose the greatest threat to the survival of the Syrian Nizari community, especially after he overthrew the Fatimids and asserted his independence from the Zangids.

It was under these circumstances that Sinan attempted to establish peaceful relations with his Christian Frankish neighbours through negotiations with King Amalric I. As a culmination of these diplomatic efforts, in 1173, Sinan sent an ambassador called Boabdelle (Abd Allah) to Amalric seeking a formal rapprochement with the Latin kingdom and expecting to be relieved from the heavy tribute which the Nizaris then paid to the Templars. The Nizari envoy had evidently received a positive response from Amalric, who had promised to send an ambassador of his own to the Nizari leader and to have the tribute cancelled in the near future. However, the Templars, who were naturally displeased by these overtures, had Sinan's emissary assassinated on his return journey by one of their knights, Walter of Mesnil. King Amalric was greatly angered by this assassination, which had been ordered by Odo of St Amand, the Grand Master of the Templars during 1171–9, and who had then refused to punish the culprit. Amalric personally led a force to Sidon, where he arrested Walter in the Templars' lodge and sent him to prison in Tyre; Amalric also conveyed his apologies to Sinan. William of Tyre further relates that it was at the time of this embassy that Sinan had informed Amalric that he and his community intended to embrace Christianity, for which reason they would expect the king to send them some Christian teachers.[32] William of Tyre had obviously misunderstood the nature of Sinan's genuine desire for improved relations with the Christian Franks. At any rate, as Amalric died in 1174, the negotiations between the Nizari leader and the king of Jerusalem proved abortive. Soon afterwards, the Nizari *fida'i*s made several unsuccessful attempts on the life of Saladin, who was then extending his hegemony over Syria; but later, lasting peace was established also between Sinan and the Ayyubid sultan.

It was also during the second half of the twelfth century that occidental travellers and chroniclers began to collect some fragmentary details and to write about the Nizari Isma'ilis. Benjamin of Tudela, the Spanish rabbi who was in the Near East during 1166–71, is probably the first European traveller to have left an account of them. Passing through Syria in 1167, Benjamin noted that there existed a people in the region called *Hashishin*, who had their principal seat at Qadmus and were a source of terror to their neighbours, killing even kings at the cost of their own lives. It is interesting to note that Rabbi Benjamin, who relates so many details on the Jewish communities of the Levant, failed to realize that the Syrian sectarians he was describing were actually Muslims. He states that these people

> do not believe in the religion of Islam, but follow one of their own folk, whom they regard as their prophet, and all that he tells them to do they carry out, whether for death or life. They call him the Sheikh Al Hashishin, and he is known as their Elder. At his word these mountaineers go out and come in.[33]

Like other westerners, Benjamin was clearly impressed by the obedience of these sectarians towards their chief. He was also the first European traveller to refer to the Nizari Isma'ilis of Persia, with some awareness of the connection between the Persian Nizaris and their co-religionists in Syria. He relates that in northern Persia, in the land of *Mulahid*, obviously a corruption of the Arabic *mulhid* (plural, *malahida*), there 'live a people who do not profess the Mohammedan religion, but live on high mountains, and worship the Old Man of the land of the Hashishin'.[34]

Another early European account of the Syrian Nizaris is to be found in the diplomatic report of Burchard of Strassburg, an envoy of Frederick I Barbarossa (1152–90), the Hohenstaufen emperor of Germany who later organized a Crusade of his own and died en route to the Holy Land in 1190. Emperor Frederick had also engaged in some diplomatic negotiations with Saladin. In 1173, the Ayyubid sultan had sent a delegation to Frederick in Germany to win the friendship of this most powerful Christian sovereign. At Strassburg, Saladin's envoys had met the *vice-dominus* Burchard, an associate of the city's bishop. Soon afterwards, when Frederick decided to reciprocate, he dispatched Burchard as his own envoy to Saladin.[35]

Burchard arrived for a short stay in Syria towards the end of 1175, soon after the first Nizari attempt on Saladin's life and the failure of the negotiations between Sinan and Amalric I. Burchard's account of the Nizaris, included in his subsequent report to Frederick Barbarossa, has been preserved in the *Chronicle* of Arnold of Lübeck.[36]

Burchard relates that

> on the confines of Damascus, Antioch and Aleppo there is a certain race of Saracens in the mountains, who in their own vernacular are called *Heyssessini*, and in Roman *segnors de montana*. This race of men live without law; they eat pork against the law of Saracens . . . They dwell in the mountains and are quasi impregnable, because they withdraw into fortified castles. Their country is not very fertile, so they live on their cattle. They have among them a lord, who inspires the greatest fear in the Saracen princes near and far, and also in the neighbouring Christian lords; because he has an astonishing mode of killing them.[37]

Burchard concludes his narrative with a story about the training of the would-be *fida'is*, which is probably the oldest written version of the Assassin legends designed to provide some explanation for the obedient behaviour of the Nizari *fida'is*. Burchard does not mention his sources; but he seems to have acquired his information orally and from the Crusader and Christian circles in the Levant.

William of Tyre is the earliest Crusader historian who a few years later, around 1180, produced his own brief description of the Syrian Nizaris and incorporated it into his *Chronicle* just before discussing Sinan's 1173 mission to King Amalric.[38]

> In the province of Tyre in Phoenicia and in the diocese of Tortosa there lives [William says,] a tribe of people who possess ten fortresses with the villages attached to them. Their number, as we have often heard, is about sixty thousand or possibly more. It is the custom of this people to choose their ruler, not by hereditary right, but by the prerogative of merit. This chief, when elected, they call the Old Man [*Senem*], disdaining a more dignified title. Their subjection and obedience to him is such they regard nothing as too harsh or difficult and eagerly undertake even the most dangerous tasks at his command. For instance, if there happens to be a prince who has incurred the hatred or distrust of this people,

the chief places a dagger in the hand of one or several of his followers; those thus designated hasten away at once, regardless of the consequences of the deed or the probability of personal escape. Zealously they labor for as long as may be necessary, until at last the favorable chance comes which enables them to carry out the mandate of the chief. Neither Christians nor Saracens know whence this name, the Assassins [Assissini], is derived.

It is interesting to note that, unlike Burchard, the well-informed William, who was equally impressed by the obedience of the sectarians, did not seek to provide any particular explanation for the unwavering loyalty of the Old Man's followers; and, consequently, he did not contribute to the formation of the Assassin legends which had then begun to appear in Crusader circles.

William of Tyre further notes that for about four centuries these people had zealously followed the law and customs of the Saracens, but that recently their chief had experienced a change of heart. Somehow he had come to possess the Christian books of the gospels and the apostolic law, which he read with interest and began to understand the Christian doctrine. As a result, he turned away from his religion and instructed his people to stop observing the practices and superstitions of that cult, also allowing the use of wine and pork. Finally he sent an ambassador to our king [Amalric], announcing that he and his community were collectively prepared to embrace Christianity.

These statements reflect an erroneous interpretation of what William of Tyre must have heard locally about certain beliefs and practices of the Syrian Nizari Isma'ilis. A learned Isma'ili leader, Sinan was also interested in establishing peaceful relations with his Christian and Sunni neighbours; as such, he must have displayed an ecumenical outlook which was in line with the general cyclical view of the Isma'ilis regarding the religious history of mankind. According to this view, the Isma'ilis believed in the common, eternal truths of all revelations, including those embodied in Judaism, Christianity and Islam, though all earlier religions had been superseded by Islam. Consequently, Jesus had been accorded an important place in Isma'ili thought as the enunciator (*natiq*) of the fifth era (*dawr*) of hierohistory, the era of Christianity. Like other highly educated Isma'ili *da'i*s, Sinan had indeed, as William relates, familiarized himself with some of the sacred scriptures of Christianity. But William evidently misunderstood these facts, which he combined with other confused rumours and reports about the alleged libertine practices of the sectarians; reports which he, like Burchard before him, must have heard locally in relation to the declaration of the *qiyama* in the Syrian Nizari community. This declaration, occurring in the mid-1160s, had been misunderstood, as noted, even by some of the Syrian Nizaris themselves. Some Syrian Muslim sources, too, relate details about the libertine practices of the dissidents in question who had gone astray.[39] At any rate, William of Tyre did not fantasize at all about the secret practices of the Syrian Nizari chief and his devoted *fida'i*s. This field soon began to be tackled by other much less informed occidental observers.

In 1187, Jerusalem and most of the other Frankish towns and castles of Outremer were seized by Saladin, who also captured a good number of Crusader princes and knights. In fact, Guy of Lusignan, then king of Jerusalem by virtue of his marriage to Amalric I's daughter Sibylla, and the Grand Masters of the knights Templar and Hospitaller spent a year in captivity before they were released by Saladin under the terms of a peace agreement. By 1189, only Tyre, saved by the efforts of Conrad of Montferrat, as well as Antioch and Tripoli were still in the hands of the Franks. It was under such circumstances that the Third Crusade was led to the Holy Land by Philip II Augustus (1180–1223) and Richard I the Lionheart (1189–99). The kings of France and England were also joined by their common nephew, count Henry of Champagne, the most powerful baron of France whose mother was half-sister to both kings. This new Crusade succeeded in July 1191 in seizing Acre, which now served as the capital of the restored kingdom of Jerusalem.

The Crusaders had always had their own internal rivalries and disputes. Marquis Conrad of Montferrat, who had played a significant part in the overall success of the Third Crusade (1189–92), had refrained from recognizing the claim of Guy of Lusignan to the throne of Jerusalem; and Guy's position was made even more difficult by the death of his wife Sibylla in October 1190. At any rate, Conrad developed his own claim to the throne of the Latin kingdom when he married Isabella, King Amalric's other daughter and Sibylla's sister, in November 1190. In April 1192, the claim of Conrad, who had meanwhile styled himself king-elect of Jerusalem and had entered into negotiations of his own with Saladin, was officially acknowledged by King Richard who was still in Outremer and by the leading Frankish dignitaries of Jerusalem. Thereupon, preparations got under way in Acre for the coronation of Conrad, who then resided in Tyre. A few days later, however, on 28 April 1192, Conrad of Montferrat fell victim in a narrow street of Tyre to the daggers of two assassins who had disguised themselves as Christian monks.

Most sources agree that Conrad's two assassins, who had waited for about six months before they finally found the opportunity to carry out their mission, were Nizari *fida'i*s sent by Sinan. There is, however, much controversy regarding the instigator of this assassination. Many Muslim sources as well as some European (especially French) ones state that Richard, King of England, who then had a quarrel with the marquis, had arranged the murder. In fact, when Richard was later briefly imprisoned in Austria, this charge was brought against him; but he denied the allegations and was released on payment of a ransom. Nevertheless, English writers felt it necessary to invent two letters supposedly written by the Old Man of the Mountain, one addressed to Leopold of Austria and the other to all the princes of Europe, which cleared Richard of any involvement in Conrad's assassination.[40] On the other hand, Ibn al-Athir, the famous Muslim historian who disliked Saladin, reports that it was the Ayyubid sultan who had commissioned Sinan to have both Conrad and Richard killed;[41] but in the event Richard's assassination had proved impossible. Finally, a late Syrian Isma'ili source attributes the initiative to Sinan himself.[42]

It is interesting to note that certain European sources, drawing on the views of the contemporary barons in Outremer, do actually provide some explanation for the Nizari leader's enmity towards Conrad. According to these sources, Conrad had offended Sinan by seizing a ship laden with a rich cargo belonging to the Syrian Nizaris, and had then refused to return the goods or the crew who were brutally drowned.

At any rate, the murder of Conrad of Montferrat greatly impressed Frankish circles and came to be discussed, usually with some notes on the 'Assassins', by most of the occidental historians of the Third Crusade.[43] The narrative of Arnold of Lübeck is of particular significance in terms of the Assassin legends; and, as we shall see later, it seems to be the earliest occidental source referring to an intoxicating potion administered by the Old Man to the would-be Nizari *fida'i*s. Henceforth, several European monarchs, such as Richard I who was charged with plotting against King Philip Augustus of France, were periodically accused of being in league with the 'Assassins' of the Latin East, or of having adopted the Old Man's methods of dealing with his enemies; all attesting to the widespread fame of the Nizaris and their methods of struggle in mediaeval Europe.[44] As the fame of the Old Man and the self-sacrificing behaviour of his *fida'i*s began to circulate more widely, the nascent legends of the 'Assassins', too, began to take more imaginative and wilder forms.

A few days after Conrad's death, his widow Isabella married Henry of Champagne, who had been favoured by King Richard I and the Frankish barons to succeed to the throne of Jerusalem; Henry became the ruler of the Latin kingdom from the time of this marriage in May 1192 until his death in 1197. In September 1192, a peace treaty was finally signed between Richard and Saladin, who had been engaged in negotiations for some time; and, at Saladin's request, the Franks also agreed to extend the peace terms to the Nizari territories in Syria. Soon afterwards, in 1192 or a year later, Sinan, who had led the Syrian Nizaris during a 30-year period to the peak of their power and fame, died at the castle of Kahf. Saladin's death occurred in 1193; and King Richard I of England finally set sail from Acre in October 1192, marking the end of the Third Crusade which had succeeded in re-establishing the kingdom of Jerusalem. With these events, an era in the complex relationships between the Syrian Nizaris, the Crusaders, and the founder of the Ayyubid state, sultan Saladin, had also come to an end.

Soon after Saladin's death, the Latins of Antioch became involved in frontier disputes with Cilician Armenia; there had also developed some deep racial and religious conflicts between the larger Greek and Armenian populations of the principality. As a result, Bohemond III (1163–1201), prince of Antioch, and Leon II (1187–98), Roupenid prince of Armenia, were soon engaged in open hostilities. On Bohemond's request, Henry of Champagne, who had now asserted some degree of hegemony over Antioch, decided to intervene in this internecine dispute which could lead to the fall of the northern principality into Armenian hands. Occidental sources relate that, in the spring of 1194, while en route to Antioch, or perhaps on the return journey to Acre, Henry passed through the territory of the Nizaris and was met by the ambassadors of the new Old Man of the Mountain who had then recently succeeded Sinan in the leadership of the 'Assassins'. On the invitation of the Old Man, who was eager to maintain a truce with the Franks in the aftermath of Conrad of Montferrat's assassination and of Saladin's peace treaty, Henry did visit the castle of Kahf, where he was entertained lavishly and was given valuable gifts by the Nizari chief, actually a Perisan *daʿi* called Nasr or Abu Mansur. In connection with this visit, a number of occidental sources, starting with the continuations of William of Tyre,[45] related variants of a story about the death leaps of the Nizari *fidaʾis* at the command of their chief; a demonstration supposedly designed to impress the Frankish king with the loyalty of the sectarians.

Sinan's successors as leaders of the Syrian Nizari community continued to exercise a certain degree of local initiative in their dealings with the Franks, though none of them achieved Sinan's relative independence from Alamut. The Nizaris now had friendly relations with Saladin's Ayyubid successors in Syria, while they continued to maintain their complex contacts and conflicts with the Crusaders and the military orders, some of which remain shrouded in obscurity. For instance, Raymond, son of Bohemond IV of Antioch, was killed in 1213 in the church of Tortosa, reportedly by some Nizari *fida'is*. And when in the following year Bohemond in an act of revenge laid siege to the Nizari fortress of Khawabi, the Nizaris received timely help from the Ayyubid rulers of Aleppo and Damascus, compelling the Franks to retreat. The circumstances surrounding Raymond's assassination remain unknown, though this act was probably rooted in hostility towards Bohemond himself. In this connection, it may be mentioned in passing that Bohemond's behaviour had also made him unpopular in Crusader circles and among the Latins of Antioch; he was even excommunicated in 1208 by patriarch Albert of Jerusalem under orders from Pope Innocent III (1198–1216). In an official report sent from Acre to Pope Innocent III earlier in 1204, this same patriarch Albert had spoken of the great fear inspired in Christians and Muslims alike by the chief of the Nizaris due to the murders committed by his *Asasis*.[46] Bohemond had also aroused the enmity of the military orders; in 1230 the Syrian Nizaris actually helped the Hospitallers in their military campaign against him. It is, therefore, not unlikely that the Hospitallers themselves may have instigated the assassination of Bohemond's youthful son.

Meanwhile, the Syrian Nizaris had somehow managed to receive tributes from some Christian rulers. In 1227, Frederick II (1211–50), Hohenstaufen emperor of Germany who led his own Crusade (1228–9) to the Holy Land, sent an embassy to the Syrian Nizari chief, Majd al-Din. The ambassadors of Frederick, who was then also the titular king of Jerusalem by virtue of his marriage to the heiress of the Latin kingdom, a granddaughter of Conrad of Montferrat and Isabella, had brought with them splendid gifts worth 80,000 dinars. Frederick himself arrived in Acre in 1228 and gained possession of Jerusalem and other localities for the Franks for a ten-year period (1229–39) under the terms of a truce signed with the Ayyubid sultan of Egypt. Emperor Frederick, too, had his own differences with papal policies, which resulted in his excommunication by Pope Gregory IX (1227–41); and his rapprochement with the Syrian Nizaris met with the disapproval of the Hospitallers, who were then attempting to make the sectarians their own tributaries. As the Nizaris refused to comply with the demands of the Hospitallers, the knights of that military order led a force into the Syrian Nizari territory and carried off much booty. By 1228, the Syrian Nizaris had in fact become tributaries to the Hospitallers under the terms of a cooperative pact, while they continued to pay tribute to the Templars. It was also around this time that the Nizaris began to lend occasional support to the military orders in their campaigns against some of the Christian rulers of the Latin states; and at least the Hospitallers reciprocated by defending the Nizaris against the encroaching forces of Antioch and Tripoli. The Nizari involvement in the Hospitaller campaign of 1230 launched from Krak des Chevaliers against Bohemond IV of Antioch represented one such instance of cooperation.

It was against this background that Bohemond V (1233–57), the next prince of Antioch and Raymond's brother, wrote to Pope Gregory IX complaining that the Grand Master of the Hospitallers was then in league with the 'Assassins'. In response to this complaint, on 26 August 1236, Pope Gregory wrote to the Archbishop of Tyre and the bishops of Sidon and Beirut insisting that the Hospitallers should terminate any compromising connections with

> the Assassins, the enemies of God and of the Christian name, who formerly dared to slay treacherously Raymond [son of Bohemond IV] . . . and many other magnates and Catholic princes, and are striving to overcome our faith by force . . . and what is far graver still the aforesaid Assassins, on account of the promise made by the aforementioned Master and brethren [of the Hospital] to support and protect them from Christian attacks, have undertaken to pay them a certain sum of money every year. Therefore we have sent them orders in writing to desist from defending these same Assassins . . . And so we now charge you that if the said Master and brethren should fail to observe this our command, you shall compel them to abandon this understanding by the censures of the Church, without right of appeal, after giving them due warning.[47]

A similar papal letter was evidently issued regarding the connections that possibly existed at the time between the Templars and the 'Assassins'.

Thus, contacts had continued to increase between the Crusaders and the Syrian Nizaris. Under such circumstances, it would not have been too difficult for the Franks to acquire more accurate knowledge about the Nizari Isma'ilis who, by the end of the twelfth century, had attracted so much public attention in Outremer, both in Crusader circles as well as among the oriental Christians of the region. But proximity to the Syrian Nizaris did not result in more accurate perceptions of the Nizari beliefs and practices; and the Crusader historians of the first half of the thirteenth century added practically nothing to the limited and distorted knowledge of the sect then possessed by Europeans. This becomes abundantly clear by analysing what James of Vitry, the most learned Frankish writer of the period, had to say on the subject.

James (Jacques) of Vitry was a cleric from Paris and an ardent preacher and supporter of the Crusading movement throughout his career. He preached the Crusade even before he was appointed, in 1216, Bishop of Acre by Pope Honorius III (1216–27); and he sustained his missionary activities during his ministry at Acre (1216–28), and after returning to Europe as the cardinal-bishop of Tusuculum. James also participated actively in the Fifth Crusade (1217–21), for which he campaigned vigorously. Indeed, he had been of the opinion that the Saracens, who had hitherto refrained from converting to Christianity because they feared the vengeance of their co-religionists, would readily convert once the Crusaders had arrived on the scene.[48] James was also the first Catholic in the Crusaders' times to have preached earnestly to the Muslims of the Levant. He travelled widely in Syria, delivering sermons to large gatherings in Christian towns and castles; he also preached in the Christian–Muslim borderland and sent numerous letters in Arabic to the Muslims living beyond the border areas.[49] In the course of the Fifth Crusade, James succeeded in different ways in obtaining control over large numbers of Muslim children who had been held as captives by the Crusaders, baptizing them and ensuring their Christian education. However, he soon realized how difficult it was to detach the Muslims from their religious background, necessitating some moderation of his earlier missionary zeal.

James of Vitry was perhaps the best informed occidental observer of Muslim affairs in Outremer after William of Tyre, although he remained extremely hostile towards Islam and does not seem to have made any special effort to learn about it. It is, therefore, not surprising that his description of the Nizari Isma'ilis is based almost entirely on that of William of Tyre. The only new factual detail he added related to the inter-connection between the Syrian and Persian Nizari Isma'ilis.[50]

In the province of Phoenicia, near the borders of the Antaradensian town which is now called Tortosa, dwells a certain people, shut in on all sides by rocks and mountains, who have ten castles, very strong and impregnable, by reason of the narrow ways and inaccessible rocks, with their suburbs and the valleys, which are most fruitful in all species of fruits and corn, and most delightful for their amenity. The number of these men, who are called Assassins [Assasini], is said to exceed 40,000. They set a captain over themselves, not by hereditary succession, but by the prerogative of merit, whom they call the Old Man (*Veterem seu Senem*), not so much on account of his advanced age as for his pre-eminence in prudence and dignity. The first and principal *abbot* of this unhappy *religion* of theirs, and the place where they had their origin and whence they came to Syria, is in the very remote parts of the east, near the city of Bagdad and the parts of the province of Persia. These people, who do not divide the hoof, nor make a difference between what is sacred and what is profane, believe that all obedience indifferently shown by them towards their superior is meritorious for eternal life. Hence they are bound to their master, whom they call the Old Man, with such a bond of subjection and obedience that there is nothing so difficult or so dangerous that they would fear to undertake, or which they would not perform with a cheerful mind and ardent will, at the command of their lord.

After offering his own version of how the Nizari *fida'is* were trained by the Old Man, which will be considered in the next chapter, James concluded his account by stating that the 'Assassins'

kept the law of Mahomet and his institutions diligently and straitly beyond all other Saracens till the times of a certain master of theirs, who, being endowed with natural genius, and exercised in the study of different writings, began with all diligence to read and examine the law of the Christians and the Gospels of Christ, admiring the virtue of the miracles, and the sanctity of the doctrine. From a comparison with these he began to abominate the frivolous and irrational doctrine of Mahomet, and at length, when he knew the truth, he studied to recall his subjects by degrees from the rites of the cursed law. Wherefore he exhorted and commanded them that they should drink wine in moderation and eat the flesh of swine. At length, after many discourses and serious admonitions of their teacher, they all with one consent agreed to renounce the perfidy of Mahomet, and, by receiving the grace of baptism, to become Christians.

Clearly, James of Vitry, like William of Tyre, had been grossly misled by confused rumours about the Nizari doctrine of the *qiyama*, which he further confounded with some misinformation about Sinan's reported desire to establish peaceful relations with the Franks of Outremer.

The last important encounter between the Franks and the Nizari Isma'ilis, prior to the loss of political power by the sect in Syria, occurred in connection with the diplomatic designs of King Louis IX (1226–70). Following the early defeat of his Crusade, which represented the culmination of the efforts of Christendom to recover the Holy Places, Louis IX (St Louis) ransomed himself from captivity in Egypt and settled down in Acre for four years (1250–54). While in Acre he exchanged embassies and gifts with the leader of the Syrian Nizari community, also obtaining some information about their beliefs. We have a detailed account of these events from the pen of the famous French chronicler John, lord of Joinville (Jean de Joinville), whose family had been in the service of the counts of Champagne. Joinville accompanied the French king on his Crusade and then stayed with him in Acre as a close companion and secretary. Joinville returned with St Louis to France in 1254, but later declined to accompany him on his Tunisian Crusade of 1270, which turned out to be even more catastrophic than the king's expedition to Egypt. In France, Joinville (d. 1317) produced a most valuable *History of Saint Louis*, with special reference to the unhappy events of the king's earlier Crusade and his dealings in Outremer.

Referring to the Nizari Isma'ilis as the Assacis and also as the Bedouins, Joinville relates that during the king's residence at Acre, probably in 1250–51, 'there came likewise to him ambassadors from the prince of the Bedouins, called the Old Man of the Mountain ... asking the king if he were acquainted with their lord ... The king said he was not; he had never seen him, although he had heard much spoken of him.' The ambassadors then told the king that he should start paying tribute to their chief 'in like manner as the emperor of Germany, the king of Hungary, the sultan of Babylon [Egypt], and many other princes, have yearly done; for they know well, that they would not be allowed to exist or reign, but during his good pleasure.' The emissaries also declared, Joinville adds, that their chief would be equally satisfied if the king were to acquit him of the tribute he then paid annually to the Grand Master of the Temple, or of the Hospital.[51]

Joinville then relates how the king promised to deliver his reply in a second meeting, which was convened later on the same day in the presence of the Grand Masters of the Templars and Hospitallers; but instead of keeping his promise, the emissaries were now pressured by the Grand Masters, Reginald of Vichier and William of Chateauneuf, into repeating their earlier request. Joinville explains that in the course

of a third meeting which took place on the following day, the Grand
Masters reprimanded the Nizari emissaries for having conveyed such an
imprudent message to the King of France, and they enjoined the
emissaries to return to their chief and 'to come back within fifteen days
with such letters from [their] prince, that the king shall be contented
with him'. According to Joinville, who may have been present at some
of these meetings, the Nizari envoys returned to Acre within the
specified period, bringing valuable gifts from their chief, including a
crystal elephant, several amber statues and other ornaments inlaid with
gold, as well as a shirt and a ring. In connection with the last two items,
the envoys reportedly told the king:

> Sire, we are come back from our lord, who informs you that as
> the shirt is the part of dress nearest to the body, he sends you this,
> his shirt, as a gift, or a symbol that you are the king for whom he
> has the greatest affection, and which he is most desirous to
> cultivate; and, for a further assurance of it, here is his ring that he
> sends you, which is of pure gold, and hath his name engraven on
> it; and with this ring our lord espouses you, and understands that
> henceforth you be as one of the fingers of his hand.

Desiring to cultivate friendly relations with the Nizari Isma'ilis, St
Louis responded to their peace initiative by dispatching his own gift-
bearing ambassadors to the Old Man of the Mountain. This Frankish
mission also included an Arabic-speaking friar, Yves the Breton, who
had conducted other negotiations with Muslim rulers on behalf of the
French king. It was in the course of his meetings with the Nizari chief,
held at the stronghold of Masyaf, that Yves evidently conversed with
the 'prince of the Bedouins' on 'the articles of his faith'. Joinville
recounts interesting details of what Yves the Breton later reported to
the king regarding his understanding of the doctrines preached by the
Nizari Isma'ilis.[52]
The Old Man of the Mountain, Friar Yves had reported,

> did not believe in Mahomet, but followed the religion of Aly, who
> was . . . the uncle of Mahomet . . . it was Aly to whom Mahomet
> was indebted for all the honours he enjoyed; and that, when
> Mahomet had made his great conquests over mankind, he
> quarrelled with and separated from Aly, who perceiving the pride
> of Mahomet, and that he wished to trample upon him, began to
> draw as many as he could to his doctrines, and retired to a part of
> the deserts and mountains of Egypt, where he gave them a

different creed from that of Mahomet. Those who support the religion of Aly call those who follow Mahomet unbelievers, as the Mahometans in like manner style the Bedouins infidels. Each party, in this respect, says the truth, for in fact they are both unbelievers.

Joinville has preserved other, equally confused and misunderstood, details of what Yves had to say on some of the more specific tenets attributed to the Nizaris. 'One of the points of the doctrine of Aly', Yves had reported, 'consists in the belief, that when any one is killed by the command or in the service of his superior, the soul of the person so killed goes into another body of higher rank, and enjoys more comforts than before'. Yves cited this alleged Nizari belief in the transmigration of souls as the main reason why the Nizari *fida'is* were so eager to be killed in the service of their chief. Having misunderstood the Isma'ili cyclical view of history, however, Yves had also misrepresented an incomplete version of this view in terms of the transmigration of the souls of prophets and their legatees. In this connection, Yves had evidently found, in the living quarters of the Old Man, a short Christian treatise which contained some sayings of Jesus addressed to St Peter. Delighted at this evidence of interest in Christianity, Yves had then told the Nizari chief to read that book frequently, 'for, small as it may be, it contains many excellent things'. The Old Man had reportedly replied that he did in fact read it frequently, adding that he held St Peter in highest esteem, because

> in the beginning of the world, the soul of Abel, after his brother Cain had murdered him, entered the body of Noah; and the soul of Noah, on his decease, went into the body of Abraham; and after Abraham it entered the body of St Peter, who is now under the earth.

Joinville himself included some information on the Nizaris in his *History of Saint Louis*, which follows closely the account of Yves the Breton.[53] He, too, notes that the Bedouins (Nizaris)

> have no great faith in Mahomet, like the Turks, but believe in the religion of Aly . . . They are persuaded that when any one of them dies for the service of his lord, or when attempting any good design, his soul enters a superior body, and is much more

comfortable than it was before; this makes them ready to die at
the command of their superiors or elders.

Joinville ends his note on the Syrian Nizaris by stating that 'their
numbers are not to be counted; for they dwell in the kingdoms of
Jerusalem, Egypt, and throughout all the lands of the Saracens and
infidels'.

It is significant that neither Joinville nor his source, Yves the Breton,
who lived in the Latin East and had contacts with the Syrian Nizaris
and their leadership, participated in the formation of the Assassin
legends. In other words, they did not fantasize about the secret
practices of the Nizaris, nor did they endorse any of the then circulating
versions of such legends purporting to explain the devotion of the
fida'is and their attachment to their chief. Joinville and Yves the Breton
were, indeed, the only thirteenth-century occidental observers of the
Nizaris who attempted to explain the devotion of the fida'is on the
basis of the sectarian beliefs, while their contemporaries in Crusader
circles and in Europe were already well embarked on their quest to
rationalize the behaviour of the fida'is in terms of their addiction to
bodily pleasures, induced with or without intoxicating potions.

St Louis, as noted, also endeavoured to forge an alliance with the
Mongols against the Muslims; and for this purpose he sent William of
Rubruck as his envoy to the Great Khan Mongke. William has several
references to the Nizaris in his account of his mission to Mongolia. In
addition to relating that a group of 'Assassins' had been sent under
different guises to Karakorum to kill the Great Khan, William is among
the earliest Europeans to have referred to the Persian Nizaris as the
'Assassins'.

William embarked on his journey to Mongolia in 1253. On passing
north of the Caspian Sea in his itinerary, he notes that 'to its south it
has the Caspian range and Persia, and to the east the mountains of the
Mulihet (that is, the Assassins)'.[54] And later, while reporting the
dispatch of a large group of 'Assassins' to Karakorum, William adds
that the Great Khan 'has sent one of the uterine brothers into the
territory of the Assassins, who are known to them as the Mulihet, with
orders for their complete extermination'.[55] In all probability, William
had heard the term 'Assassins', or its variants such as 'Axasins' and
'Hacsasins' which appear in other manuscripts of his itinerary, from the
Crusaders and was to some extent aware, like James of Vitry, of the ties
between the Syrian and the Persian Nizaris. William used the words
Assassins and Mulihet (a corruption of the Arabic mulhid or malahida)
interchangeably; in addition to applying the term 'Assassins' to both

the entire Persian Nizari community and the group of the Nizari *fidā'is*. At any rate, William of Rubruck did not succeed in his diplomatic mission and returned to Europe in 1256. St Louis himself, having accomplished none of his designs for Christendom during his stay in Outremer, had returned to France a year earlier. Meanwhile, Mongke's own designs against the Muslim powers were carried out with catastrophic precision.

By 1258, the Mongols had achieved their twin objectives of destroying the Nizari state in Persia and the Abbasid caliphate. The Mongol armies then advanced into Syria, where they had some initial successes before being decisively defeated in 1260, in Palestine, by the Mamluks who were now establishing their own rule over Egypt and Syria, in succession to the Ayyubids.

The Syrian Nizari Isma'ilis were, thus, spared the horrific fate of their Persian co-religionists. But the extinction of the political power of the parent sect in Persia had dealt a devastating blow to the Syrian Nizaris who soon lost their own, now essentially fragile, independence. By 1267, the Syrian Nizaris had become tributaries to Baybars I (1260–77), the Mamluk sultan who expelled the Mongols from Syria and inflicted decisive defeats on the Crusaders. Meanwhile, as a result of a treaty signed between the Mamluk sultan and the Hospitallers, the latter had renounced the tribute which they themselves had hitherto received from the Nizaris. The Syrian Nizaris had now, in fact, placed themselves under the suzerainty of the Mamluk state; and by 1273 they had lost even their nominal independence. However, the Syrian Nizaris were allowed to remain in their fortresses in the Jabal Bahra under the strict surveillance of Mamluk lieutenants. The legendary accounts of the *fidā'is* and their activities also continued to circulate, even though the Nizaris were now devoid of any political power and no longer had any prominent political enemies. There are also some scattered reports suggesting that Baybars and his successors in the Mamluk dynasty may have employed the services of the Syrian Nizaris against their own enemies. For instance, the assassination of Philip of Montford, lord of Tyre and an important baron of Jerusalem, in 1270, and the unsuccessful attempt on the life of Prince Edward of England in 1272, are reported to have been instigated by Baybars with the help of the Nizari *fidā'is*.

With the loss of their independence and political power, the Nizaris no longer played any important part in the political events of the Near East; and there no longer occurred any direct contact between them and the Franks. Under these conditions, the Franks learned nothing new about the Nizaris during the later Middle Ages, enabling the highly embellished and imaginative tales of Marco Polo and other westerners to fall on fertile ground. Tales of the 'Assassins' now derived 'legitimacy' or pseudo-historicity from the fanciful heritage of several generations.

In sum, mediaeval Europeans learned very little about Islam and Muslims, and their less informed knowledge of the Isma'ilis found expression in a few superficial observations and erroneous perceptions scattered in Crusader histories and other occidental sources. Yet by the middle of the thirteenth century, many of these sources claimed to possess intricate details about the secret practices of the Isma'ilis and their chief, the Old Man of the Mountain; the Assassin legends had by then truly come into being.

Notes and References

1. See, for instance, Edward W. Said, *Orientalism* (London, 1978), pp 59 ff.
2. N. Daniel, *Islam and the West: The Making of an Image* (Edinburgh, 1966); and R.W. Southern, *Western Views of Islam in the Middle Ages* (Cambridge, MA, 1962). See also M. Th. d'Alverny, 'La Connaissance de l'Islam en Occident du IXe siècle au milieu du XIIe siècle', in *L'Occidente e l'Islam nell' alto medioevo* (Spoleto, 1965), pp 577–602; M. Rodinson, 'The Western Image and Western Studies of Islam' in J. Schacht and C.E. Bosworth (eds), *The Legacy of Islam* (2nd edn, Oxford, 1974), pp 9–62; A. Hourani, *Europe and the Middle East* (London, 1980), pp 1–73; and *Islam in European Thought* (Cambridge, 1991), pp 7–60; and W.M. Watt, *Muslim–Christian Encounters* (London, 1991), especially pp 59–88.
3. For a modern view on the Judaeo-Hagarene origins of Islam, see P. Crone and M. Cook, *Hagarism: The Making of the Islamic World* (Cambridge, 1977), a controversial study which contains numerous interesting insights and hypotheses.
4. See Steven Runciman, *A History of the Crusades*, 3 vols (Cambridge, 1951–54).
5. The early history of the Frankish states is investigated by different scholars in *A History of the Crusades*, ed. Setton, Vol 1, pp 368–462, 528–61.
6. There are different editions of the Latin text of William of Tyre's *Historia rerum in patribus transmarinis gestarum*; in the most recent and best edition of this work by R.B.C. Huygens, used here, its title is stated simply as *Chronicon* (Turnhout, 1986).
7. See William of Tyre, *Chronicon*, p 100.
8. For more details, see Peter W. Edbury and John G. Rowe, *William of Tyre: Historian of the Latin East* (Cambridge, 1988), pp 32–58.
9. *Gesta Francorum et aliorum Hierosolimitanorum*, ed. and tr. R. Hill (London, 1962).
10. See Runciman, *A History of the Crusades*, Vol 2, pp 291–324; Urban T. Holmes, 'Life among the Europeans in Palestine and Syria in the Twelfth and

Thirteenth Centuries', in *A History of the Crusades*, ed. K.M. Setton: Vol IV, *The Art and Architecture of the Crusader States*, ed. H.W. Hazard (Madison, WI, 1977), pp 3–35; and P.M. Holt, *The Age of the Crusades* (London, 1986), pp 31–7.

11. Southern, *Western Views*, pp 27–8.

12. See, for instance, Walter of Compiègne, *Otia de Machomete*, ed. R.B.C. Huygens, in *Sacris Erudiri*, 8 (1956), pp 286–328.

13. Pedro de Alfonso, *Dialogi in quibus impiae Judaeorum confutantur*, in J.P. Migne (ed.), *Patrologia Latina* (Paris, 1844–64), Vol 157, pp 527–672, with the *Dialogus* dealing with Islam on pp 597–606.

14. See M. Th. d'Alverny, 'Deux traductions latines du Coran au Moyen Age', *Archives d'histoire doctrinale et littéraire du Moyen Age*, 22–23 (1947–48), pp 69–131; and James Kritzeck, *Peter the Venerable and Islam* (Princeton, 1964).

15. For a list of the individual items in this collection, see Daniel, *Islam and the West*, pp 399–400.

16. See M. Th. d'Alverny, 'Notes sur les traductions médiévales d'Avicenne', *Archives d'histoire doctrinale et littéraire du Moyen Age*, 27 (1952), pp 337–58; M. Fakhry, *A History of Islamic Philosophy* (2nd edn, London, 1983), pp 66–94, 107–62; and H. Corbin, *History of Islamic Philosophy*, tr. L. Sherrard (London, 1993).

17. On this embassy, see Matthew Paris, *Chronica Majora*, ed. Henry R. Luard (London, 1872–83), Vol 3, pp 488–9; English trans. *Matthew Paris's English History*, tr. John A. Giles (London, 1852–54), Vol 1, pp 131–2.

18. William of Rubruck, *The Mission of Friar William of Rubruck: His Journey to the Court of the Great Khan Möngke 1253–1255*, tr. P. Jackson (London, 1990), pp 226–35.

19. Ibid., p 222.

20. On the missionary aspects of the Crusading movement, see Benjamin Z. Kedar, *Crusade and Mission: European Approaches toward the Muslims* (Princeton, 1988), especially pp 97–203.

21. Watt, *Muslim–Christian Encounters*, pp 85–6; and *The Influence of Islam on Medieval Europe* (Edinburgh, 1972), pp 73–7.

22. Southern, *Western Views*, p 103.

23. See P. Kraus, 'Hebräische und syrische Zitate in isma'ilitischen Schriften', *Der Islam*, 19 (1931), pp 243–63; S.M. Stern, 'Fatimid Propaganda among Jews according to the Testimony of Yefet b. Ali the Karaite', in his *Studies in Early Isma'ilism* (Jerusalem–Leiden, 1983), pp 84–95; and J.T.P. de Bruijn, 'al-Kirmani', EI2, Vol 5, pp 166–7.

24. William of Tyre, *Chronicon*, Book 1, ch 4, pp 109–10, and Book 19, ch 21, pp 890–2; English trans. *A History of Deeds Done Beyond the Sea*, tr. Emily A. Babcock and A.C. Krey (New York, 1943), Vol 2, pp 323–5.

25. James of Vitry, *Historia Orientalis*, in *Gesta Dei per Francos*, ed. J. Bongars (Hanover, 1611), Vol 1, pp 1060–1. See also Daniel, *Islam and the West*, p 318.

26. Ricoldo da Monte Croce, *Itinerarium*, in *Peregrinatores medii aevi quatuor* J.C.M. Laurent (ed.), (2nd edn, Leipzig, 1873), ch 8, p 127; and *Il Libro della*

Peregrinazione nelle parti d'Oriente di frate Ricoldo da Montecroce, ed. U. Monneret de Villard (Rome, 1948), p 111; Daniel, *Islam and the West*, p 319; and E. Kohlberg, 'Western Studies of Shi'a Islam', in M. Kramer (ed.), *Shi'ism, Resistance, and Revolution* (London, 1987), pp 31 ff., reprinted in his *Belief and Law*, article II.

27. See William of Tyre, *Chronicon*, Book 13, ch 26, pp 620–2, and Book 14, ch 19, pp 656–7; tr. Babcock and Krey, Vol 2, p 77.

28. See Runciman, *A History of the Crusades*, Vol 2, pp 362–400; and Marshall W. Baldwin, 'The Latin States under Baldwin III and Amalric I, 1143–1174', in *A History of the Crusades*, ed. Setton, Vol 1, pp 548–61.

29. William of Tyre, *Chronicon*, Book 19, chs 18–19, pp 887–9; tr. Babcock and Krey, Vol 2, pp 319–21; it is after the account of this embassy that William explains the differences between Sunni and Shi'i Islam.

30. Ibid., Book 17, ch 9, pp 770–2; tr. Babcock and Krey, Vol 2, pp 196–8.

31. Ibid., Book 17, chs 18–19, pp 785–7; tr. Babcock and Krey, Vol 2, pp 214–15.

32. Ibid., Book 20, chs 29–30, pp 954–6; tr. Babcock and Krey, Vol 2, pp 392–4. See also J. Hauziński, 'On the Alleged Attempts at Converting the Assassins to Christianity in the Light of William of Tyre's Account', *Folia Orientalia*, 15 (1974), pp 229–46.

33. Benjamin of Tudela, *The Itinerary of Benjamin of Tudela*, ed. and tr. Marcus N. Adler (London, 1907), text pp 18–19, trans. pp 16–17.

34. Ibid., text p 50, trans. pp 53–4.

35. P. Scheffer-Boichorst, 'Der kaiserliche Notar und der Strassburger Vitztum Burchard', *Zeitschrift für die Geschichte des Oberrheins*, 43 (1889), pp 456–77.

36. Arnold of Lübeck, *Chronica Slavorum*, in G.H. Pertz et al. (eds), *Monumenta Germaniae Historica: Scriptores* (Hanover, 1826–1913), Vol 21, pp 235–41.

37. Ibid., p 240; English trans. in Lewis, *The Assassins*, pp 2–3.

38. William of Tyre, *Chronicon*, Book 20, ch 29, pp 953–4; tr. Babcock and Krey, Vol 2, p 391.

39. See *Bustan al-jami*, ed. Claude Cahen, in his 'Une chronique Syrienne du VIe/XIIe siècle: Le *Bustan al-Jami*', *Bulletin d'Études Orientales*, 7–8 (1937–38), p 136; Abu'l-Fada'il Muhammad al-Hamawi, *al-Ta'rikh al-Mansuri*, ed. P.A. Gryaznevich (Moscow, 1963), p 176; and Lewis, 'Kamal al-Din's Biography of Rašid al-Din Sinan', pp 230, 241–2, 261.

40. See, for instance, Joseph F. Michaud, *Michaud's History of the Crusades*, tr. W. Robson (London, 1852), Vol 3, pp 434–5.

41. Ibn al-Athir, *Kitab al-kamil fi'l-ta'rikh*, ed. Carl J. Tornberg (Leiden, 1851–76), Vol 12, p 51.

42. See Abu Firas, *Fasl min al-lafz al-sharif*, in S. Guyard, 'Un Grand Maître des Assassins au temps de Saladin', *Journal Asiatique*, 7 série, 9 (1877), trans. pp 408–12, text pp 463–6; English trans. in F. Gabrieli, *Arab Historians of the Crusades*, tr. E.J. Costello (Berkeley, 1969), pp 242–5.

43. See, for instance, the following accounts, some of which also relate Conrad's act of piracy against the Nizari cargo: Ambroise, *L'Estoire de la Guerre Sainte*, ed. and tr. G. Paris (Paris, 1897), pp 235 ff.; *L'Estoire de Eracles Empereur*, in *Recueil des Historiens des Croisades: Historiens Occidentaux* (Paris, 1844–

95), Vol 2, pp 192–4; *Chronique d'Ernoul et de Bernard le Trésorier*, ed. L. de Mas Latrie (Paris, 1887), pp 288–9; William of Newburgh, *Historia rerum Anglicarum*, ed. H.C. Hamilton (London, 1870), Vol 3, p 181; *Itinerarium peregrinorum et gesta regis Ricardi*, ed. W. Stubbs, in *Chronicles and Memorials of the Reign of Richard I* (London, 1864), Vol 1, pp 337 ff.; and *Chronicles of the Crusades; being Contemporary Narratives of the Crusade of Richard Coeur de Lion and of the Crusade of Saint Louis* (London, 1848), pp 276–7.

44. See Charles E. Nowell, 'The Old Man of the Mountain', *Speculum*, 22 (1947), pp 508 ff.; and L. Hellmuth, *Die Assassinenlegende in der österreichischen Geschichtsdichtung des Mittelalters* (Vienna, 1988), pp 9–22, 116–65, tracing the roots of some such mediaeval Austrian legends about Frederick II, as contained especially in the writings of Jans Enikel who flourished in the second half of the thirteenth century, to eastern models and Nizari influences.

45. See, for instance, *L'Estoire de Eracles*, pp 216, 230–1; and *Chronique d'Ernoul*, pp 323–4.

46. See *Chroniques gréco-romanes inédites ou peu connues*, ed. C. Hopf (Berlin, 1873), p 31.

47. The English translation of this papal letter of 1236, expressing objections to the relations between the Hospitallers and the 'Assassins', is cited in E.J. King, *The Knights Hospitallers in the Holy Land* (London, 1931), pp 234–5.

48. James of Vitry, *Lettres de Jacques de Vitry, évêque de Saint-Jean d'Acre*, ed. R.B.C. Huygens (Leiden, 1960), pp 88–9, 95.

49. Ibid., pp 91–4.

50. The Latin text of James of Vitry's account of the 'Assassins' is contained in his *Historia Orientalis*, in *Gesta Dei per Francos*, Vol 1, pp 1062–3; English trans. in *Secret Societies of the Middle Ages* (London, 1846), pp 117–19.

51. Joinville's account of the exchange of embassies between St Louis and the Nizari leader is contained in his *Histoire de Saint Louis*, ed. N. de Wailly (Paris, 1868; reprinted, Lille, n.d.), pp 218 ff.; English translation in Jean de Joinville, *Memoirs of John Lord de Joinville*, tr. T. Johnes (Hafod, 1807), Vol 1, pp 194 ff., reprinted in *Chronicles of the Crusades*, pp 470 ff.

52. Joinville, *Histoire*, pp 222–4, and *Memoirs*, pp 195–7, reprinted in *Chronicles of the Crusades*, pp 472–4.

53. Joinville, *Histoire*, pp 121–3, and *Memoirs*, pp 148–9, reprinted in *Chronicles of the Crusades*, pp 420–1.

54. William of Rubruck, *The Mission*, p 128.

55. Ibid., p 222.

4

Origins and Early Formation
of the Legends

The Isma'ilis organized a dynamic, revolutionary movement against the Abbasids who, like the Umayyads before them, had, in the eyes of the Shi'a, usurped the legitimate rights of the Alids to the leadership of the Muslim community. The Isma'ili *da'wa* or religio-political propaganda achieved its crowning success in 909 in the establishment of the Fatimid caliphate; the first Shi'i caliphate ruled by the Isma'ili imam from the progeny of Ali and the Prophet's daughter Fatima.

The Isma'ilis, generally perceived as belonging to a single homogeneous community, were targeted for a hostile literary campaign by different groups of Muslim writers. In time, the seminal anti-Isma'ili 'black legend' came to be accepted by the Muslim majority as an accurate description of the motives, teachings and practices of the Isma'ilis. However, their political fortunes continued to rise and the movement survived the Nizari–Musta'li schism of 1094. The Nizari Isma'ilis were quick to retrieve the revolutionary zeal and ideals of the pre-Fatimid Isma'ilis; and they launched an armed revolt against the Sunni Saljuq Turks in Persia and Syria. Confronted by the overwhelmingly more superior and decentralized military power of the Saljuqs, the Nizari Isma'ilis also resorted to assassinating their prominent enemies in particular localities. This policy proved very effective, and before too long most political assassinations of any importance, at least in the central Muslim lands, were attributed to the daggers of the Nizari *fida'is*, who rarely survived their own missions. The eastern assassinations of the Alamut period, whether or not actually committed by the *fida'is*, played an important part in shaping anti-Nizari opinion in Muslim society. Hostile reports and misinformation about the alleged Nizari abrogation of the *shari'a* further contributed to the Nizaris' negative image.

In time, the reports of the assassinations attributed to the Nizaris also caught the attention of the Crusaders and their historians. Westerners were particularly impressed by the self-sacrificing behaviour of the Nizari devotees. By the final decades of the twelfth century, the Crusaders and their occidental observers had already begun to resort to imagination in order to explain to their own satisfaction the motives behind the unwavering devotion of the *fida'i*s belonging to the sect of the 'Assassins'.

The Nizaris were also the target of the official wrath of the Sunni establishment, in addition to inheriting the defamations levelled against the earlier Isma'ilis. Mediaeval Muslim writers sometimes designated the Nizaris by religious terms such as the Batiniyya and the Ta'limiyya, when not referring to them as the Isma'iliyya, and the Nizariyya.[1] However, the Nizaris, like other Isma'ilis, were more commonly designated as the 'Malahida' (or 'Mulhidun') by their Muslim enemies during the Alamut period and later, especially from the second half of the twelfth century. Much less frequently, the Nizaris were referred to by other abusive terms and expressions such as 'al-Hashishiyya', or 'Jama'at al-Hashishiyya', which supposedly meant the community of hashish users.

The earliest written application of the term *hashishiyya* to the Nizaris, representing the first known instance of its use in Islamic sources, occurs in the highly anti-Nizari polemical epistle issued around 1123 by the Fatimid chancery in Cairo on behalf of the caliph al-Amir, who was then recognized as an imam by the Musta'lian Isma'ilis. As noted already, this epistle, the *Iqa' sawa'iq al-irgham*, sent to the Musta'lians of Syria, was a second official attempt, after the earlier *al-Hidaya al-Amiriyya*, to refute the claims of Nizar, al-Amir's uncle, to the Isma'ili imamate while reasserting the legitimacy of the Musta'lian line of imams. In the *Iqa' sawa'iq al-irgham*, the term *hashishiyya* is used twice in reference to the Syrian Nizaris without any explanation.[2] This implies that the term had already, by the early decades of the twelfth century, acquired a generally-known meaning in the Muslim world, or at least in Egypt and Syria.

The Syrian Nizaris are again referred to as 'Hashishiyya' in the earliest known Saljuq chronicle, written in 1183 by Imad al-Din Muhammad al-Katib al-Isfahani (d. 1201) whose history, the *Nusrat al-fatra*, is now extant only in an abridged version compiled in 1226 by al-Bundari.[3] It is also interesting to note that these early Saljuq chroniclers use the terms *hashishiyya*, *malahida* and *batiniyya* interchangeably.[4] Only a few other contemporary Muslim historians, notably Abu Shama and Ibn Muyassar, occasionally used the term *hashishiyya* (singular, *hashishi*) in reference to the Nizaris of Syria

(Sham),[5] while none of these Muslim authors provided any derivative explanation for their use of this term. Ibn Muyassar, for instance, merely states that in Syria they are called 'Hashishiyya'; in Alamut, they are known as Batiniyya and 'Malahida'; in Khurasan, they are called Ta'limiyya, and they all are Isma'ilis. Subsequently, the term seems to have fallen into disuse; Ibn Khaldun (d. 1406) is among the rare Muslim authors writing after the thirteenth century who states that the Syrian Nizaris, once called as 'al-Hashishiyya al-Isma'iliyya', were known in his time as the Fidawiyya.[6]

The Persian historians of the Ilkhanid period, including Juwayni and Rashid al-Din, who are the main sources for the history of the Persian Nizari community during the Alamut period, do not use the term *hashishiyya* in reference to the Persian Nizaris. In fact, the term *hashishi* and its variants do not appear at all, to this author's knowledge, in any of the Persian texts of the Alamut or post-Alamut period which have references to the Nizari Isma'ilis. Mediaeval Persian authors generally designated the Nizaris as *malahida* or *mulahida* when desiring to employ abusive terms. But W. Madelung, the foremost western authority on the Isma'ilis and the Zaydis, has recently discovered that the Persian Nizaris, too, were called 'Hashishis' in some contemporary Zaydi sources written in the Arabic language in the Caspian region during the first half of the thirteenth century. In these hostile Zaydi texts, the Isma'ili community at large is often referred to as 'Malahida', while 'Hashishi' is more specifically applied to the Nizari *fida'i*s sent from Alamut on assassination missions.[7] Thus, the argument of Bernard Lewis that the term *hashishi* was local to Syria, and that it was never used by Muslims in reference to the Persian Nizaris, has proved to be erroneous.[8] It is safe to assume, however, that the term *hashishi* did originate in the Arabic-speaking Muslim countries, but it failed, unlike the word *mulhid* (plural, *malahida*), to acquire currency in the Persian language, which was also chosen as the religious language of the Persian Nizari community.

Hashish, or *hashisha*, is the Arabic name for a product of hemp, a cultivable plant whose Latin name is *cannabis sativa*. This plant, and its more common variety Indian hemp (*cannabis Indica*), have been known and used in the Near East since ancient times as a drug with intoxicating effects. The seeds and leaves of the hemp plant, as well as the products derived from it, have acquired different names and nicknames in India, Persia and the Arab world, including *banj* (*bang*), *shahdanaj*, *qinnab* and *kif*.[9] But it is not known how and when the Arabic word hashish, which originally meant 'dry herb', came to be applied as a nickname to the hemp plant, or rather to its resin which contains the active element of hemp. At any rate, this hallucinatory drug must have been rather widely used by the time of the adoption of the word hashish as its nickname. Subsequently, the nickname itself led to the derivation of terms designating a person (or persons) using or being addicted to this product, notably *hashishi* (plural, *hashishiyya*; colloquial plurals *hashishiyyin* and *hashishin*) and, less commonly, *hashshash* (plural, *hashshashin*). The earliest known written attestation of the designation *hashishiyya* occurred, as noted, in reference to the Syrian Nizaris in the Musta'lian polemical epistle issued around 1123. This document did not explain why the term was applied to the Nizaris, although it may be assumed that its application implied the idea but not the fact that the Nizaris were actually hashish users. At any rate, it is evident that by the beginning of the twelfth century, the word *hashishiyya* had already been a term familiar to the Muslims for some time, dating at least to the second half of the eleventh century and preceding the Nizari–Musta'lian schism.

The use of hashish grew significantly in Syria, Egypt and other Muslim countries during the twelfth and thirteenth centuries, especially among the lower strata of society. It was at this time that the harmful effects of hashish began to be discussed extensively throughout Muslim society; and, starting in the thirteenth century, numerous tracts were written by Muslim authors who described these effects in terms of different physical, mental, moral and religious categories.[10] In particular, Muslim writers stressed that the extended use of hashish would have extremely harmful effects on the user's morality and religion, relaxing his attitude towards those duties, such as praying and fasting, specified by the sacred law of Islam.[11] As a result, the hashish user would qualify for a low social and moral status, similarly to that of a *mulhid* or heretic in religion. It was particularly in this sense that the Muslim jurists argued against hashish users, and strongly demanded their punishment as criminals and heretics.

As Professor Franz Rosenthal has observed, one thing stands out clearly in the entire mediaeval discussion of hashish by Muslim writers:

> a certain class distinction was made between confirmed addicts and the rest of the people ... Hashish eaters were believed to be low-class people either by nature or by being reduced to that state through their habit which impaired all their faculties but in particular those moral and character qualities that determine the individual's standing in society.[12]

Thus, hashish users were plainly regarded as social outcasts and criminals, and the *hashishiyya* were branded as dangerous to Islam and society, and condemned as such by majority opinion at least from the latter part of the eleventh century.

It was in the abusive senses of 'low-class rabble' and 'irreligious social outcasts' that the term *hashishiyya* seems to have been used metaphorically in reference to the Nizari Isma'ilis during the twelfth and thirteenth centuries, and not because the Nizaris or their *fida'is* secretly used hashish in a regular manner, which in any event would not have been public knowledge. Needless to add that addiction to a debilitating drug like hashish would have been rather detrimental to the success of the *fida'is* who often had to wait patiently for long periods before finding a suitable opportunity to carry out their missions. Even abstracting from the ascetic character of Hasan Sabbah, who personally instituted the sect's revolutionary policies, the obedience and discipline of the Nizari *fida'is* was not without its antecedents among earlier Shi'i groups which were similarly imbued with elitism and a unique sense of group solidarity and devotion. In modern times, too, similar behaviour has been manifested by certain Muslim groups espousing martyrology. At any rate, the fact remains that neither the Isma'ili texts which have been recovered so far nor any contemporary non-Isma'ili Muslim texts, which were generally hostile towards the Nizaris, attest to the actual use of hashish by the Nizaris. Indeed, the major Muslim historians of the Nizaris, such as Juwayni, who generally attribute all types of sinister motives and beliefs to the Isma'ilis, do not even refer to the Nizaris as 'Hashishis'. The few Arabic sources which do refer to the Nizaris as 'Hashishis' never explain this appellation in terms of the use of hashish, even though they were prepared to heap all sorts of defamatory accusations upon the heads of the Nizaris.

Muslims who were familiar with Shi'i martyrology did not require an explanation in order to understand the self-sacrificing behaviour of the *fida'is*. As a result, Muslim authors, unlike western writers, did not fantasize about the sect's secret practices. The available evidence indicates that it was the name Hashishiyya that in time led to the unfounded suggestion that the Nizaris, or their *fida'is*, used hashish in a regular manner; a myth which was accepted as reality during the Middle Ages and was essentially endorsed by Silvestre de Sacy and other orientalists of the nineteenth century. The hashish connection proved particularly appealing to mediaeval western observers who needed 'simple' explanations for the seemingly irrational behaviour of the Nizari *fida'is*.

Under such circumstances, beginning in the second half of the twelfth century, Arabic variants of the term *hashishi* were heard and picked up locally in Syria by the Crusaders, who received their information about Muslims mainly through oral channels. This information served as the basis for a number of terms, such as Assassini, Assissini and Heyssessini, by which the Nizari Isma'ilis of Syria came to be designated in base-Latin sources of the Crusaders and in different European languages, resulting in the more familiar name 'Assassins'. The Nizari 'assassinations' later received further exaggeration in western popular lore and literature when the term 'assassin' entered the western languages as a new common noun meaning 'murderer'. At any rate, by the end of the fourteenth century the epithet *hashishi* was evidently no longer regarded as a term of abuse in Muslim society. Al-Maqrizi (d. 1442), the famous Egyptian historian who has an informative section called 'the hashish of the poor' (*hashishat al-fuqara*) in his well-known book dealing with the antiquities of Cairo,[13] relates that by his time the use of hashish had indeed reached a peak; it was discussed and utilized, even among the better classes of Cairo and Damascus, publicly and without inhibition. Nevertheless, al-Maqrizi, too, related an anecdote about hashish and the Isma'ilis, stating that around the year 1392 a Persian Isma'ili, whom he now designates as a 'Mulhid' and not a 'Hashishi', prepared electuaries made of hashish, honey and spices which were sold under the name of *uqda* to members of the upper classes in Cairo.

It is, therefore, not surprising that none of the variants of the Assassin legends can be found in Muslim sources produced during the twelfth and thirteenth centuries; the period of the political prominence of the Nizaris in Persia and Syria which partially coincided with the formative period of these legends found in European sources. The Muslim authors of the pre-Mongol times, who had socio-cultural and religious affinities with the Isma'ilis, did not find it necessary to fantasize about the secret practices of the Nizari *fida'is*. The legends make their original appearance in the western sources in connection with the Syrian Nizaris whose activities and reputation had attracted the attention of the Crusaders and other occidental observers. The Crusaders had no contacts with the Nizari community in Persia, and consequently they did not produce comparable 'imaginative' descriptions of the Persian Nizaris of the Alamut period. It was only starting with Marco Polo's account of the 'Assassins' that the Assassin legends began to be extended to the parent Nizari community in Persia, despite the fact that at least some of the occidental sources had earlier recognized the supremacy of the Persian Nizaris over their Syrian co-religionists.

It is my contention, as argued below, that westerners themselves were responsible for fabricating the Assassin legends in their familiar, popular forms, and putting them into circulation in the Latin East as well as in Europe. These legends, rooted essentially in the 'imaginative ignorance' of the mediaeval Europeans, did nevertheless draw on some important bits and pieces of information or disinformation as well as misunderstood rumours, hostile allegations and exaggerated half-truths which were picked up locally and orally. Such oral channels, as noted, were readily available to the Franks, not only through direct encounters with the Muslims but also through the close relations existing in Crusader times between the Frankish circles and oriental Christians who had their own contacts with the Muslims.

The Syrian Nizaris, who possessed a vulnerable and small princi-pality in a hostile milieu, made an important impact, quite dispro-portionate to their numbers or political power, on the regional politics of the Latin East. This was particularly the case when they were led by Rashid al-Din Sinan, their most famous leader and the original 'Old Man of the Mountain'. Indeed, it was Sinan who reorganized the Syrian Nizari community and led them to the peak of their power and fame. Other factors, too, contributed to the Crusaders' impressions of the Syrian Nizaris. These sectarians, detested by many of their Muslim neighbours, were singled out for all types of defamation and the matter could not have escaped the attention of the Crusaders who, in a rare instance of its kind, adopted a special appellation, 'Assassins', in reference to the Nizaris, echoing the names such as 'Hashishiyya' applied to them abusively by their Muslim enemies. Then there were the assassinations attributed to the Nizaris in a highly exaggerated manner by their Muslim adversaries; altogether fewer than five Frankish personalities may have actually been killed by the *fida'is* during the entire period of the Crusaders' presence in Outremer. Nevertheless, it was the exaggerated reports of the alleged Nizari assassinations and the daring behaviour of the real *fida'is*, who usually carried out their missions in public places and rarely survived their victims, which greatly impressed the Crusaders, who would rarely endanger their own lives for other than worldly rewards. This explains why the Assassin legends came to revolve entirely around the *fida'is*, especially in connection with their recruitment and training.

The stage was thus set, from the time of Sinan's leadership in the second half of the twelfth century, for the formation of the Assassin legends, which provided satisfactory explanations for behaviour that seemed irrational or superhuman to the mediaeval western mind, then generously endowed with imaginative powers for interpreting all things Oriental or Islamic. The Assassin legends, consisting of a number of separate but connected stories, developed gradually, and not strictly in terms of clearly identifiable stages, although they followed an ascending tendency or trend towards more elaborate versions. They culminated in the version popularized by Marco Polo who combined a number of such legends in a fully integrated form, also adding his own original contribution in the form of a secret 'garden of paradise' where earthly delights were procured for the *fida'is*. Different legends or components of particular legends were 'imagined' sometimes independently and at times concurrently by different authors; while, in a general sense, most authors used the accounts of their predecessors as the basis for making their own contributions. In the event, from the latter part of the twelfth century, the occidental chroniclers, travellers and envoys to the Latin East who had something to say on the 'Assassins' participated, as if in tacit collusion, in the process of fabricating, transmitting and legitimizing the Assassin legends. A century later the legends had acquired wide currency and had come to be accepted as reliable descriptions of Nizari practices, in much the same way as the earlier anti-Isma'ili 'black legend' formulated by Muslim writers had in time come to be accepted as the true expression of Isma'ili motives and teachings.

An exhaustive survey of different categories of mediaeval European sources bearing on the 'Assassins' is beyond the scope of this study.[14] For our purposes it will suffice to review the origins and some of the early developments and milestones in the formation of the major European myths of the 'Assassins', from the second half of the twelfth century to the turn of the fourteenth century.

The earliest known European account purporting to explain the self-sacrificing behaviour of the *fida'is* was produced by Burchard of Strassburg who had visited Syria in the autumn of 1175. Burchard included this account, as part of his description of the 'Heyssessini' ('Assassins'), in his report to Frederick I Barbarossa who had sent him on a diplomatic mission to Saladin.

After relating that the Assassins have a prince or lord who strikes the greatest fear into the Saracen princes and the neighbouring Christian lords, because he has a habit of killing them in an astonishing way, Burchard adds:

> the method by which this is done is as follows: this prince possesses in the mountains numerous and most beautiful palaces, surrounded by very high walls, so that none can enter except by a small and very well-guarded door. In these palaces he has many of the sons of his peasants brought up from early childhood. He has

them taught various languages, as Latin, Greek, Roman, Saracen as well as many others. These young men are taught by their teachers from their earliest youth to their full manhood, that they must obey the lord of their land in all his words and commands; and that if they do so, he, who has power over all living gods, will give them the joys of paradise. They are also taught that they cannot be saved if they resist his will in anything. Note that, from the time when they are taken in as children, they see no one but their teachers and masters and receive no other instruction until they are summoned to the presence of the Prince to kill someone. When they are in the presence of the Prince, he asks them if they are willing to obey his commands, so that he may bestow paradise upon them. Whereupon, as they have been instructed, and without any objection or doubt, they throw themselves at his feet and reply with fervour, that they will obey him in all things that he may command. Thereupon the Prince gives each one of them a golden dagger and sends them out to kill whichever prince he has marked down.[15]

It is certain that Burchard must have heard some oral traditions about the Nizaris during his brief stay in Syria in 1175, when the memory of the first unsuccessful Nizari attempt on Saladin's life, which had taken place a few months earlier, was still fresh in local circles. This may, indeed, explain why he chose to include a description of the Nizaris in his diplomatic report. But it is not clear to what extent Burchard merely repeated details heard by him locally from oral sources. At any rate, it may be safe to assume that, being an uninformed observer of the East, he fully believed the authenticity of what was related to him in Syria, probably by Frankish and local Christian sources; and, in the absence of earlier written reports, he personally acted imaginatively in combining the pieces, or the building blocks which appear in his tale, into what seemed to him to be a complete and sensible whole. This becomes all the more plausible if Burchard's account is compared with the much more factual description of the 'Assassins' written a few years later by the well-informed William of Tyre, who spent some three decades in the Holy Land and possibly had personal contacts with the local Nizaris. As noted, William may even have been present when, in 1173, Sinan's ambassadors met with King Amalric I in Jerusalem; to Burchard, Sinan was merely a remote lord of a strange people living in impregnable mountains. As a result, William, equally impressed by the devotion of the Nizaris to their chief, neither reproduced any local tales which by then must have been circulating in Crusader circles nor did he give free rein to his own imagination in a matter that was to perplex the Franks for a long time to come. Similarly, Benjamin of Tudela, the Spanish rabbi who travelled extensively in the Near East and was in Syria earlier in 1167, did not fantasize about the secret practices of the Nizaris. Indeed, with very few exceptions, Europeans who were long-term residents of the Holy Land during Crusader times did not contribute in any important fashion to the formation of the Assassin legends.

In Burchard's account of the Nizaris, we have the earliest written statement of the secret procedures utilized for the recruitment and training of the Nizari *fida'is*, which may be designated here as the 'training legend'. Would-be *fida'is* were allegedly recruited in child-hood and then trained by special teachers in complete isolation until they were ready to be dispatched on their missions. The training was designed to prepare the youthful recruits to become unconditionally responsive to any command of their lord. However, Burchard also cites an inducement factor in the form of a reward: a promise by the Nizari chief to bestow 'paradise' on them if they always acted obediently. This, too, may be regarded as the first, rudimentary statement of the 'paradise legend', which in different forms was to become an integral component of the Assassin legends.

The Nizari sources which have been recovered so far do not contain any details on the organization and training of the *fida'is* during the Alamut period, if ever such information existed; nor can such details be found in contemporary Sunni and non-Isma'ili Shi'i sources dealing with the Nizaris. In Persia, the *fida'is* do not seem to have been organized into any special group, while in Syria they were evidently organized, at least temporarily, in the time of Sinan. Most of Burchard's details about their rigorous training programme, adopted or conjectured independently by later occidental writers, may be regarded as gross exaggeration or a fictitious portrayal of what may have actually taken place, especially regarding the young age of the recruits and their prolonged training in isolation. Also, there is no evidence to suggest that the *fida'is* received specific instructions in languages. Even if the Syrian *fida'is* did receive any training, it would more probably have been of a technical nature, designed to ensure the success of their performance in the field rather than to condition and shape their mental disposition from an early age; at any rate, all matters related to the activities of the *fida'is* would have been among the Nizaris' most closely guarded secrets. Therefore, it is safe to assume that no factual information would have been available to outsiders, local Christians and Muslims alike. Burchard's detailed account of the recruitment and training of the *fida'i*s should, thus, be taken to represent an 'imaginative' and exaggerated construction based on rumours.

In contrast to his 'imaginary' description of the training programme, Burchard's brief reference to the paradise promised to the *fida'i*s is essentially based on distorted Nizari beliefs of the time; its sources, therefore, can be identified more readily. By the twelfth century, Muslims had long been familiar with the Islamic traditions, rooted in the Quran, which held that pious believers, those who feared God and followed the right path, as well as martyrs of Islam, would be guaranteed an eternal place in Paradise as their deserved reward in the afterlife. Paradise was described rather vividly in the Quran. For the Shi'i Muslims, their imams would also ensure through their intercessionary role on the Day of Judgement that their followers would receive their just reward by being admitted into Paradise. The Nizari Isma'ilis, as the partisans of the only rightful imam of the time, certainly expected to qualify as a saved community for the paradisal state in the afterlife.

There were, however, more specific reasons why the Nizaris in general and their *fida'i*s in particular expected to be deserving of Paradise. Ever since the martyrdom of the imam Husayn and his companions in 680, the theme of martyrology had occupied a particular place in the Shi'i ethos, which accorded a unique status, comparable to that of the pious believers, to those devotees who gave their lives in the service of their creed and imam. This was, indeed, the manner in which the *fida'i*s were viewed by the rest of the Nizari community during the Alamut period. The *fida'i*s, whether they returned safely from their missions or lost their lives as martyrs, were held in high esteem, attested to by the rolls of honour kept at Alamut and other major Nizari fortresses. As a rare instance of its kind, we also have the already-noted poem by Ra'is Hasan, a Persian Nizari historian, poet and functionary of the early thirteenth century, in which the three *fida'i*s who had killed a Turkish *amir* are praised for their self-sacrificing behaviour which had entitled them to the joys of the otherworldly paradise.[16] Similar ideas are echoed in the scattered and brief references to the *fida'i*s found in Muslim historical sources; they reveal, for instance, that the mothers of the *fida'i*s would happily expect their sons to become martyrs and as such enter Paradise. Burchard could easily have heard such local traditions regarding the Nizaris' hope of access to Paradise.

There were even more immediate reasons for the appearance of the paradise connection in Burchard's account. He visited Syria in 1175, a few years after the declaration of the *qiyama* or Resurrection in the Nizari community. This declaration, initiated in Persia in 1164, had been repeated shortly afterwards in Syria by Sinan. The Muslim sources relate that Sinan himself had to deal personally, in 1176, with a group of the Syrian Nizaris who had somehow misunderstood the *qiyama* doctrine, indulging in libertine practices. Such episodes also provided further suitable excuses for Muslim opponents of the Nizaris to accuse them of the outright abandonment of the law and of exercising antinomianism. Traces of these accusations, preserved by some Syrian historians, are clearly reflected in the account of Burchard who states that the 'Heyssessini' (Nizaris) 'live without law; they eat swine's flesh against the law of the Saracens, and make use of all women'. Similar accusations are reported in William of Tyre's account; all this reveals that by the 1170s the Syrian Nizaris were already being accused by other Muslims of practices incorrectly associated with the declaration of the *qiyama*. It is equally clear that such accusations, in those early post-*qiyama* years, were prevalent enough to have attracted Burchard's attention during his short stay in Syria.

In a distorted fashion, Burchard seems to have heard something else, too, about one of the central ideas of the *qiyama* doctrine then preached within the Syrian Nizari community. As noted, the *qiyama*, or the awaited Day of Judgement, was interpreted spiritually for the Nizaris on the basis of the well-known Isma'ili method of esoteric interpretation. On this basis, it was explained that only the Nizaris, as the sole community of true believers acknowledging the rightful imam of the time, were capable of understanding the spiritual reality and the true meaning of all religions and, as such, Paradise had now been created for them in this world. In other words, by contrast to other religious communities, both Muslim and non-Muslim, the Nizaris were henceforth collectively admitted into Paradise and their *da'wa* implied an invitation into that paradisal state. Burchard must have heard about the important 'paradise' of the Nizaris in such a way as to have warranted its inclusion in his account in a key role. Like other mediaeval Europeans with some limited and distorted knowledge of Islam, Burchard may also have been familiar with the ideas, then current in certain Christian circles, about the 'sensual' nature of the paradise promised to the Muslims. The Latin translation of the Quran, produced in 1143, had already introduced the Islamic paradise to mediaeval Europe, and Pedro de Alfonso and others after him in the twelfth century had dwelled polemically on the hedonistic delights of the Islamic 'garden of paradise' to prove that Islam was not a spiritual religion, and, therefore, not comparable to Christianity. In time, the

European conceptions of the Islamic paradise, rooted in Quranic descriptions, were incorporated into the Assassin legends, culminating in Marco Polo's detailed account of the Nizari 'garden of paradise'.

It is also important to note that the notion of 'paradise' is utilized in Burchard's account in a highly legendary and metaphysical manner, in so far as the access to it was placed, in an unexplained fashion, under the full control of the Nizari chief who was, thus, portrayed as a superhuman figure. He was to be feared and obeyed by the *fida'is* just as the Quran had specified the behaviour of the believers towards God. This should not cause any surprise, however, because Burchard's account purported to explain the puzzling obedience of the *fida'is* precisely in terms of the extraordinary hold exercised over them by their chief. In this connection it should be recalled that the Nizari chief to whom Burchard is referring in his account was Rashid al-Din Sinan, who did indeed enjoy unprecedented popularity and veneration in the Syrian Nizari community. This is clearly reported by the contemporary Andalusian traveller Ibn Jubayr, who passed through Syria shortly before his death in 1184.[17] In a Syrian Nizari hagiographical work produced later in the sixteenth century, by an obscure Nizari author known as Abu Firas, Sinan is actually exalted as a saintly hero and different wonders and miraculous acts are attributed to him.[18] A few Sunni authors of the Mamluk period, too, ascribe extraordinary powers and acts to Sinan, presumably drawing on oral traditions.[19] All this may be taken to reflect Sinan's popular reputation for the spectacular; a reputation which was evidently circulating already in his lifetime in Syria and which also came to be reflected, though in a distorted fashion, in Burchard's contemporary account.

At any rate, the 'paradise legend' is already distinguishable in an embryonic form in Burchard's account; henceforth, it became a permanent component of the Assassin legends. In line with the general trend of these legends towards more exaggerated versions during the early period of their formation, the 'paradise legend' became gradually more removed from the actual beliefs of the Nizaris concerning Paradise; progressing from the initial depiction of the sectarians' hope to gain the celestial paradise to cravings for the carnal delights of a terrestrial garden of paradise, constructed secretly by the Nizari chief to simulate the delights of the promised Paradise. Burchard's account of the recruitment and training of the *fida'is* also contains the central aspects of another legend, which were subsequently adopted, modified and elaborated in different ways by successive generations of European writers. Thus, by 1175, the stage had been set for the formation and widespread circulation of the Assassin legends in Crusader circles and

European sources. Burchard's account itself, included in his diplomatic report to Emperor Frederick I, was already available in Germany by the late 1170s; and it was seen and utilized by others in northern Europe, especially Arnold of Lübeck.

Almost all the European writers, after Burchard, who had something to say about the 'Assassins', also fantasized about the recruitment and training of the *fida'i*s, repeating with minor modifications the details contained in Burchard's account. All these sources essentially aimed to show the ingenious methods utilized by the Old Man of the Mountain, who cleverly combined indoctrination with psychological deceit based on the promise of Paradise, to condition and control the disciplinarian behaviour of the *fida'i*s. As noted, William of Tyre does not relate any details on the alleged training of the would-be *fida'i*s; but all other European sources of the later decades of the twelfth and the thirteenth centuries, including the old French continuations of William of Tyre's *Historia*, with minor variations state that the Old Man recruited his future *fida'i*s at an early age, or even in childhood, sometimes separating them by force from their parents, and then had them trained by special teachers in his own house, palace, or in certain secluded places, always deceiving them by promising them the joys of Paradise.[20] In this connection, James of Vitry's account is of particular importance, representing a further development, or a subsequent stage, in the early formation of the Assassin legends.

'The Old Man, their lord', explains James of Vitry,

> causes boys of this people to be brought up in secret and delightful places [*locis secretis et delectabilibus*], and having had them diligently trained and instructed in the different kinds of languages, sends them to various provinces with daggers, and orders them to slay the great men of the Christians, as well as of the Saracens . . . promising them, for the execution of this command, that they shall have far greater delights, and without end, in paradise, after death [*in paradiso post mortem*], than even those amidst which they had been reared. If they chance to die in this act of obedience they are regarded as martyrs by their companions, and being placed by that people among their saints, are held in the greatest reverence. Their parents are enriched with many gifts by the master, who is called the Old Man [*Senex*] . . . Whence these wretched and misguided youths . . . undertake their deadly legation with such joy and delight.[21]

As noted, James of Vitry, the Bishop of Acre (1216–28), was the best

informed Frankish observer of Muslim affairs in the Latin East, after
William of Tyre. His account of the Nizari Isma'ilis is basically
modelled on what William had written a few decades earlier, although
he added his own embellishments. At any rate, the account of James,
produced during the first half of the thirteenth century, is independent
of Burchard's account; and in terms of its legendary content falls
somewhere between the rather sober description of the Archbishop of
Tyre and the imaginative narrative of Burchard. Unlike William, James
seems to have been more readily influenced by some of the tales he had
heard locally; but, in contradistinction to Burchard, some of the central
beliefs of the contemporary Nizaris and their *fida'i*s are more clearly
and accurately reflected in his account. Thus, James correctly relates
that the Nizaris held that 'all obedience indifferently shown by them
towards their superior is meritorious for eternal life', and that the
*fida'i*s who did not return from their missions would be regarded as
martyrs by their companions and as such they were held in greatest
reverence.

James of Vitry, too, has something to say on the training programme
of the *fida'i*s, which he must have heard locally. But he omits many of
the intricate details found in Burchard's account, revealing that he had
not blindly believed his local oral sources. Like other Frankish writers
before him, except William of Tyre, James also connects the obedience
of the *fida'i*s to their hope of gaining Paradise in the afterlife, which
had been promised to them. It should be emphasized here that this form
of the paradise connection, rooted in actual Nizari beliefs, appears in
all the western accounts of the Nizaris, from Burchard to Marco Polo.
During this period, only William of Tyre and Thietmar do not connect
the devotion of the *fida'i*s to the promised Paradise. Thietmar, a
German traveller who visited the Holy Land during the early decades of
the thirteenth century and was thus a contemporary of James, merely
states that the 'Assassins' obeyed their master until death.[22] Furthermore, in all the western accounts before Marco Polo, one does not find
any causal connection between the places where the *fida'i*s were
trained and the celestial paradise whose delights awaited them.

James of Vitry's account differs in one significant aspect from all
other western accounts produced before Marco Polo. He is the earliest
western author to refer to the training places of the would-be *fida'i*s as
the *locis secretis et delectabilibus*, the secret and delightful places, as if
vaguely anticipating the terrestrial 'secret garden of paradise' elaborated later by Marco Polo. James does, in fact, imply that the future
*fida'i*s enjoyed certain delights in the course of their training, which
presumably would have made them even more eager for experiencing

the greater otherworldly pleasures, promised all along as their ultimate reward. However, James does not provide any details on these alleged 'secret and delightful places', and the delights that the would-be *fida'is* supposedly enjoyed as trainees. It is quite possible that such ideas and insinuations were developed on the basis of some misunderstood, or imaginatively distorted, local rumours then circulating among the Crusaders in the Latin East. Accordingly, during his long ministry at Acre in close proximity to the Nizari territory in Syria, James of Vitry could easily have heard about the gardens and the water conduits of Masyaf, Qadmus, Kahf and other Nizari fortresses in Syria. In his account, James does, in fact, speak of the Syrian Nizari castles 'with their suburbs and the valleys, which are most fruitful in all species of fruits and corn, and most delightful for their amenity'.

It is a known fact that Hasan Sabbah planted numerous trees in the Alamut valley, and also improved the cultivation and irrigation systems there. His future successor, Buzurg-Ummid, adopted similar measures and completely changed Lamasar into a 'delightful place' during his long governorship of that castle in northern Persia. Other Nizari leaders, too, including Sinan in Syria, concerned themselves with such matters, which transformed the major Nizari fortresses into delightful sites and agriculturally self-sufficient enclaves, guaranteeing their survival under long sieges. It is, thus, possible that by his 'secret and delightful places' James may have been merely referring to the Nizari castles themselves. Be that as it may, for James these delightful places were clearly distinguished from the celestial paradise promised to the *fida'is* as a reward for their obedience. As in other accounts, here, too, the behaviour of the *fida'is* is essentially motivated by their desire to enter the metaphysical, celestial paradise; and their 'delightful' training places merely served to give them a foretaste of the delights that awaited them in the afterlife. This is why James explains that the otherworldly delights, expected by the *fida'is*, would be superior to the delights which the *fida'is* had already enjoyed in this world during their training. According to James, the obedience of the *fida'is* was not motivated, as in Marco Polo's account, by their desire to return to their earlier delightful training places or to a 'garden'; it was rather the expectation of the bliss of the celestial paradise that prepared the *fida'is* for self-sacrifice.

Thus, in terms of its essential points, James of Vitry's account is a more accurate portrayal of the actual Nizari beliefs than what the much less-informed Burchard had earlier said on the subject. Furthermore, James does not depict the Nizari chief as a superhuman figure; although here, too, he is represented as a deceitful character. Nevertheless,

James of Vitry made his own important contribution to the development of the Assassin legends, in so far as he introduced the idea of the 'secret and delightful places', and in doing so he anticipated, in a crude and partial manner, the Old Man of the Mountain's terrestrial secret 'garden of paradise', which was to become fully elaborated in Marco Polo's account. James of Vitry may, therefore, rightfully be regarded as one of the major early proponents of the Assassin legends, and his account represents an important milestone in the early formation of these legends.

Another milestone can be traced to the German writer Arnold of Lübeck (d. 1212), who wrote his *Chronicle* before 1210 as a continuation of Helmond of Bosau's *Chronicle of the Slavs*. While reporting Conrad of Montferrat's assassination in 1192, Arnold produces his own account of the 'Heissessin' ('Assassins'). It should be recalled that the same Arnold of Lübeck had access to the diplomatic report of his contemporary countryman, Burchard of Strassburg, and used this report as one of his sources. However, Arnold also had his own direct oral sources in the Latin East, which he seems to have visited briefly in 1172.

Admitting at the outset that the things he had heard about the Old Man might appear ridiculous (*ridiculosum*), and then dismissing such doubts on the account of the reliability of his witnesses, Arnold of Lübeck relates:

> 'this Old Man has by his witchcraft so bemused the men of his country, that they neither worship nor believe in any God but himself. Likewise he entices them in a strange manner with such hopes and with promises of such pleasures with eternal enjoyment, that they prefer rather to die than to live. Many of them even, when standing on a high wall, will jump off at his nod or command, and, shattering their skulls, die a miserable death. The most blessed, so he affirms, are those who shed the blood of men and in revenge for such deeds themselves suffer death. When therefore any of them have chosen to die in this way, murdering someone by craft and then themselves dying so blessedly in revenge for him, he himself hands them knives which are, so to speak, consecrated to this affair, and then intoxicates them with such a potion that they are plunged into ecstasy and oblivion, displays to them by his magic certain fantastic dreams, full of pleasures and delights, or rather of trumpery, and promises them eternal possession of these things in reward for such deeds.[23]

Arnold of Lübeck's account is important in several respects. First, by summarily dismissing his own doubts about the authenticity of what had been related to him by his oral sources and affirming the reliability of these same sources, Arnold attests that from early on the Assassin legends had come to enjoy a reputation for authenticity in Crusader circles. This, of course, greatly facilitated the subsequent elaboration and transmission of these legends in mediaeval Europe. Secondly, and much more significantly, this is the earliest western source referring to an unexplained intoxicating potion administered by the Old Man to the *fida'is*; the first statement of a new legend which may be designated as the 'hashish legend', and which was later adopted by Marco Polo and other western sources. This new legend about the hashish dreams of the *fida'is* was, in all probability, invoked by the abusive designations, connected with hashish, which were at the time applied to the Syrian Nizari Isma'ilis by their Muslim opponents. These designations were now interpreted literally. Thirdly, Arnold's account gave a new twist to the 'paradise legend', allowing the *fida'is* to enjoy the delights of the celestial paradise in yet another, hallucinatory, fashion in this world.

Arnold of Lübeck's account of the Nizari *fida'is* is even more removed from the reality than those of Burchard and James of Vitry. Like other Frankish authors, Arnold too depicts the Old Man of the Nizaris as a scheming manipulator of the *fida'is'* motivations; a deceitful leader who beguiles the gullible *fida'is* by promising them the delights of Paradise in the afterlife. But in Arnold's account the Old Man's deception takes on a new and more sinister form in so far as he now diabolically motivates them into self-sacrifice by simulating in them, under the double influences of a drug and his own magical powers, a delusion of the delights of Paradise. Thus, the otherworldly reward expected by the *fida'is* has, in Arnold's account, acquired a terrestrial dimension in that the *fida'is* are deluded, through hallucinatory dreams invoked by a narcotic drug, with the visions of Paradise and its delights. However, Arnold stops short of talking about any actual experimentation with such delights in a terrestrial 'garden of paradise' designed specifically for that purpose by the Old Man; another variant of the 'paradise legend' implied in James of Vitry's account and fully incorporated into the Assassin legends by Marco Polo.

Finally, it is to be noted that Arnold's account alludes to yet another of the famous Assassin legends, the 'death-leap legend'. This most impressive story of how the Nizari *fida'is* would instantly leap to their death, from high towers or walls, at the command of their chief in order to demonstrate their loyalty and enable their chief to intimidate his enemies, was repeated with slight variations in many mediaeval European sources. It was first related in the old French continuations of

William of Tyre's chronicle in connection with Henry of Champagne's reported visit, in 1194, to the Old Man of the Mountain.[24] Count Henry, it will be recalled, had then recently succeeded Conrad of Montferrat to the throne of the Latin kingdom. The Nizari chief had, according to these occidental sources, staged the suicide demonstration in Henry's presence in order to dissuade him from contemplating any ill designs against the Syrian Nizari community. This legend had become quite famous in Europe by the end of the thirteenth century. It is, for instance, included in the Latin history of Marino Sanudo, the Venetian historian who himself travelled several times to the East and presented his historical work to Pope John XXII (1316–34) in 1321. Referring to the Nizari chief as *Rex Arsasidarum*, Marino places the suicide demonstration, which supposedly took place in the presence of Henry of Champagne, in the year 1193.[25] In some versions of this legend, including one appearing in the famous Italian collection of 100 old stories, the German emperor Frederick II replaces Henry of Champagne as the European dignitary in whose presence the Old Man (*Il Veglio*) demonstrates the absolute obedience of his *fida'i*s;[26] while Arnold of Lübeck presents the legend as a customary demonstration of loyalty in the Nizari community.

There is little doubt, however, that such death-leap demonstrations did not take place in the presence of Henry of Champagne or any other European dignitary. This legend may have been closely related to the hashish connection in that the *fida'i*s under the influence of that drug would presumably leap more readily to their death. At any rate, Arnold of Lübeck, who does not name any European monarch in his version, seems to have preserved this legend more faithfully as it had then evidently acquired popularity in the East. Like Arnold, Ibn Jubayr mentions this story as a customary practice of the Syrian Nizari community of Sinan's times.[27] A few other eastern sources, too, contain the death-leap legend. Georgius Elmacin (Jirgis al-Makin), an Arabic-speaking Coptic historian who died in 1273, even transposes the scene of this legend to the Persian Nizari community of Hasan Sabbah's time. According to Elmacin, it was Hasan's son who had commanded the suicides of some *fida'i*s in order to intimidate an ambassador of the Saljuq sultan Malikshah who had demanded obedience from the Nizari community.[28] Elmacin's entire account lacks historicity.

L. Hellmuth has forwarded an interesting hypothesis regarding the origin of the death-leap legend.[29] He argues that the eastern versions of this legend were in all probability based either directly on the ancient Alexander romance, which was well known in the East as well as in Europe, or on popular stories derived from that romance. According to a late version of the Alexander romance, Alexander the Great had intimidated the envoys of the Jews, whose country he was then invading, by ordering some of his soldiers to jump into a ravine.[30] Western writers, as was their custom, added their own embellishments and included European dignitaries in their Nizari death-leap accounts to make them more attractive to their European audiences.

The contacts between the Franks and the Syrian Nizaris continued during the first half of the thirteenth century. But these contacts, culminating in the dealings between King Louis IX of France and the Old Man of the Mountain, did not in any way dispel the Assassin legends, which had continued to circulate. Joinville and his source Yves the Breton, who personally held discussions on doctrinal matters with the chief of the Syrian Nizaris, were perhaps the only thirteenth-century occidental authors who wrote about the sectarians without contributing to the Assassin legends. Both of them, as noted, merely attributed the obedience of the *fida'i*s to the alleged Nizari belief in the transmigration of souls, allowing for the soul of a martyred *fida'i* to be reincarnated in a body of higher rank which would be capable of enjoying greater comforts and pleasures.

By 1256 the Persian Nizari state had collapsed under the onslaught of the Mongols. Soon afterwards, in the early 1270s, the Syrian Nizaris lost whatever authority and independence they had precariously retained after the fall of Alamut, becoming obedient subjects of the Mamluk state. By 1277, the Mamluk armies had also succeeded in reducing the Crusader dominions of Outremer to a small strip of coastland in Syria; and, in 1291, Acre itself, the last remaining stronghold of Christendom in the Holy Land, surrendered to the Mamluks. These developments, as noted, marked the end of the political power and prominence of the Nizari Isma'ilis as well as the termination of the Frankish–Nizari encounters in the Latin East, encounters which were to be immortalized by the Assassin legends.

With the loss of their political prominence, the Nizaris disappeared from the historical stage and henceforth survived as a peaceful religious community. In no small measure, this was also due to the fact that the Nizari communities of Syria, Persia and elsewhere now made a deliberate effort to live clandestinely under different guises in order to safeguard their survival. As a result, there are only some scattered references to the Nizaris in the Muslim historiography of the early post-Alamut centuries. Under such circumstances, Europeans had even less reason to write or speculate about the Nizaris, with whom they no longer had any contacts. In fact, westerners had remained unaware of the continued existence of the Nizaris after the thirteenth century; and it was not until the early decades of the nineteenth century that Europeans rediscovered them, once again in Syria. That the Nizaris were remembered at all by the Europeans during the later Middle Ages and subsequent centuries, was due to their past reputation and, indeed, to the wide currency of the Assassin legends in Europe.

By the turn of the thirteenth century, the name 'Assassins' in its different forms, and the varied stories about the remote people who bore that name, had been made famous throughout Europe by the Crusaders and other Franks who had travelled to the East. These stories, especially those related to the obedience of the *fida'is* and the mysterious ways of the Old Man of the Mountain, had made such a deep impression that Provençal poets frequently made comparisons between their own romantic devotion to their ladies and the loyalty of the 'Assassins' to the 'Old Man'.[31] The Assassin legends had now truly acquired an independent life of their own, especially in Italy, to where such legends had been constantly transmitted by members of the Venetian and other Italian trading communities of the Levant.

With the disappearance of direct contacts between the Europeans and the Nizaris, the Assassin legends began to be further embellished; indeed, myths rooted in 'imaginative ignorance' could now come into full play. It was under such circumstances that the Venetian Marco Polo (1254–1324), the most famous of all the mediaeval European travellers, gave the Assassin legends a new lease of life under his own authority.

Marco Polo's father and uncle, Niccolò and Maffeo, had already spent some seven years in the 1260s travelling in the East as far as the court of the Great Khan Qubilai (1260–94) in China. Qubilai, it will be recalled, was the brother and successor of Mongke (d. 1259) who had a few years earlier ordered the destruction of the Nizari fortresses in Persia. On their second journey to China, the Polo brothers had decided to take along Niccolò's young son Marco, then 17 years old. The Polo party left Venice in the summer of 1271, and in November 1271 they embarked on their eastward itinerary from Acre. In 1273, the three Venetian travellers traversed Persia through Kirman and Khurasan, about 17 years after the collapse of the Nizari state there. From Persia, the Polos proceeded to Balkh, Badakhshan and Pamir in the upper Oxus region, which since then have had important Nizari communities. Crossing the Pamir highlands, they descended to Kashgar and Yarkand, where lesser Nizari communities have been located. The party then crossed the Great Gobi Desert and finally reached the summer court of Qubilai in May 1275. The young Marco Polo immediately won the favour of Qubilai and served the Great Khan in different capacities during his 17-year stay in China. Charged with one last mission to accompany a Mongol princess to the Ilkhanid court in Persia, Marco Polo and the other two Venetian travellers embarked on their return journey in 1292, arriving in Venice three years later in 1295, after an absence of some 25 years.

There was only one major upheaval in Marco Polo's final decades spent quietly in Venice as a wealthy and highly honoured citizen. In 1298 he had taken command of one of the Venetian galleys which in that year participated in yet another of the then recurrent battles between Venice and Genoa. This time, the Genoese completely defeated the Venetian fleet, and captured some 7000 Venetians, among them Marco Polo. In prison in Genoa, Marco Polo had the account of his earlier travels committed to writing; he dictated his memories of 'the kingdoms and marvels of the East' to a fellow-prisoner known as Rusticiano or Rustichello of Pisa, a man of some literary talent and evidently a professional romance-writer. By the time Marco Polo was released from prison in August 1299, Rustichello had completed what may be regarded as the original version of Marco Polo's travels. This original version, written in a peculiar old French mingled with Italian, has never been recovered, but the work was soon translated into a number of Italian dialects as well as Latin. The complex problems related to the authenticity of the manuscripts of this famous travelogue have been analyzed by Sir Henry Yule (1820–89), H. Cordier (1849–1925), Arthur C. Moule (1873–1957) and other modern scholars. It merely suffices to note here that all the early manuscripts of Marco Polo, produced during the fourteenth century, suffer from various defects, including omissions and scribal revisions and interpolations. Marco Polo himself seems to have revised his travelogue during the latter part of his life in Venice, while Rustichello must have undoubtedly added his own emendations to the original Franco-Italian text which was subsequently translated into Venetian and other dialects.

Marco Polo interrupts his itinerary in eastern Persia to report what he claims to have heard there from several natives, some 30 years earlier, concerning the Old Man of the Mountain and his Assassins.[32] The Venetian traveller, or rather his scribe Rustichello, relates:

The Old Man was called in their language Alaodin . . . He dwelled in a most noble valley shut in between two very high mountains where he had made them make the largest garden and the most beautiful that ever was seen in this world . . . And here he had made them make the most beautiful houses and the most beautiful palaces that ever were seen, of wonderful variety, for they were all

gilded and adorned in azure very well with all the fair things of
the world, both with beasts and with birds, and the hangings all of
silk. And besides he had made them make in that garden many
beautiful fountains which corresponded on different sides of these
palaces, and all these had little conduits there . . . through some of
which it was seen ran wine and through some milk and through
some honey and through some the clearest water. There were set
to dwell ladies and damsels the most beautiful in the world, who
all knew very well how to play on all instruments and sing
tunefully and sweetly dance better than other women of this
world round these fountains . . . Their duty was to furnish the
young men who were put there with all delights and pleasures.
There were plenty of garments, couches, food, and all things
which can be desired. No sad thing was spoken of there, nor was
it lawful to have time for anything but play, love, and pleasure.
And these damsels most beautifully dressed in gold and silk were
seen going sporting continually through the garden and through
the palaces; for the women who waited on them remained shut up
and were never seen abroad in the air. And the Old Man made his
men understand that in that garden was Paradise. And for this
reason he had it made in such a way, that Mahomet in his time
made the Saracens understand about it that those who did his will
should all when they died go to Paradise where they would find all
the delights and pleasures of the world and will have there as
many fair women as they wish at their pleasure and that they will
find there beautiful gardens and full of rivers which run separately
in fullness of wine and of milk and of honey and of water, in the
same way as that of the Old Man; and therefore had he made
them make that garden like Paradise of which Mahomet had
spoken to the Saracens. And therefore the Saracens of that
country believe truly that that garden is Paradise, because of its
beauty and delectable pleasure. He wished to give them to
understand that he was a prophet and companion of Mahomet,
and that he could make whoever he wished go into the said
Paradise.

And into this garden entered no man ever except only those
base men of evil life whom he wished to make satellites and
Assassins. Because he had indeed a castle at the entry of that
garden at the mouth of the valley so very strong and impregnable
that he was not afraid of a man in the world; and it could be
entered by a secret way; and it was very carefully guarded, and in
other parts it was not possible to enter into this garden but only

there. And the Old Man kept with him at his court all the young men of the inhabitants of those mountains of the country from twelve years to twenty; they were those who seemed to wish to be men of arms and brave and valiant, who knew well the hearsay, according as Mahomet their most unhappy prophet had told them, that their Paradise was made in such manner as I have told you, and so they believed in truth as Saracens believe it. And every day he preached to them of this garden of Mahomet, and how he was able to make them go therein. And what shall I tell you about it? Sometimes the Old Man, when he wished to kill any lord who made war or was his enemy, made them put some of these youths into that Paradise by fours and sixes and by tens or twelves and by twenties together just as he wished, in this way. For he had opium to drink given them by which they fell asleep and as if half dead immediately as soon as they had drunk it, and they slept quite three days and three nights. Then he had them taken in this sleep and put into that garden of his, into different rooms of the said palaces, and there made them wake, and they found themselves there.

Relating yet further details on how the Old Man of the Mountain trained his Assassins to become perfectly obedient, Marco Polo states that

and when the youths were waked up and they find themselves in there and see themselves in so fine a place and they see all these things which I have told you, made just as the law of Mahomet says . . . they believe that they are most truly in Paradise. And the ladies and the damsels stayed with them all day playing and singing and causing great enjoyment, and they did with them as they pleased, so that these youths had all that they wished, and never will they go out from thence of their own will.

And the Old Man lord, of whom I have told you, holds his court very beautiful and great and lives very nobly, and makes those simple people of the mountains who are about him believe that it is so as I have said and that he is a great prophet, and so they all truly believe . . . And after four or five days when the Old Man wishes any of them his Assassins to send to any place and to have any man killed, then he has the drink of opium given again to as many as pleases him of these youths to make them sleep, and when they are asleep he has them taken into his palace which was outside the garden. And when these youths are awaked and they find themselves out of their garden in that castle in the palace, they make great marvel at it and are not very glad of it, that they find themselves outside of the Paradise, for from the Paradise from which they came they would never of their own will be parted. The Old Man makes them come before him, and they go immediately before the Old Man and behave themselves very humbly towards him and kneel as those who believe that he is a great prophet. The Old Man asks them whence they come, and those say that (by thy goodness) they come from Paradise. And they said indeed in the presence of all that in truth that is Paradise, as Mahomet told our ancestors in their law, recounting to them all the things which they find there, and how they had great desire to return there. And the others who hear this and had not been there and have seen none of it wondered extremely to hear it and had great wish to go to Paradise, and many had a wish to die that they might be able to go there, and much desired that day when they should go there. And the Old Man answered them, Son, this is by the commandment of our prophet Mahomet, that whoever defends his servant he will grant to him Paradise; and if thou art obedient to me thou shalt have this favour. Through this means he had so inspirited all his people to die that they might go to Paradise that he whom the Old Man ordered to go to die for his name reckoned himself happy, with sure hope of deserving to go to Paradise, so that as many lords or others as were enemies of the said Old Man were killed with these followers and Assassins, because none feared death if only he could do the commandment and will of the said Old Man, and they exposed themselves like madmen to every manifest danger, wishing to die together with the king's enemy and despising the present life. And for this reason he was feared in all those countries as a tyrant.

And when the Old Man wished to have any lord or any other man killed he took some of these his Assassins and sends them where he wished, and told them that he wished to send them carried by his angels to Paradise, and that they go to kill such a man, and if they should die that they will go immediately to Paradise. Those to whom this was commanded by the Old Man did it very willingly more than anything that they could do; and they went and did all that the Old Man commanded them for the great desire that they had that they might come back to Paradise. And in this way no man escaped who was not killed when the Old Man of the Mountain wished.

At the end of Marco Polo's account, it is explained that the Old Man had had two deputies in Damascus and Kurdistan who observed all his manners and customs. And that the end of the Old Man of the Mountain, known as Alaodin, came when, after being besieged for three years, he with all his men and all those Assassins were killed by the Mongols who also destroyed his castle and its garden of paradise.

Marco Polo's description of the Old Man of the Mountain and his Assassins represents the most elaborate synthesis of the Assassin legends; only the death-leap legend is absent here. He added his own original contribution in the form of the Old Man of the Mountain's secret 'garden of paradise'. According to Marco Polo, the Old Man had specially designed this garden at his residence for the sole purpose of deceiving the would-be *fida'is*, because the otherworldly paradise promised to them as a reward was nothing but a deception. Thus, the training of the *fida'is* involved a most crucial last phase in which the misguided and duped youngsters spent a brief time in the garden of paradise, where they became deeply addicted to various bodily pleasures procured for them in a most sumptuous manner. In this account, the hashish connection or legend is given a role subservient to that of the 'paradise legend', which itself now appears essentially in a terrestrial form. The *fida'is*, rather than being deluded with hallucinatory dreams of paradise as in Arnold of Lübeck's account, are actually put to sleep under the influence of opium or some such drug while being carried to and from the garden of paradise. This secret garden bears a close resemblance to the Paradise described in the Quran and promised by Mahomet (Prophet Muhammad) to pious believers. Indeed, according to Marco Polo, the Old Man styled himself closely on the pattern established by the Prophet in order to enhance the appeal of his mischievous machinations.

In sum, in Marco Polo's account, the *fida'is'* hope for gaining the otherworldly paradise, rooted in reality, is completely transformed into a desire for perpetually enjoying a variety of carnal delights in this world. The *fida'is* become the devotees of the Old Man simply because they wish to return to that 'garden', where they had intensely, but alas only too briefly, experienced all the unthinkable joys which could be attained only in the otherworldly paradise described in the Quran. Having experienced a foretaste of the delights of the Old Man's 'garden', the *fida'is* are no longer concerned with the celestial paradise; it is the terrestrial 'garden' of delights hidden in the Old Man's compound of palaces and castle which they now incessantly seek. Admission to this 'garden' is under the strict control of the Old Man, who admits for a second time, and indeed for ever, only those

'Assassins' or *fida'is* who have actually performed murderous missions for him. This is why the 'Assassins' feared no danger and remained obedient servants of the Old Man until their death.

The heritage of the earlier European versions of the Assassin legends is clearly manifest in Marco Polo's original synthesis, which soon after its compilation began to circulate as the standard and the most popular version. The Venetian traveller does not acknowledge any debt to his European predecessors, nor does he allude to his own original contribution to the Assassin legends. But his account does appear as a digressionary note, one of several such digressions in his travelogue, implying that he was quoting other sources. In the case of his account of the Old Man of the Mountain and his Assassins, Marco Polo claims to have heard the tale in Persia from some local informants. At any rate, with Marco Polo, the scene of the Assassin legends, which had hitherto developed only in connection with the Syrian Nizaris, was transposed to Persia; and the legends were now recounted for the first time also in reference to the Persian Nizari community of the Alamut period. Furthermore, it is important to bear in mind that this important innovation received the endorsement of the renowned Venetian traveller, whose 'eyewitness' accounts of the Asian kingdoms and events were taken rather seriously by his European readers.

It is known that Marco Polo passed through southern Khurasan in eastern Persia, the former Nizari territory of Quhistan, on his way to China. There he evidently saw a ruined castle, one of many such castles which formerly belonged to the Persian Nizaris of that region. However, his itinerary did not take him to Alamut, which appears to be the castle alluded to in his account. If this account is at all to be credited to Marco Polo then it must be assumed that he had heard from his Persian informants some details about Alamut and the Persian Nizari community of the earlier times, as his account of the 'Assassins' is admittedly not based on personal observation. Citing the name of Alaodin in reference to a Persian Nizari chief and alluding to the fact that the 'Old Man' in Persia had a deputy in Syria, must have been among such details picked up by the youthful Marco Polo while passing through Persia. But his Old Man Alaodin was in fact Ala al-Din Muhammad III (1221–55), the penultimate ruler of the Nizari state in Persia. The last ruler was Ala al-Din's son Rukn al-Din, who surrendered to the Mongols in 1256 and was killed by them a few months later in Mongolia. The watchful Juwayni, who visited Alamut in 1256 shortly before that fortress was partially demolished by the Mongols, did not find any sign of Marco Polo's 'garden' there; nor is the existence of any such Isma'ili garden in Persia attested by Rashid al-Din or any other Muslim source. However, Juwayni was greatly impressed by the water conduits, cisterns and storage facilities which he did find at Alamut.

It cannot be denied that Marco Polo's account bears a distinctly European imprint, revealing the influences of different traditions which are ultimately traceable to Burchard of Strassburg, Arnold of Lübeck and James of Vitry. Therefore, it seems that Marco Polo knowingly mixed the information he had gathered some 30 years earlier in Persia, concerning the Nizari chief there, with the Assassin legends then circulating in Europe in connection with the Syrian Nizaris; legends which he must have heard in Venice after returning from his travels in 1295. It is also possible that Marco Polo may have added the account of the Old Man and his Assassins to one or more manuscripts of his travelogue after leaving his Genoa prison; as noted, he did in fact make such revisions and emendations during the last 20 years of his life. Rustichello and other scribes, too, may have played a part in this connection. All this points to the conclusion that the Venetian traveller could not have heard his account in its entirety from his Persian informants. There are further proofs for this inference, aside from the fact that many essential points of his account are traceable to European antecedents developed in connection with the Syrian Nizaris.

Marco Polo, like William of Rubruck before him, uses corrupted forms of the name 'Mulhid' (plural, 'Malahida'), such as 'Mulecte' and 'Mulehet', in reference to the Persian Nizaris in general, as the contemporary Muslim opponents of the Nizaris called them in Persia. Thus, in the introductory sentences to his account he says:

> Mulecte is a country where, as is told, a certain very evil prince who was called the Old Man of the Mountain used to live long ago; in which country heretics according to the Saracen law used to dwell. For this name of Mulecte means to say a place where heretics stay, in the tongue of Saracens. And from the said place the men are called Mulehetici, that is heretics of their law, like Patarini among the Christians.[33]

Marco Polo also adopts the name 'Assassin', which appears in different forms in his manuscripts, such as the Italian variant 'Asciscin', as an appellation for the Persian *fida'is*, the Old Man's Assassins. As noted, the term Assassins had originally acquired currency in the Crusader circles in reference to the Syrian Nizaris; and the term had been derived from the variants of the word *hashishi* used abusively, in the Arabic language, to designate the Nizaris. However, *hashishi* or its different variants had never gained popularity in the Persian language or in Persia, where the Nizaris were commonly called *malahida* by their Muslim opponents. Therefore, Marco Polo could not have heard the name 'Assassins' from his Persian informants.

There is also Marco Polo's curious application of the title of the 'Old Man of the Mountain' to the Persian Nizari chief. This title, as noted, had been utilized by the Franks in reference to the Nizari chief in Syria. The Syrian Nizaris themselves, but not their Persian co-religionists, did evidently refer to their local leader with the common Muslim term of respect *shaykh*, lord or master, also having the secondary meaning of 'old man' or 'elder'. However, as Bernard Lewis has observed,[34] the Crusaders rendered this term into Latin, old French and Italian on the basis of its secondary meaning of 'old man' as *vetus, vetulus, senex, viel, veglio*, etc., rather than by its more relevant equivalents such as *senior, segnors* and *dominus*. Furthermore, this erroneous rendition of *shaykh* was linked with the mountain fortresses in which the Syrian Nizari leader lived, resulting in full titles such as 'Vetus de Montanis', or 'Viel de la Montaigne', meaning the 'Old Man of the Mountain'. Thus, it seems that these titles were coined, in reference to the Syrian Nizari chief, by the Crusaders themselves, because their full Arabic equivalent, namely 'Shaykh al-Jabal', has not been found in any contemporary Arabic or Persian source. The Spanish rabbi and traveller Benjamin of Tudela, who passed through Syria in 1167, speaks of the Syrian Nizari chief as 'Shaykh al-Hashishin', adding that he is known as their elder (*zagen*).[35] It is, therefore, safe to assume that the Arabic title of 'Shaykh al-Jabal', found in some modern historical novels, represents an Arabic translation from the mediaeval and later European equivalents of this title, coined and used by the Crusaders and their occidental chroniclers. At any rate, Marco Polo could not have heard the title 'Old Man of the Mountain' in Persia where neither the Nizaris nor their contemporary opponents used titles such as *shaykh* or *shaykh al-jabal*, or its full Persian equivalent, namely, *pir-i kuhistan*, in reference to the central leader of the Nizari community.

There is little doubt, then, that Marco Polo's account of the Old Man and his Assassins represents an original admixture of some details heard in Persia and the Assassin legends then circulating in Europe, to which he added his own imaginative component in the form of the Old Man's secret garden of paradise. And this 'garden', not found in any earlier European source before Marco Polo, was essentially modelled on the Quranic description of Paradise then available. Aware of the connection between the Persian and Syrian 'Assassins', it seems that

Marco Polo, perhaps aided by Rustichello or a later scribe, used the opportunity of compiling his travelogue to present his own 'complete' version of the Assassin legends, as a digressionary note from his itinerary in Persia, where he had seen a ruined castle and had been told some local tales about the Nizari Isma'ilis of that country. And he relates what he claims to have heard in Persia in 1273, only 17 years after the downfall of the Persian Nizari state there, as if the Nizaris and their Old Man had by then already become nothing but long forgotten memories.

Marco Polo's travelogue stirred the imagination of his contemporaries, and by the second half of the fourteenth century numerous manuscripts of it in Latin, old French and Italian dialects were circulating in Europe. In like manner, his tale of the Old Man's garden of paradise soon began to exercise such fascination on European minds that it came to overshadow the earlier accounts. Indeed, Marco Polo's version of the Assassin legends came to be adopted, to various extents, by successive generations of European writers as the standard description of the 'Assassins'.

The account of Odoric of Pordenone (d. 1331), the Franciscan friar from northern Italy and another famous European traveller who visited China during 1323–7, is perhaps the earliest European account of the 'Assassins' based almost entirely on Marco Polo, even though Odoric claims to be relating his own observations and experiences. On his return journey to Italy, in 1328 Odoric passed through the Caspian coastland in northern Persia, a region he calls Melistorte and by which he may have been referring to the Alamut valley. It is in connection with this part of his itinerary that Odoric presents his account of the Old Man of the Mountain.[36]

> And in this country there was a certain aged man called *Senex de Monte* [Old Man of the Mountain], who round about two mountains had built a wall to enclose the said mountains. Within this wall there were the fairest and most crystal fountains in the whole world: and about the said fountains there were most beautiful virgins in great number, and goodly horses also, and in a word, everything that could be devised for bodily solace and delight, and therefore the inhabitants of the country call the same place by the name of Paradise. The said old *Senex*, when he saw any proper and valiant young man, he would admit him into his paradise. Moreover by certain conduits he makes wine and milk to flow abundantly.
>
> This *Senex*, when he hath a mind to revenge himself or to slay

any king or baron, commandeth him that is governor of the said paradise, to bring thereunto some of the acquaintance of the said king or baron, permitting him a while to take his pleasure therein, and then to give him a certain potion being of force to cast him into such a slumber as should make him quite void of all sense, and so being in a profound sleep to convey him out of his paradise: who being awaked, and seeing himself thrust out of the paradise would become so sorrowful, that he could not in the world devise what to do, or whither to turn him. Then would he go unto the foresaid Old Man, beseeching him that he might be admitted again into his paradise: who saith unto him, You cannot be admitted thither, unless you will slay such or such a man for my sake, and if you will give the attempt only, whether you kill him or not, I will place you again in paradise, that there you may remain always; then would the party without fail put the same in execution, endeavouring to murder all those against whom the said Old Man had conceived any hatred. And therefore all the kings of the East stood in awe of the said Old Man, and gave unto him great tribute.

And when the Tartars had subdued a great part of the world, they came unto the said Old Man, and took from him the custody of his paradise: who being incensed thereat, sent abroad diverse desperate and resolute persons out of his forenamed paradise, and caused many of the Tartarian nobles to be slain. The Tartars seeing this, went and besieged the city wherein the said Old Man was, took him, and put him to a most cruel and ignominious death.

It is interesting to note that the Assassin legends also appear, in a version closely modelled on Marco Polo's account, in a portion of a curious historical novel in Arabic which contains an anachronistic biography of the Fatimid caliph al-Hakim (996–1021). In 1813, the Austrian orientalist Joseph von Hammer-Purgstall announced his discovery, at the Imperial Library (now National Library) in Vienna, of the unique manuscript of this novel, entitled the *Sirat amir al-mu'minin al-Hakim bi-Amr Allah*, and he published the fragment containing the Assassin legends together with its French translation in a short notice.[37] The authorship of this work, completed in 1430, had been wrongly but deliberately attributed to the famous Muslim biographer Ibn Khallikan (d. 1282), probably in order to enhance its prestige and circulation. This novel was probably written in Syria some time in the late Mamluk period, by a local Sunni Muslim or more probably an Arab Christian, who was familiar with the Assassin legends, especially the version handed down by Marco Polo and Odoric of Pordenone.

According to this novel, a certain Isma'il, the leader of the Isma'ilis, once landed at Tripoli, laden with plundered jewels and surrounded by *fidawi*s (*fidā'is*). Subsequently, he went to Masyaf, in Syria, where he was received most hospitably by the inhabitants of the castles and fortresses of that region. There, in order to win more *fidawi*s, he built a vast garden with water conduits, and constructed a magnificent four-storey pavilion in its midst. The windows of the pavilion were painted with stars of gold and silver, and its rooms filled with luxuries. This was the retreat of the finely dressed and perfumed young slaves (*mamluk*s) of both sexes he had brought with him from Egypt. He filled the garden with all types of beautiful plants, fruits and flowers, and with animals and birds. Isma'il also had a two-storey house built for himself there, whence secret passages led to the garden which was all enclosed with walls. In his house, Isma'il entertained his people all day long. And in the evening, he would choose some young men, whose firmness of character had impressed him, to sit by his side. While talking to these young men about the excellent qualities of the imam Ali he would secretly give them *bang* (*banj*), or some such intoxicating drug, mixed in their drink, which would soon sink them into a death-like sleep. Isma'il would then carry one of the drugged men to the garden pavilion, leaving him in the care of the male and female slaves who were commanded to fulfil his every desire. When the drugged man awoke confused, the slaves assured him that he was indeed in Paradise; and that he would return there even after his death; for this place was destined for him. The young man would be so overwhelmed by the beauty of the pavilion and the delights he experienced there that he would no longer know whether he was awake or dreaming. Soon, the slaves would tell him that he had been dreaming about Paradise. When two hours of the night had gone by, Isma'il would return and make the young man pledge silence about his experience in the garden, also telling him that he owed his blissful vision to a miracle of Ali. Then Isma'il would have delicious dishes served to him in containers of gold and silver as well as drinks which were again mixed with *bang*. As soon as the young man fell asleep again, he would be carried out of the garden and taken to Isma'il's house where he was assured, after waking up, that he had not dreamed but had been really in Paradise. He was, furthermore, told that Ali had admitted him among his friends and that if he kept his secret and served Isma'il and died a martyr, he would received that same place in Paradise permanently; but if he told anyone about that secret he would be an enemy of the imam and would be chased away. This was how Isma'il surrounded himself with devoted *fidawi*s until his reputation was established.

It may be noted that von Hammer-Purgstall, who a few years later published his own hostile tract on the Nizaris, took this novel seriously. He, in fact, used it in conjunction with Marco Polo's account as sufficient evidence that such Nizari gardens of paradise had actually existed in both Syria and Persia;[38] an inference which should now be summarily dismissed as utterly groundless. On the contrary, as the Old Man's secret 'garden of paradise' does not appear in any known source before Marco Polo, who could not have acquired his information on the 'Assassins' from Arabic sources in Syria, it can more plausibly be hypothesized that the legend contained in this Arabic novel was itself influenced, perhaps directly, by the European Assassin legends, especially the versions traceable to Marco Polo and Odoric. The late Arabic version in question also attests to the indirect impact that the Assassin legends circulating in the Crusader and Christian circles of the Latin East may have had on eastern popular lore and literature, especially in Syria where the Nizaris had acquired political prominence and where the inhabited Nizari fortresses had continued to be a reminder of the past glories of the sect. However, it is by no means impossible that both the accounts of Marco Polo and the *Sira* might have been at least partially based on a common earlier oriental source not related to the Nizaris, such as some of the tales contained in the famous *Book of a Thousand Nights and a Night*. Be that as it may, it is not possible at this time to say anything more with any degree of certainty regarding the origin of the Assassin legends contained in the fictitious *Sirat al-Hakim*.

By the end of the Middle Ages, and indeed until the nineteeth century, European knowledge of the Nizari Isma'ilis had not progressed much beyond what the Crusaders and their chroniclers had transmitted on the subject; and the field continued to be dominated by such fanciful impressions and fictitious accounts, including especially the Assassin legends. During the Renaissance, the Nizaris were occasionally referred to by a traveller or pilgrim to the Holy Land, resulting in brief notices that did not contain any new information. For instance, the Dominican friar Felix Fabri, who visited the Holy Land twice in 1480 and 1484, mentions the 'Assassins' among the peoples of the region, and merely reiterates some of the earlier tales; he relates:

There are there Assassins, who are Mahometans, and are exceedingly obedient to their own captain, for they believe that it is by obedience alone that they can win happiness hereafter. Their captain causes their young men to be taught diverse languages, and sends them out into other kingdoms to serve the kings thereof, to the end that, when the time requires it, each king's servant may kill him by poison or otherwise. If after slaying a king the servant makes good his escape to his own land, he is rewarded with honours, riches and dignities; if he is taken and put to death, he is worshipped in his own country as a martyr.[39]

In the meantime, by the middle of the fourteenth century, the word assassin, instead of signifying the name of a sect in Syria, had acquired a new meaning in Italian, French and other European languages; it had become a common noun describing a professional murderer. The earliest European example of this usage, retained to the present day, evidently occurred in Italy. The renowned Italian poet Dante (1265–1321), in the 19th canto of the *Inferno* in his *La Divina Commedia*, speaks of the treacherous assassin (*le perfido assassin*); and the Florentine historian Giovanni Villani (d. 1348) relates how the lord of Lucca sent 'his assassins' (*i suoi assassini*) to Pisa to kill an enemy.[40] Thus, it was the methods of struggle associated with the 'Assassins' rather than the fidelity and spirit of self-sacrifice of the Nizari Isma'ili *fida'i*s that ultimately impressed the Europeans and gave the word assassin its new meaning in European languages. With the advent of this usage, the origin and significance of the term 'Assassins' was slowly forgotten, while the sect continued to arouse some interest in Europe, due mainly to the popularity of the Assassin legends.

The first western monograph devoted entirely to the history of the Nizaris was published in France in 1603; its author was a certain Denis Lebey de Batilly, a French official at the court of King Henry IV of France.[41] The author had become deeply concerned about the revival of political murders in Europe, including that of Henry III of France at the hands of a Jacobin friar, whom he refers to as '*un religieux assasin-porte-couteau*'. Apprehensive about the activities of such assassins in the religious orders of Christendom, the author had set out in 1595 to compose a short treatise on the true origin of the word *assasin*, which had then acquired new currency in France, and the history of the sect to which it had originally belonged, calling these sectarians '*les anciens Assasins*'. This work combined in a highly confused and anachronistic manner the accounts of a number of occidental sources with Marco Polo's narrative, and it did not add any new details to what had been known in Europe about the 'Assassins' in the thirteenth century.

Indeed, by Lebey de Batilly's time the origin of the word assassin had long been forgotten in Europe; and his attempt at an etymological explanation of the term did not solve the mystery, but it did start a new trend of enquiry. Henceforth, an increasing number of European philologists and lexicographers began to collect the variants of this term occurring in mediaeval occidental sources, such as *arsasini*, *assassini* and *heyssessini*, also proposing many new etymologies.[42] Meanwhile, the Isma'ilis themselves were identified more correctly within the broader context of Islam in a pioneering work of western Orientalism compiled by d'Herbelot (1625–95). This French orientalist showed clearly that the Isma'ilis were in fact one of the main sects of Shi'i Islam, and that the Isma'ilis themselves had been split into two main groups, namely, the Isma'ilis of Africa and Egypt (the Fatimids), and those of Asia (also called 'Malahida'), centred at Alamut and founded by Hasan Sabbah.[43] By the eighteenth century, many strange etymologies of the term 'Assassin' had become available, while the sectarians had received a few more notices from the pens of travellers and missionaries to the East. The utterly confused picture of the Nizaris then circulating in Europe is well reflected in two memoirs read in 1743 by a French scholar, Camille Falconet (1671–1762), before the Académie Royale des Inscriptions et Belles Lettres. In these memoirs, published in 1751 in Paris, Falconet reviewed the notices of his European predecessors, including those of Benjamin of Tudela, William of Tyre, Arnold of Lübeck, James of Vitry as well as Marco Polo, and then presented his own brief account of the history and doctrines of the Persian and Syrian 'Assassins', an account permeated with erroneous statements and the Assassin legends; he also proposed yet another absurd etymology of the name 'Assassin'.[44]

It remained for Silvestre de Sacy (1758–1838), the doyen of nineteenth-century orientalists, finally to solve the mystery of the name 'Assassin'. In a *Memoir*, translated for the first time into English in the Appendix to this book, he showed, once and for all, that the word assassin was connected with the Arabic word hashish. He cited Arabic texts, notably by the Syrian historian Abu Shama (1203–67), in which the Nizaris are called 'Hashishi' (plural, 'Hashishiyya'). In this famous *Memoir*, de Sacy also produced what may be regarded as the first scholarly account of the Nizari Isma'ilis in modern times, utilizing all the major occidental studies as well as a number of Muslim chronicles then available in Paris. However, in conjecturing why the Nizaris had been called 'Hashishiyya', de Sacy partially endorsed the Assassin legends, which under his authority were now reintroduced into the orientalist circles of Europe.

It was under such circumstances that the mediaeval tales about the Nizaris, the Assassin legends, began to reappear in different forms in the studies of the eminent orientalists of the nineteenth century dealing with the Isma'ilis. The most widely read among such studies, published in 1818, was a book written by the Austrian orientalist-diplomat Joseph von Hammer-Purgstall (1774–1856). In his book, devoted to the Nizaris of the Alamut period, von Hammer accepted Marco Polo's account in its entirety as well as all the sinister acts and heresies attributed to the Nizaris. Fully convinced of his scholarship on the Nizaris, he found it sufficient to state that

> what the Byzantines, the Crusaders, and Marco Polo related of them, was long considered a groundless legend, and an oriental fiction. The narrations of the latter have not been less doubted and oppugned, than the traditions of Herodotus concerning the countries and nations of antiquity. The more, however, the east is opened by the study of languages and by travel, the greater confirmation do these venerable records of history and geography receive; and the veracity of the father of modern travel, like that of the father of ancient history, only shines with greater lustre.[45]

That von Hammer should have subscribed to such a fanciful and hostile view concerning the Nizaris is not, however, surprising, because his narrative was in fact based on what Crusader chroniclers and mediaeval Sunni authors had gathered or fabricated on the subject. It is also worthy of note that von Hammer's book achieved great success in Europe; it was soon translated into French and English and continued to be utilized, until recent decades, as the standard interpretation of the mediaeval Nizari history.

The Assassin legends, thus, defied dispellment by the scientific Orientalism that had begun in Europe during the nineteenth century. In the East, too, a host of tales on the Nizaris, some drawing closely on European antecedents, had acquired wide popularity through a number of historical novels. These legends with forgotten origins were now accepted, to various degrees, also by the Muslims themselves, as factual descriptions of some of the secret practices of the mediaeval Nizaris; after all they had been circulating for more than seven centuries.

In the meantime, the general progress in Islamic studies, together with the recovery and study of a large number of authentic Isma'ili sources, was preparing the ground for the initiation of modern scholarship in Isma'ili studies. These Isma'ili manuscript sources had hitherto been guarded secretly in many private collections in Yaman, India, Persia, Syria and Central Asia. Many of these Isma'ili texts have now been critically edited, published and studied. Modern progress in

Isma'ili studies, which has continued unabated since the 1930s, has already necessitated drastic revisions of our ideas concerning the true nature of Isma'ili history and thought during mediaeval times; it has also made it possible for scholars to evaluate critically different categories of non-Isma'ili sources dealing with the Isma'ilis, including the Crusaders' sources.

The breakthrough in Isma'ili studies has been particularly rewarding in the case of the Nizaris of the Alamut period, whose history had been shrouded in so much mystery and obscurity, long providing a suitable ground for imaginative tales and legends. It is, indeed, due to the modern revaluation of the Nizaris, resulting mainly from the pioneering studies of Wladimir Ivanow (1886–1970), Marshall G.S. Hodgson (1922–68) and Bernard Lewis, that the Nizaris of the Alamut period who patronized learning and spiritualized their mission can no longer be judged as an order of drugged Assassins trained for senseless murder and mischief.

Rooted in fear, hostility, ignorance and fantasy, however, the exotic tales of hashish, daggers and earthly gardens of paradise, have proved too sensational to be totally relegated to the domain of fiction by more sober investigations of modern times. That such legends have continued to fire the popular imagination of so many generations, and that they are still believed in many quarters, attest to the unfortunate fact that in both western and eastern societies the boundaries between fact and fiction, and reality and fantasy, are not always clearly definable. Now, finally, the time has come to recognize, once and for all, that the Assassin legends are no more than absurd myths; the products of ignorant, hostile 'imagination', and not deserving of any serious consideration; even though they have circulated for centuries as reliable narratives. Could the Nizari *fida'i*s really have been the gullible characters portrayed in these legends; the blind devotees of a deceitful leader who easily made them addicted to hedonistic pleasures and then demanded of them nothing less than self-sacrifice for his own diabolically selfish motives? And how truthful an image could this possibly be of Hasan Sabbah, the founder of the Nizari revolutionary movement? Hasan Sabbah was an austere and highly pious Muslim who in the 30 years of his leadership never set foot outside the Alamut castle, did not hesitate to execute his own son when he was accused of drinking wine, and sent his wife and daughters to live permanently in another distant fortress where they were to earn their simple life by spinning. It was on the basis of a Shi'i ideology and such harsh principles that he founded and directed an independent movement and a cohesive territorial state in the midst of a highly hostile ambience.

The challenge posed to the existing order by Hasan Sabbah and retained by other Nizari leaders in Persia and Syria did naturally call forth a campaign, both military and literary, against the Nizaris who already had been targeted as Isma'ilis for the hostility of Muslim society at large. And in time, the anti-Isma'ili traditions of the Muslims, in which the myths of the earlier Isma'ilis had been rooted, found their full 'imaginative' development in the Assassin legends of the Crusaders, who did not know much about Islam and knew even less about the Nizaris. In a sense, then, the Assassin legends were generated as a result of an extraordinary type of tacit cooperation between the Christians and the Muslims during Crusader times.

It was, thus, that a mythical journey started by Ibn Rizam at Baghdad was eventually completed, via China, Persia, Syria and many other lands, by Marco Polo in a Genoa prison; and the anti-Isma'ili 'black legend' of the Muslim authors found its successor in the 'Assassin legends' of the Christian Crusaders. The Assassin legends, lacking in historicity, have indeed had a fascinating mythical ancestry and history.

Notes and References

1. See, for instance, Muhammad b. Abd al-Karim al-Shahrastani, *Kitab al-milal wa'l-nihal*, ed. W. Cureton (London, 1842), p 147; partial English trans. *Muslim Sects and Divisions*, tr. A.K. Kazi and J.G. Flynn (London, 1984), p 165.
2. Al-Amir bi-Ahkam Allah, *Iqa' sawa'iq al-irgham*, pp 27, 32.
3. See al-Bundari, *Zubdat al-nusra*, pp 169, 195.
4. Ibid., pp 144, 145, 146, 177, 180.
5. See Abu Shama, *Kitab al-rawdatayn fi akhbar al-dawlatayn*, Vol 1, pp 240, 258; and Ibn Muyassar, *Akhbar Misr*, p 102.
6. Ibn Khaldun, *Muqaddima* (3rd edn, Beirut, 1900), p 68; English trans. *The Muqaddimah: An Introduction to History*, tr. F. Rosenthal (2nd edn, Princeton, 1967), Vol 1, p 143.
7. See Madelung (ed.), *Arabic Texts*, pp 146, 329.
8. See B. Lewis, 'Assassins of Syria and Isma'ilis of Persia', in Accademia Nazionale dei Lincei, *Atti del convegno internazionale sul tema: Persia nel medioevo* (Rome, 1971), p 574, reprinted in his *Studies in Classical and Ottoman Islam*, article XI; and 'Hashishiyya', EI2, Vol 3, pp 267–8.
9. See F. Rosenthal, *The Herb: Hashish versus Medieval Muslim Society* (Leiden, 1971), pp 19–40.
10. For details on some of the most famous works of this genre, see Rosenthal, *The Herb*, pp 5–18.
11. This problem is discussed at length, for instance, in the *Zahr al-arish fi tahrim al-hashish*, written by al-Zarkashi (d. 1392). This treatise is edited by Rosenthal in his *The Herb*, pp 176–97.
12. Rosenthal, *The Herb*, p 140.
13. See Taqi al-Din Ahmad b. Ali al-Maqrizi, *Kitab al-mawa'iz wa'l-i'tibar*

bi-dhikr al-khitat wa'l-athar (Bulaq, 1270/1853), Vol 2, pp 126–9; also edited
with French translation and commentary in Silvestre de Sacy's *Chrestomathie
Arabe* (Paris, 1806), Vol 1, pp 121–31 (text), and Vol 2, pp 120–55
(translation and commentary).

14. For the only study on this subject, written in the Polish language, see J.
Hauziński, *Muzułmańska sekta asasynów w europejskim piśmiennictwie
wieków średnich* (Poznan, 1978). Much relevant information is also contained
in L. Hellmuth's *Die Assassinenlegende in der österreichischen Geschichtsdichtung des Mittelalters.*

15. Burchard of Strassburg's report is preserved in Arnold of Lübeck's *Chronica
Slavorum*, p 240; reproduced in Hauziński, *Muzułmańska*, p 148; English
trans. in Lewis, *The Assassins*, p 3.

16. See Ivanow, 'An Ismaili Poem in Praise of Fidawis', pp 66–72.

17. Ibn Jubayr, *Rihla*, ed. W. Wright, 2nd revised edn by M.J. de Goeje (Leiden-
London, 1907), p 255; English trans. *The Travels*, tr. R.J.C. Broadhurst
(London, 1952), p 264.

18. Shihab al-Din Abu Firas, *Fasl min al-lafz al-sharif*, ed. and tr. S. Guyard in his
'Un grand Maître des Assassins au temps de Saladin', *Journal Asiatique*, 7
série, 9 (1877), pp 387–489.

19. See, for instance, Ibn al-Dawadari, *Kanz al-durar*, ed. S.A. Ashur (Cairo,
1972), Vol 7, pp 120–1.

20. See, for instance, Burchard of Mount Sion, *Descriptio Terrae Sanctae*, in
J.C.M. Laurent (ed.), *Peregrinatores medii aevi quatuor*, (Leipzig, 1864), pp
88–9; English trans. *A Description of the Holy Land*, tr. A. Stewart (London,
1897), pp 105–6; Ambroise, *L'Estoire de la Guerre Sainte* pp 235–7;
Continuation de Guillaume de Tyr, dite du Manuscrit de Rothelin, in *Recueil
des Historiens des Croisades: Historiens Occidentaux*, Vol 2, pp 523 ff.;
Itinerarium peregrinorum et gesta regis Ricardi, in *Chronicles and Memorials
of the Reign of Richard I*, Vol 1, p 339; *Itinéraire de Londres à Jérusalem*,
attributed to Matthew Paris, in H. Michelant and G. Raynaud (eds), *Itinéraires
à Jérusalem et descriptions de la Terre Sainte* (Geneva, 1882), pp 128–9.
Relevant excerpts of some of these and other texts are reproduced in
Hauziński, *Muzułmańska*, pp 149 ff., 161 ff.

21. James of Vitry, *Historia Orientalis*, pp 1062–3; reproduced in Hauziński,
Muzułmańska, pp 159–61; English trans. in *Secret Societies*, pp 118–19. See
also von Hammer-Purgstall, *History of the Assassins*, pp 125–6, which
completely endorses the authenticity of such mediaeval Crusader accounts,
attesting to the lasting role of the Assassin legends in influencing western
scholarship on the Nizaris until the present century.

22. Thietmar, *Magistri Thietmari Peregrinatio*, ed. J.C.M. Laurent (Hamburg,
1857), p 52.

23. Arnold of Lübeck, *Chronica Slavorum*, pp 178–9; reproduced in Hauziński,
Muzułmańska, p 88; English trans. in Lewis, *The Assassins*, pp 4–5.

24. *L'Estoire de Eracles*, p 216; and *Chronique d'Ernoul*, pp 323–4.

25. Marino Sanudo Torsello, *Liber Secretorum Fidelium Crucis*, in *Gesta Dei per
Francos*, ed. J. Bongars (Hanover, 1611), Vol 2, p 201.

26. *Cento novelle antiche* (Florence, 1572), p 92, and *Il Novellino*, ed. G. Favati

(Genoa, 1970), p 352. See also Leonardo Olschki, *Storia letteraria delle scoperte geografiche* (Florence, 1937), pp 215–16.

27. Ibn Jubayr, *Rihla*, p 255; trans. p 264.

28. Georgius Elmacin, *Historia Saracenica*, ed. and tr. Th. Erpenius (Leiden, 1625), p 286, and Hammer-Purgstall, *History of the Assassins*, p 135.

29. Hellmuth, *Die Assassinenlegende*, pp 113–16.

30. See *Alexandri historia fabulosa*, ed. C. Mueller (Paris, 1867), Vol 2, p 24.

31. See F.M. Chambers, 'The Troubadours and the Assassins', *Modern Language Notes*, 64 (1949), pp 245–51.

32. Marco Polo, *Marco Polo: The Description of the World*, ed. and tr. A.C. Moule and P. Pelliot (London, 1938), Vol 1, pp 128–33; this is a critical English edition based on a Latin version, also containing collated passages derived from other principal manuscripts of this work. See also Marco Polo, *The Book of Ser Marco Polo*, ed. and tr. H. Yule, 3rd revised edn by H. Cordier (London, 1929), Vol 1, pp 139–46, containing a briefer account of the Old Man of the Mountain and his Assassins.

33. Marco Polo, *Marco Polo: The Description of the World*, Vol 1, pp 128–9.

34. Lewis, *The Assassins*, p 8; and 'Assassins of Syria', p 575.

35. Benjamin of Tudela, *The Itinerary*, text p 19, trans. p 17.

36. Odoric of Pordenone, *The Journal of Friar Odoric*, in *The Travels of Sir John Mandeville*, ed. A.W. Pollard (London, 1915), pp 356–7; also in *Cathay and the Way Thither: Being a Collection of Medieval Notices of China*, ed. and tr. H. Yule, revised by H. Cordier (London, 1911–14), Vol 2, pp 257–8; and in coontemporaries of Marco Polo: Consisting of the Travel Records of the Eastern Parts of the World of William of Rubruck . . ., ed. M. Komroff (New York, 1928), pp 246–7.

37. J. von Hammer-Purgstall, 'Sur le paradis du Vieux de la Montagne', *Fundgruben des Orients*, 3 (1813), pp 201–6. See also *Secret Societies*, pp 74–8.

38. See von Hammer-Purgstall, *History of the Assassins*, pp 136–8.

39. Felix Fabri, *Evagatorium in Terrae Sanctae*, ed. C.D. Hassler (Stuttgart, 1843–49), Vol 2, pp 496–7; English trans. *The Book of the Wanderings of Brother Felix Fabri*, tr. A. Stewart (London, 1897), Vol 2, p 390.

40. Cited in Lewis, *The Assassins*, p 2.

41. Denis Lebey de Batilly, *Traicté de l'origine des anciens Assasins porte-couteaux* (Lyon, 1603), reprinted in C. Leber (ed.), *Collection des meilleurs dissertations, notices et traités particuliers relatifs à l'histoire de France* (Paris, 1838), Vol 20, pp 453–501.

42. See Daftary, *The Isma'ilis*, pp 15 ff.

43. See the entries 'Bathania', 'Fathemiah', 'Ismaelioun', 'Molahedoun' and 'Schiah', in Barthélemy d'Herbelot de Molainville, *Bibliothèque orientale* (Paris, 1697).

44. C. Falconet, 'Dissertation sur les Assassins, peuples d'Asie', *Mémoires de Littérature, tirés des Registres de l'Académie Royale des Inscriptions et Belles Lettres*, 17 (1751), pp 127–70; English trans. 'A Dissertation on the Assassins, a People of Asia', tr. T. Johnes, as an appendix in Joinville, *Memoirs of John Lord de Joinville*, Vol 2, pp 287–328.

45. Von Hammer-Purgstall, *History of the Assassins*, p 2.

Appendix:

Silvestre de Sacy's Memoir
on the 'Assassins'

Translated by Azizeh Azodi
Edited and introduced by Farhad Daftary

Introductory Note

Baron Antoine Isaac Silvestre de Sacy was the most eminent orientalist of the nineteenth century and, indeed, the founder of modern Orientalism in Europe. Through his scholarship and distinguished career, de Sacy's name is associated with almost every field of oriental studies; and through a wide circle of students, disciples and correspondents, he also acquired the distinction of being the teacher or mentor of the most prominent orientalists of his time.[1]

Born in Paris on 21 September 1758, de Sacy was privately tutored at a Benedictine abbey, where he initially studied Classics. Later, while training as a Biblical scholar, he became interested in studying the Orient. It did not take de Sacy long to master a rare combination of ancient and modern oriental languages, including Syriac, Chaldean, Hebrew, Arabic and Persian. By the age of 30, he had concerned himself with every sacred and profane aspect of the Orient, including its geography, ancient monuments and inscriptions, history, religions and literature. He published pioneering studies in all these fields, many of them long memoirs, anthologies and critical editions of original texts. In particular, de Sacy's mastery of Arabic and Persian remained unrivalled in the Europe of his time; and he composed a number of textbooks, chrestomathies and books of grammar for these languages which provided the needed foundations for the initiation of their scientific study in Europe.

De Sacy became the first professor of Arabic in the École des Langues Orientales Vivantes on the establishment of that important School of Oriental Languages in 1795, and in 1806 he was appointed to the new chair of Persian at the Collège de France; later, he became the director of both these institutions, and the president and permanent secretary of the Académie des Inscriptions, as well as the curator of oriental manuscripts at the Bibliothèque Royale. He was one of the founders of

131

the Société Asiatique and was nominated as its first president when this, the oldest of the European oriental societies, was established in 1822; he also involved himself in the redaction of the society's *Journal Asiatique*, in which many of his own shorter studies appeared. Earlier, de Sacy had actively supported the publication of the *Fundgruben des Orients*, the first oriental periodical in Europe which appeared during 1809–18. Silvestre de Sacy's scholarship and eminence were fully recognized in his lifetime. In 1832, he was made a new peer of France, and was a grand officer of the Légion d'Honneur, an honour then recently instituted by Napoléon Bonaparte; he was also the recipient of many foreign honours and titles. He died on 21 February 1838 and was buried in the Père Lachaise cemetery in Paris.

De Sacy maintained a lifelong interest in investigating the religion of the Druzes, and this kindled his original interest in studying the history of the Isma'ilis, required as background knowledge for a better understanding of the origins of the Druze movement. What was to become known as the Druze religion, it may be recalled, was initially an Isma'ili schismatic movement, organized during the final years of the Fatimid caliph al-Hakim's reign (996–1021) by a few dissident *da'is* who propounded a number of extremist doctrines, including especially al-Hakim's divinity. But in time, the Druzes came to represent a separate religious community, beyond the confines of Isma'ilism or perhaps even Shi'i Islam.

De Sacy's study of the Druzes dated back to the early 1790s, the years of the French Revolution when he temporarily retreated to his country house outside Paris. As in other areas of his scholarly endeavours, de Sacy began his study of the Druzes on the basis of their own literature, a sacred scripture comprised mainly of the writings and letters of the founders of the Druze religion, notably Hamza and al-Muqtana. Such Druze texts, unlike those of the Isma'ilis, had been available in Europe since 1700, when a Syrian physician had come to France and presented King Louis XIV (1643–1715) with a collection of four Druze manuscripts. De Sacy's first contact with Druze literature was, in fact, through the same four manuscripts, which he translated from Arabic into French, during his years of seclusion outside Paris. Henceforth, he devoted himself to studying the literature and doctrines of the Druzes. De Sacy's scholarship on the Druzes eventually culminated, after some 40 years and several memoirs and shorter studies, in his monumental *Exposé de la religion des Druzes*, a two-volume work published in 1838, the last year of his life. One of de Sacy's principal works, this remains the classic treatment of the early history and doctrines of the Druzes; it also describes the Druze literature then available in European libraries.

In the long introduction to his *Exposé*, de Sacy also elaborated his views on the early history and doctrines of the Isma'ili movement, including what he had been able to gather on the Qarmatis.[2] Relying exclusively on the writings of Sunni authors, however, he naturally espoused their anti-Isma'ili stance. In particular, he adopted the polemical 'black legend' concerning the origins of Isma'ilism. This legend, it will be recalled, had been put into circulation by Ibn Rizam and Akhu Muhsin, whose anti-Isma'ili polemics had been fragmentarily preserved by a few later authors, notably al-Nuwayri. By drawing extensively on al-Nuwayri's historical work, then available in manuscript form at the Bibliothèque Royale, de Sacy, too, presented the controversial Abd Allah b. Maymun al-Qaddah as the real founder of Isma'ilism. Furthermore, he reiterated al-Nuwayri's nine-stage initiation process into Isma'ili religion, leading allegedly to atheism.[3]

De Sacy's defective study of the Isma'ilis did, however, lead to an important etymological discovery. It was due to his combined interest in Isma'ilism and philology that de Sacy finally solved, after many abortive attempts of earlier European scholars, the mystery of the name 'Assassin'. De Sacy prepared an important *Memoir* on the 'Assassins' and on the origin of their name, which he read before the Institut de France in 1809;[4] and he had its full version published later in 1818.[5] This full version of de Sacy's *Memoir* has been translated for the first time into English in this Appendix. Suffice it to say that in this *Memoir*, de Sacy examined and rejected all the previous etymological explanations, and then showed that the variant forms of the word assassin occurring in base-Latin documents of the Crusaders and in different European languages, were connected with the Arabic word hashish. He further suggested that all these variant forms, such as *assissini*, *assassini*, etc., were derived from two alternative Arabic forms, namely, *hashishi* (plural, *hashishiyya* and *hashishiyyin* or *hashishin*) and *hashshash* (plural, *hashshashin*). In support of his hypothesis, de Sacy was able to cite Arabic texts, notably by the Syrian chronicler Abu Shama, in which the Nizari Isma'ilis were in fact called 'Hashishi' (plural, 'Hashishiyya'), but he could not produce similar substantiating quotations for the second Arabic form of his suggested etymology, namely *hashshash* (*hashshashin*), a more modern word and the common term for a hashish taker. Therefore, as B. Lewis has argued, the second part of de Sacy's etymological explanation, with all that it implies, must be rejected.[6]

In his *Memoir on the Dynasty of the Assassins*, de Sacy also included a brief history of the Nizaris of Persia and Syria during the Alamut period, summarizing all that he had been able to extract from the Islamic sources and the chronicles of the Crusaders. In this pioneering study, de Sacy definitely placed the 'Assassins' in the frame of Islamic history as Nizari Isma'ilis, ending numerous fanciful hypotheses, proposed by European authors since the times of the Crusaders. But he himself fell under the spell of the 'Assassin legends' transmitted through the occidental sources. As a result, in conjecturing on the reason why the Nizaris had been called 'Hashishis', de Sacy, too, arrived at the conclusion that the Nizaris must have actually used hashish, or a hashish-containing potion, in some manner; though he did exclude the possibility of any habitual use of this drug by the *fida'i*s. As explained in his *Memoir*, de Sacy believed that hashish, or an electuary of it, was at the time the secret possession of the Nizari chief, who used it sparingly and in a regulated manner on the *fida'i*s to procure them with ecstatic dreams of Paradise, a foretaste of the eternal bliss that awaited them if they obeyed their chief. Thus, de Sacy linked his etymological explanation to the tales told by the occidental authors of mediaeval times, notably Arnold of Lübeck, Marco Polo and Odoric of Pordenone, of how the young *fida'i*s were deluded by their scheming chief.

De Sacy's *Memoir* proved to be a landmark in Nizari studies; and it did pave the ground for a few more 'scholarly' writings on the subject by the later orientalists, notably Étienne M. Quatremère (1782–1852) and Charles F. Defrémery (1822–83); but it did lend the seal of approval of this doyen of nineteenth-century orientalists to the Assassin legends. That an eminent savant of the calibre of Silvestre de Sacy should so readily have fallen victim to the twin influences of the anti-Isma'ili campaign of the Sunni polemicists and the 'Assassin' fantasies of the Crusaders is once again a reminder of how the Isma'ilis had been studied, until recent times, almost exclusively on the basis of evidence collected or fabricated by their enemies and by ignorant observers.

Notes and References

1. See J. Reinaud, 'Notice historique et littéraire sur M. le baron Silvestre de Sacy', *Journal Asiatique*, 3 série, 6 (1838), pp 113–95; A.C.L. Victor, 'Éloge de Silvestre de Sacy', in Silvestre de Sacy, *Mélanges de littérature orientale* (Paris, n.d.), pp 3–32; H. Derenbourg, *Silvestre de Sacy (1758–1838)* (Paris, 1895); H. Dehérain, *Silvestre de Sacy, 1758–1838: Ses contemporains et ses disciples* (Paris, 1938); and Académie des Inscriptions et Belles Lettres, *Centenaire de Silvestre de Sacy (1758–1938)* (Paris, 1938).

2. A. Silvestre de Sacy, *Exposé de la religion des Druzes* (Paris, 1838), Vol 1, introduction pp 1–246.

3. Silvestre de Sacy, *Exposé*, Vol 1, introduction pp 70–138; see also his 'Recherches sur l'initiation à la secte des Ismaéliens', *Journal Asiatique*, 1 série, 4 (1824), pp 298–311, 321–31.

4. A brief version of this *Memoir* was originally published in the *Moniteur*, 210 (July, 1809), pp 828–30; English trans. in von Hammer-Purgstall, *History of the Assassins*, pp 227–35; and it also appeared as 'Mémoire sur la dynastie des Assassins et sur l'origine de leur Nom', *Annales des Voyages*, 8 (1809), pp 325–43.

5. A. Silvestre de Sacy, *Mémoire sur la dynastie des Assassins, et sur l'étymologie de leur Nom*, in *Mémoires de l'Institut Royal de France*, 4 (1818), pp 1–84.

6. Lewis, *The Assassins*, pp 11–12.

Memoir on the Dynasty of the Assassins, and on the Etymology of their Name[*] by Silvestre de Sacy

In a work I lately submitted to the Class,[1] I gave a detailed account of the doctrines of the Isma'ili sect, going back, as far as possible, to the origin of this sect and of the religious or rather philosophical system which specifically characterizes it. There is convincing proof that the secret doctrine of the Isma'ilis, into which only a small number of adepts were initiated, aimed at substituting philosophy for religion, reason for faith, and unlimited freedom of thought for the authority of revelation. This freedom, or rather this licence, could not long remain a simple speculation of the mind; it went to the heart, and its pernicious moral influence soon made itself felt. Thus the Isma'ilis had groups emerging from their midst who attained all the immorality of which their doctrine had laid the foundations, and who shook off not only the restraints of faith and public worship, but also those of decency and the most sacred laws of nature. What went on during the orgies of the Qarmatis, what the Druzes were more than once accused of, what certain sects practise even today in Mesopotamia and in some parts of Syria, would perhaps have made the original authors of this doctrine blush; the authors who, no doubt, had failed to foresee all the consequences of their system.

However, neither the unlimited freedom of thought, which essentially formed the ultimate stage of the Isma'ili teachings, nor the licentiousness characterizing several branches of this sect, were common to all those who professed the allegorical doctrine and recognized the transmission of the imamate to Isma'il, the son of Ja'far Sadiq. Even the admission and initiation of new proselytes was carried out in stages

---

[*] Originally published as *Mémoire sur la dynastie des Assassins, et sur l'étymologie de leur Nom*, in *Mémoires de l'Institut Royal de France*, 4 (1818), pp 1–84. F. Daftary's notes and annotations to this *Memoir* are indicated by the initials F.D.

136

and with great discretion. For as it pursued both a political aim and ambitious views, the sect was above all interested in having a large number of partisans in all places and among all social classes. So it had to adapt itself to the character, the temperament and the prejudices of vast numbers: what could be revealed to some would have shocked and permanently estranged less daring minds and more easily alarmed consciences. As long as the allegorical doctrine could serve as a means to intimate the necessity of recognizing the legitimate succession to the caliphate in the person of Ali and of the imams issued from his blood through Isma'il, the son of Ja'far; and as long as its followers were obliged to submit blindly to the commands of the *da'is* or missionaries, acting as the ministers and interpreters of the will of the imam, who remained hidden under the veils of mystery, waiting for the right time to manifest himself, not much trouble was taken to acquaint the new convert with further secrets. It is not surprising, therefore, that the Isma'ilis were divided into several sects with their doctrines differing in various degrees from those of Islam. These were the Qarmatis, the Nusayris, the Fatimids or Batinis of Egypt, the Druzes, the Isma'ilis of Persia, known by the name of *Mulhid* (plural, *Malahida*) or impious, and those of Syria, to whom the name *Assassins* especially applies.

I have elsewhere shown that the Qarmatis were a branch of the Isma'ilis, and that the allegorical doctrine was established in their midst with all its consequences. Whence the insurrection against authority, the pillage of pilgrim caravans, the desecration of places sacred to Islam, the profanation of Mecca, the removal of the Black Stone, etc. The Nusayris, who exist even today in the mountains of Lebanon are, to all appearances, a branch of the Qarmati faction.[2] The Fatimids or Batinis of Egypt consider themselves as Isma'ilis. Their dynasty was first founded in Africa, around the end of the third century of Hegira, by a *da'i* of the Qarmatis. However, having attained their political aims, Mahdi and his successors realized that they had better use a somewhat different language; and, after having preached rebellion against the Abbasid caliphs, they began to preach submission to authority. The allegorical doctrine also had to be mitigated; for had they accepted its consequences, had they abolished public worship and eliminated prayer, fasting and pilgrimage, they would have outraged people and overthrown by their own hands the throne they had just ascended. Acting in their own interests, they thus became tolerant, followed external practices and protected the hierarchy; and they contented themselves with introducing in Egypt, after their conquest, a few of the external signs characterizing the Shi'ites or partisans of Ali, whom Arab historians call *shi'ar al-tashayyu, the devotees of Shi'ism.*

But although they outwardly acted in conformance with the doctrine and customs accepted by the common Muslims and founded on the letter of the Koran and on tradition, they nevertheless preserved and secretly propagated their allegorical doctrine. They had their *da'i*s, headed by the supreme chief of the sect, called *da'i al-du'at* or *Da'i* of *da'i*s, who often combined these functions with those of the *qadi al-qudat* or supreme judge. Meetings of the sect were regularly held once or twice a week in the palace of the caliphs. The sect propagated itself through the admission of new initiates, men and women. At each meeting, mystical instructions, called the *Lectures of Wisdom, majalis al-hikma*, were read; these were specifically composed for the purpose, read and approved at the special reunions of the *da'i*s, which also took place in the palace, and then submitted to the caliph for his approval. All these practices belonged to the sect of the Isma'ilis and that of the Qarmatis.[3] Besides, various facts conclusively prove that the Qarmatis and Fatimids, who stemmed from a common origin, had the same doctrine and the same philosophical aim, and actually formed one and the same sect, though divided by their political interests.

In the year 317 of the Hegira, Abu Tahir, the chief of the Qarmatis, had flooded Mecca and its holy temple with the blood of pilgrims and had removed the Black Stone. He died in 332, and so did his brother Abu Mansur Ahmad;[4] but they had two brothers who succeeded them, Abu'l-Qasim Sa'id and Abu'l-Abbas. It was under their government that the Black Stone was returned to Mecca. This restitution was induced, according to Nuwayri, by a letter from Ubayd Allah, the first caliph of the Fatimid dynasty, addressed to the Qarmati chief to reproach him for his conduct on this occasion.

> You have justified the reproaches levelled against us, you have revealed the secret and the true spirit of our doctrine which leads to incredulity and immorality. Unless you restore to the Meccans what you took from them, unless you replace the Black Stone, and unless you return the cloth that covered the Ka'ba, I no longer have anything in common with you, neither in this world nor in the next.

Hamza Isfahani, quoted by Reiske in his notes on Abu'l-Fida (*Abulfedae Annales Moslemici*, Vol 2, p 752), reports that Abu Tahir, having returned to Hajar after the pillage of Mecca, acknowledged Ubayd Allah as his sovereign, had public prayers recited in his name, and informed him about them in a letter, but he subsequently ceased showing these marks of obedience once he received reproaches and threats instead of the rewards and expressions of gratitude he had expected.

The Qarmatis had made themselves so feared in the empire of the Abbasid caliphs through their repeated forays in Syria, that they were granted, at the time of the Ikhshidid emirs who reigned in Egypt and Syria in the name of the caliphs, an annual tribute of 300,000 gold coins to be disbursed by the public treasury of Damascus. When Jawhar had subjugated Egypt for the Fatimids, and when Syria was also conquered for them by another general, Ja'far bin Fallah, the Qarmatis found this a favourable occasion to expand their power. Hasan, the son of Abu Mansur Ahmad, who was then governing them, first advanced to Kufa, with the intention of entering Syria.[5] Hatred against the Fatimids prompted Bakhtiyar, a prince of the Buwayhid or Buyid family, who at the time held the office of *amir al-umara* in Baghdad, to support his venture by giving him all the arms of the Baghdad arsenal and 400,000 gold coins to be paid by Abu Taghlib, son of Nasir al-Dawla of the Hamdan family. Abu Taghlib, who welcomed this opportunity to avenge himself for the insulting and threatening tone in which he had been addressed by Ja'far bin Fallah, the general of the Fatimids in Syria, paid the 400,000 gold coins to the Qarmati prince, and also supplied him with provisions and troops. His army was further enlarged by all the soldiers of the Ikhshidids, who had been driven out of Egypt and had flooded into Syria and Palestine. Thus finding himself at the head of a strong army, Hasan the Qarmati advanced to Damascus, of which he gained possession, and, after several other conquests, he marched towards Egypt. Jawhar, who was the commander there, was greatly alarmed by this move and strongly urged Mu'izz, who had not yet left Qayrawan, to come to Egypt. Mu'izz actually arrived there in 363,[6] and wrote from there to the Qarmati prince, pointing out that they both belonged to the same sect, and that it was from the Isma'ilis that the Qarmatis had received their doctrine. Hasan, adds the author from whom Nuwayri borrowed this story, was well aware that the two sects were one and the same; and, in fact, the Isma'ilis and Qarmatis agreed in professing atheism and complete licence as regards people and property, and in denying the prophetic mission. But even though they agreed about the doctrine, when one of the two parties had an advantage over the other it would not spare the lives of those who followed the opposing party and would show them no mercy.

Hasan took no heed of Mu'izz's approach; he entered Egypt, went as far as Ayn Shams, besieged Cairo and took possession of the moat. The defeat of Mu'izz would have been inevitable had he not won over to his side one of the chiefs of the Qarmati army, who abandoned the latter in the thick of the fight. Hasan was forced to flee. Soon he also lost Damascus. After Hasan's death, which occurred in 366, the Qarmatis had a few more quarrels with neighbouring princes, until the year 375, when they disappeared from history, as it were. Yet I have learned from books of the Druzes that they were still ruling in Lahsa in 422.[7]

What I just said about the close links that existed, at least from the point of view of a common origin and doctrine, between the Isma'ilis of Egypt or Fatimids and Qarmatis, applies with no less certainty to the Isma'ilis of Persia and Syria, known by the names of *Mulhids* and *Assassins*.[8] It is well known that the Assassins of Syria, who were so famous in the history of the Crusades, depended on the Isma'ilis of Persia; but not enough is known about the liaisons that existed between them and the Fatimids, and it is even possible that this idea was abandoned as a result of what one reads about the murder of Amir bi-Ahkam Allah, one of these caliphs, who was killed by the Batinis or Isma'ilis.

De Guignes (*Histoire des Huns*, Book X, Vol 3, pp 221, 222) has nevertheless pointed out this connection by saying that Hasan Sabbah, the founder of the Isma'ili dynasty of Persia, had spent some time with Mustansir billah, the caliph of Egypt, and that the religion he founded was somehow related to the sect to which the Fatimids belonged. The author of the *Tableau général de l'empire Othoman* (Vol 1, p 36) also mentions this, albeit inaccurately, by saying that Hasan Humayri, the founder of the Isma'ili sect in Persia, was a depraved sheikh who, having preached in Persia and Syria in favour of the Fatimids of Egypt and against the Abbasids of Baghdad, ended up making false commentaries on the Koran and founding a new sect. In a dissertation I shall mention below, the abbot S. Assemani of Padua also says that according to the author of the *Nigaristan*, Hasan preached in favour of the caliphs of Egypt, and against the Abbasids. But these slight indications are not sufficient to prove the close relationship that existed between the Fatimids of Egypt and the Isma'ilis of Persia. This relationship is more clearly pointed out by the author of the *Nizam al-tawarikh*, a chronological summary of the history of the oriental dynasties, of which I provided an excerpt in Volume IV of the *Notices et Extraits des Manuscrits* (p 686). This writer says that Mustansir, the Fatimid caliph of Egypt, sent Hasan patents making him a governor and his lieutenant.

The history of the dynasty founded by Hasan, which lasted 170 years, is as yet little known. D'Herbelot, and after him Marigny in his

Révolutions des Arabes, and de Guignes in the first volume of his *Histoire des Huns*, have listed the succession of princes of this dynasty, but with very little detail. The prelate Et. Évode Assemani, in his *Catalogue des Manuscrits Orientaux de la Bibliothèque des Médicis à Florence* (p 242), also included the succession of these princes, based on the chronological tables of the oriental dynasties, written in the Turkish language; but he added no facts to it. In my note on the *Nizam al-tawarikh* to which I have already referred, I included what information this brief summary offered on that dynasty. And finally, abbot S. Assemani of Padua has published, in the June 1806 issue of the journal printed in that town and entitled *Giornale dell'Italiana letteratura*, a dissertation containing a few more details about this family. He used the *Nigaristan* as his source. It all comes to four or five pages, and can hardly be said to contribute to an adequate knowledge of the history of the Isma'ilis.

It is easy to make up for the inadequacy of these materials by referring to Mirkhwand's *Rawdat al-safa*, which contains a very long and very detailed history of this dynasty, and particularly of its founder Hasan bin Sabbah. Adding to that the contributions of Elmacin, Abu'l-Fida, Abu'l-Faraj and a few other writers, the progress of this power can be traced from its origin to its destruction.

Mr Falconet, in his two memoirs on the Isma'ilis or Assassins published in the collection of the Académie des Belles Lettres (Vol XVII, pp 127 ff.), has very aptly discussed a number of facts concerning this subject. He showed that the Assassins of Syria were a branch of the Isma'ilis of the Jibal or of Persia, that the head of the sect, *le Vieux de la Montagne* (*the Old Man of the Mountain*), lived in Alamut, and that the Isma'ilis of Syria came under his jurisdiction. He also discussed the origin of the name *Assassins*: but as he did not know any oriental languages, his research was exclusively based on those oriental writers of whom printed translations were available, and on a few excerpts from Abu'l-Fida communicated to him by de Guignes, who was very young at the time. Thus Falconet's work remains very incomplete. However, since he rightly established the identity of the Isma'ilis of Persia and the Assassins of Syria, I shall not dwell on a discussion of this historical point; I shall mainly try to describe the relationship of this branch of Isma'ilis with the branch to which the caliphs of Egypt belonged; and then I shall proceed to discuss the origin of the name *Assassins*. I shall also add a few observations on the various names given to the Isma'ilis by oriental historians.

The history of the Isma'ilis of Persia provided by Mirkhwand is interesting enough to deserve a complete translation. However, as this task is extraneous to the work of the Class, I reserve it for the collection of the *Notices [et Extraits]*[9] and will only give a brief outline of their beginnings here.[10]

Shahrastani and Ibn Khaldun tell us that the Isma'ilis are divided into two branches or sects, or to use their own expression, into two *preachings, da'wa,* an old one and a new one. The old one goes back to the period of imam Isma'il, son of Ja'far Sadiq, or rather to that of his son Muhammad, around the middle of the third century of the Hegira; the new one starts with Hasan bin Sabbah, around the year 483 of the same calendar.

These authors say that each of these two Isma'ili branches has its own particular dogmas and tenets, but they both agree on several important points forming the essence of their system. Thus all Isma'ilis recognize the rights of Ali and of his children after him to the *imamate,* that is, to the sovereign spiritual and temporal power, and consider as usurpers all princes who exercised this sovereignty in disregard of the rights of Ali's family. Unlike many other sects that are partisans of Ali, they do not accept a succession of twelve imams.[11] The imams they recognize are seven in number, and the seventh one is Isma'il, son of Ja'far Sadiq: this is why they call themselves Isma'ilis. They believe that after Isma'il the imamate remained hidden, and that its function was filled by obscure personages not known to men: the true faith was then entrusted, like a deposit, to the *da'is* or other ministers until such time as the imam reappeared. This manifestation occurred in the person of Ubayd Allah, surnamed the *Mahdi,* who, with the assistance of the *da'i* Abd Allah, first founded the dynasty of the Ubaydite or Fatimid caliphs in North Africa. Under the fourth prince of this dynasty, Egypt was added to their dominions; it became the seat of power of these pontiffs, who rivalled those of Baghdad and had an infinite number of partisans in the latter's dominions, where they secretly maintained *da'is* or missionaries, eager to propagate their doctrine and ready to take advantage of every opportunity to promote their rights.

Hasan bin Sabbah was one of these *da'is.* His father's name was Ali; and if he is sometimes called *son of Sabbah,* or *son of Muhammad bin Sabbah,* it is because he claimed descent from a person who was famous for his virtues and for the miracles attributed to him, called *Muhammad bin Sabbah Humayri* [Himyari].

Hasan's father, Ali, lived withdrawn from the world and was given to mortification, but was thought to harbour opinions that were hardly religious and of very doubtful orthodoxy. To ward off such suspicions, he sent his son to Nishabur, to study with a sheikh who was well known for the pureness of his faith, as well as his enlightened mind and virtues, the imam Muwaffaq Nishaburi. Here Hasan came into close contact with a person who was to become very famous under the name of *Nizam al-Mulk*. This connection later brought him the advantage of becoming attached to the service of Saljuqid sultan Malikshah, to whom he was introduced by his erstwhile fellow-student, who had become a vizier under the name of *Nizam al-Mulk*. He subsequently tried to supplant his benefactor; but having failed in this project due to the vizier's intrigues and shrewdness, he saw himself obliged to leave the court, and retired first to Rey, and then to Ispahan, where he went into hiding at the house of the *ra'is* Abu'l-Fadl.

Hasan himself said:[12]

I was brought up from my youth in the doctrine of the Shi'ites who recognize the succession of the twelve imams: I had struck up an acquaintance with one of those sectarians called *rafiq* (I shall explain this word below); his name was *Amira Darrab*. I was convinced that the doctrine of the Isma'ili sect corresponded with that of the philosophers: so I always argued with Amira when he stood up for the Isma'ili sect, or when he attacked my faith. Nevertheless these discourses impressed themselves on my mind; and having fallen dangerously ill, I came to realize that the doctrine of the Isma'ilis was the true one; that the reason I had not adopted it was stubbornness; and that, were I to die in this condition, I would be hopelessly lost. Having recovered from my illness, I became acquainted with another Isma'ili, and then with a *da'i* whom I asked to admit me to the sect. Later, I myself was promoted to the rank of *da'i* and sent to Egypt to enjoy the privilege of seeing the imam Mustansir.

Mustansir, no doubt delighted by a circumstance that could make him expand his power in Asia, showered Hasan with honours, without, however, admitting him to his presence. The caliph kept abreast of all of Hasan's activities and talked about him in such favourable terms that everyone believed he would soon rise to the most prominent position. At this juncture, there occurred a heated altercation between Hasan and the *amir al-juyush* or commander-in-chief of the caliph's armies, who directed the Isma'ili sect, about Mustansir's designation of Nizar,[13] one of his sons, as his successor. The caliph had revoked this decision, and the *amir al-juyush* had approved of his doing so.[14] Hasan, on the other hand, supported the irrevocability of the first designation. Mustansir was urged by the *amir al-juyush*, who may have been jealous of Hasan's influence, to have him arrested and imprisoned in the

Damietta fortress; but, as the caliph was not willing to do so, Hasan's enemies put him on board a ship with some Franks and sent him to the Maghrib. After a few adventures that seemed something of a miracle, Hasan landed in Syria, went to Aleppo, then to Baghdad, and then to Khuzistan, Ispahan, and finally to Yazd and Kirman, performing his functions as a *da'i* all along and sparing no efforts for the propagation of his sect. He subsequently returned to Ispahan, then went to Khuzistan where he spent three years. From there he went to Damghan, where he also spent three years, converting many people. Afterwards he travelled to Gurgan, and from there by way of Damawand and Qazwin, he entered Daylam. He finally settled at Alamut, where he spent his time meditating and leading a religious life.

We need hardly describe the ways in which Hasan bin Sabbah managed to seize the fortress of Alamut, a place situated in the Qazwin region and belonging to sultan Malikshah. It was governed by a *kutwal* or commandant called *Mahdi*. In these parts, the preachings of the *da'i*s, particularly those of Husayn Qa'ini, had brought about such an increase in the number of partisans of the Isma'ili doctrine who recognized as their sovereign the imam established in Egypt, that Hasan had no difficulty in forcing the *kutwal* to sell him, for 3000 dinars, a stretch of land the size of an ox-hide. But this bargain enabled Hasan, who was as shrewd as Dido, to take possession of a vast site comprising the entire citadel. He gave Mahdi a draft for 3000 dinars drawn on the governor of Girdkuh, who had secretely embraced his party, and forced him to leave. Having become master of Alamut,[15] he sent the *da'i* Husayn Qa'ini with other *rafiq*s on a mission to convert and subject the peoples of Kuhistan, a country belonging to Khurasan and situated near the south-eastern end of this large province.

Here an important circumstances should be noted. I shall translate Mirkhwand's text literally.

> When Hasan, son of Sabbah, became master of Alamut, he ordered a canal to be dug, and had water brought from far away to the foot of the fortress. He had fruit trees planted outside the place and encouraged the inhabitants to cultivate and develop the soil. This is how the air of Alamut, which was previously very unhealthy, became pure and salubrious.

Could this not have served to accredit the idea of the delightful gardens of the Assassins, which I shall mention below? But let us go back to the sequence of historical facts.

Malikshah sent troops against Hasan, but it was in vain that they laid siege to Alamut. Hasan, who at the time had no more than 70 *rafiq*s with him, stood his ground against the assailants, and, having received a reinforcement of 300 men from outside, he fell upon the sultan's troops by night, made a great carnage and took an enormous booty. The death of Malikshah, which occurred in the year 485 of the Hegira (AD 1092), subsequently contributed to extending and consolidating Hasan's power.

Hasan had two sons, whom he killed, one for having drunk wine, the other because he was suspected of having been responsible for Husayn Qa'ini's assassination. Hasan's aim in doing so was to show everybody that he had no intention of establishing a sovereignty which he would pass on to his children. He devoted himself with such zeal to administering his dominions and gave so much time to replying to the questions addressed to him regarding the dogmas of the sect that, throughout the 35 years he spent at Alamut, he left his apartment only twice to climb to the terrace of his palace, and never set foot outside the fortress.

I shall not go any further with this historical excerpt. Suffice it to say that before his death, which happened in 519 of the Hegira,[16] Hasan designated as his successor Kiya Buzurg-Ummid, whose descendants, under the title of *muqaddim*, preserved the sovereignty of Alamut and of the other places conquered by the Isma'ilis, and that, under the reign of Kiya Buzurg-Ummid himself, the Isma'ilis took arms against a descendant of Ali, called Abu Hashim, who wanted to be recognized as an imam in Gilan. On this occasion, too, Mirkhwand refers to the Isma'ilis as *rafiqan*.

Let us end with a few events in the history of the Isma'ilis.

In 498, they pillaged and massacred a caravan near Rey, consisting of a group of pilgrims travelling to Mecca from India and the Mawara al-Nahr or Transoxania.

In 500, they suffered a defeat from sultan Malikshah.[17]

In 502, they almost took possession of Shayzar in Syria.

The year 519[18] saw the death of Hasan, son of Sabbah, who, according to Abu'l-Fida, forbade common men to cultivate the sciences, and more enlightened men to read the books of ancient philosophers.

The first conquest of the Isma'ilis in Syria was Baniyas; they took possession of it in 523.[19]

In 525, they captured Masyat[20] in Syria; this place became their chief locality.[21]

In 559, Hasan, the son of Muhammad and grandson of Kiya Buzurg-

Ummid, abolished all the Islamic practices and, in the name of a hidden imam, from whom he claimed to have received a special order to this effect, gave his subjects complete freedom to drink wine and to indulge in everything that was forbidden by Muslim law. He proclaimed that knowledge of the allegorical meaning of these precepts rendered their literal observance useless, and thus earned the sect the name of *Mulhids* or impious.[22]

According to Mirkhwand and the author of the *Nigaristan*, Hasan reigned for a few years only: he died in 561 (1165), and his son Muhammad, who imitated his impiety, reigned for 46 years and died in 606 (1209).[23] However, according to the author of the *Nizam al-tawarikh*, Hasan reigned for 50 years and died in 607 (1210). It was his son whose reign was very short. Depending on which one of these accounts we accept, the embassy of the Old Man of the Mountain to the King of Jerusalem, Amalric I, coincided either with Hasan's or with his son's reign.[24] It is thus true, as William of Tyre reports, that the prince who sent the embassy had abolished all the practices of the Muslim religion, destroyed the mosques, and allowed the consumption of wine and pork, as well as incestuous unions. Those who are familiar with the books of the Druzes find it easy to believe that this prince may have read the holy books of the Christians and conceived the desire, not to embrace Christianity, but to learn more about its doctrine and practices.

Sinan, the head of the Isma'ilis in Syria and the founder of the sect's power in that country, died in 588.

In 608, all the Isma'ilis, both of Syria and of Persia, followed the orders of Jalal al-Din Hasan, the emir of Alamut and sixth prince of this dynasty, to observe the external signs of the Muslim religion which they had abandoned by order of the ancestor of this prince, Hasan, son of Muhammad and grandson of Kiya Buzurg-Ummid.

In 644, ambassadors of Ala al-Din, the emir of the Isma'ilis of Persia, attended a *couriltai* or general assembly of Mongol tribal chiefs for the election of a Khan of the Tartars.

In 668, sultan Baybars entered the Isma'ili territories in Syria and captured Masyat from them.

Finally in 670, this same prince put an end to their power in Syria.[25]

This power had already collapsed in Kuhistan in 653, through the submission of the prince of the Isma'ilis, Rukn al-Din Khurshah, to Hulagu, the destruction of Alamut, and the massacre of Rukn al-Din's family and of a large number of *Mulhids*.[26]

When I say that the Isma'ilis were exterminated, both in Persia and in Syria, before the end of the seventh century of the Hegira, what I mean is not their sect, but the sovereignty they had founded. They often reappear in history at a later period and continue practising their profession of assassins which had made them so fearsome. One such instance about which oriental historians have handed down to us the most ample details is their repeated conspiracy against Qarasunqur. This emir, who had been governor or viceroy of Aleppo for the sultan of Egypt, Malik al-Nasir Muhammad, son of Qala'un, had been forced to leave the dominions of this sultan and take refuge with the Mongols of Persia, the descendants of Hulagu, who were at that time under the command of Uljaytu Khan, also called Khudabanda. The sultan, who resented his being protected from his vengeance, tried several times to have him assassinated by Isma'ilis whom he had sent for that purpose. On one single occasion, he dispatched 34 of them to this effect. They were people living at Masyat, the former capital of the Isma'ilis in Syria. Qarasunqur escaped their attempts and resorted to the same method, but with equal lack of success, to have the sultan killed. A hundred and twenty-four Isma'ili assassins subsequently sent by Malik al-Nasir to kill Qarasunqur perished as victims of his vengeance without being able to carry out their project. The Isma'ilis still had a chief at Masyat, even at that period. For Maqrizi tells us that the sultan appealed to him and gave him a large sum of money so that he would send him some of his people. In the report about these events, Masyat still appears to be the residence and refuge of these Assassins. The sultan then negotiated with Qarasunqur and the vizier of the Mongol prince and promised not to send any more Isma'ilis to assassinate them; but he did not keep his word. He again entrusted the execution of his project to an Isma'ili who had been sent to him from Masyat, and whom he fed for 34 days before giving him his orders and dispatching him, supplying him with enough food and drink for several persons each day. This man killed another emir, mistaking him for Qarasunqur. Several of these murderers were tortured in vain, they never confessed anything.

The Isma'ili sect still survives today, as I shall mention below.

I shall now discuss the origin of the name *Assassins*.

I mentioned at the beginning of this *Memoir* that the Isma'ilis or Batinis were known in the histories of the Crusades under the name of *Assassins*. This name was pronounced and written in different ways, either, as Falconet says, due to the mistakes of copyists, or because of the ignorance of the authors themselves. Among these variants, those that are most authoritative are the following: *Assassini, Assessini, Assissini* and *Heissessini*. The latter, stemming from Arnold of Lübeck, has the advantage of keeping the aspirate which the original word must have contained, since Benjamin of Tudela writes *Hashishin* with a *heth* in Hebrew, and since the Greek authors write it with a *x* (*khi*), calling these sectarians *Xasisioi*.[27] Renaudot (*Hist. patr. Alex.*, p 470) also writes *Hassissini*, and sometimes *Hassassini*; but he does not give the etymology of this word.[28]

Various etymologies of the word *assassins* have been suggested. I would not have mentioned the opinion of M. de Caseneuve (*Dictionnaire étymologique de la langue Françoise*, 1750), who proposes to derive the name *Assassins* from the ancient Teutonic word *sahs, sachs, saehs*, meaning cutlass, because this derivation is obviously spurious, nothing being less natural than to look for the origin of an oriental denomination in the language of the Teutons; however, this scholar thought he could prove that the name did not come from the languages of Asia and was unknown to the Saracens, quoting as his authority William, archbishop of Tyre, who said: *Hos tam nostri quam Saraceni nescimus unde deducto vocabulo, Assissinos vocant* (*Gesta Dei per Francos*, Vol 1, p 994). De Caseneuve obviously reads far too much into this passage, in which William admits that he does not know the origin of this name, but by no means states that it was unknown to the Saracens.

Court de Gébelin (*Dictionnaire . . .*) also derives the word *assassin* from the Teutonic *sachs*; but the same word, signifying the *dynasty of the Assassins*, appears to him to stem from *shahi shah, king of kings*.

Th. Hyde (*Veterum Persarum religionis historia*, p 493), who had doubtless never come across the denomination in any Arab author, thought that it must be the word *hassas* derived from the root *hassa*, meaning, among other things, *to kill, to exterminate*. This opinion was followed by Ménage and by Falconet. De Volney also adopted this etymology without citing any evidence (*Voyage en Égypte et en Syrie*, 3rd edn, Vol 1, p 404).

Benjamin of Tudela mentions the Assassins in two passages (*Itiner. D. Benjaminis*, pp 32, 89): he writes their name the first time, when talking about the Assassins of Syria, with a *heth*; in the second passage, referring to the Ismaʿilis of Persia, whom he calls *Molahat*, a corruption for *Malahida*,[29] he says that they acknowledged the authority of the old man residing in the land of the *Cashishin*, as Baratier rightly rendered it, and not, as Constantin Lempereur ludicrously translated, *seniorem suae regionis Alcaschischin, quasi senes dicas appellantes*. I am noting this so that no one should imagine, on false authority, that Benjamin of Tudela interpreted the word *Assassins* as meaning *old man*. For all I know, some manuscripts of this Jewish writer may also have *Hashishin* in the second passage written with a *heth* instead of a *caf*; in any case, the substitution of *caf* for *heth* should not surprise anyone familiar with oriental languages. I would add that when quoting Benjamin of Tudela, I do not claim to guarantee the reality of his journey. However, although he probably never set eyes on many of the countries he described, it cannot be denied that his sources were quite reliable.

The learned author of the *Bibliotheca Orientalis Clementino Vaticana* (Vol 2, pp 214, 215, 320), Joseph-Simon Assemani, having found a town, called *Hasasa* by the Arabs and *Beth-hasosonoye* or *Hasosonitho* by the Syrians, in the Takrit region in Mesopotamia, imagined that this was the place from which the *Assassins* mentioned by the historians of the Crusades had derived their name. This conjecture is not based on any historical foundation and was not worthy of being adopted by the author of the *Oriens Christianus* (Vol 2, col 1584). The spelling of this name bears no similarity with that of the real Arabic name of the *Assassins*. Falconet has rejected this conjecture of Assemani's; but through another error, he confused *Hassasa*[30] with *A'zaz*, or *Izaz*, a town in Mesopotamia, although these two names have no consonants in common (*Mémoires de l'Académie des Inscriptions*, Vol XVII, p 163).

Falconet mentioned another origin for the name of the *Assassins*, an origin he himself rejects, but I must not omit it because it might find supporters, and it actually had the approval of D. Carpentier, the author of the *Glossarium ad scriptores medii aevi*. Besides, this will provide me with an opportunity to make a few useful observations. Abu'l-Fida, in his *Description of Syria* (*Tab. Syriae*, p 19), mentions that *Masyat*, a town that was the headquarters of the Isma'ili sect in Syria, is situated on a mountain called *Jabal assikkin* (*Jabal al-sikkin*). As *sikkin* means *knife, dagger*, the name of this mountain may mean *mountain of the Knife*, and there seems to be some analogy between this designation, the atrocities of which the Assassins were accused, and their being called *Assassins*.

'We have seen', says Falconet (*Mémoires de l'Académie des Inscriptions*, Vol XVII, p 163),

> that the *Assikkin* mountain, the *mountain of the Dagger*, was the residence of the commander of the *Assassins* in Syria; the knives used by the *Assassins* were called *sikkin*; their sovereign was attributed the title *magister cultellorum* by Jacques de Vitry; his subjects were called *cultelliferi* by Matthew Paris, and even *sicarii* by William of Newburgh . . . But all these concordances, however felicitous they may be, merely form one of those far too often

misleading clues in the search for the origin of words, without prevailing against the etymology we first proposed.

The etymology favoured by Falconet is, as I mentioned before, the one proposed by Hyde.

Falconet's reflections are highly justified. But we can add, in order to give them more weight, first, that there is in fact no great resemblance between the word *alsikkin* or *assikkin* and the name *Assassins*; secondly, that it is doubtful whether *Jabal assikkin* means *mountain of the Dagger* (*la montagne du Poignard*). Abu'l-Fida does not mention it. It is true that Koehler's translation says: *De hac denominatione montis, qua Assekkin vocatur, quod cultrum significat, mirifice commentus est Ibn Said.* But the words *quod cultrum significat* were added by the translator, and we do not know the special origin attributed to this term by Ibn Sa'id, whose work has not come down to us (*Michaelis Descriptio Aegypti*, p 36; Reiske in d'Herbelot's *Bibliothèque orientale*, The Hague, 1779, Vol 4, p 754; Rommel, *Abulf. Arab. Desc.*, p 7). Perhaps *Sekkin* in this case is the name of a man, so that we should translate *Sekkin's mountain* (*la montagne de Sekkin*). What is at least certain is that a person called *Sekkin* played an important part in this country around the time of Hakim and in the establishment of the religion of the Druzes, and that we have, in the collection of sacred books of this sect (Arabic Manuscript of the Bibliothèque du Roi, no 158), a diploma dating from the tenth year of the Hamza era, 418 of the Hegira, in which Sekkin is appointed superintendent or inspector general of a diocese, or an ecclesiastical province, designated as the *peninsula of the upper Syria* and apparently having as its borders Arabia to the south, Hamat and its territory to the north, Iraq to the east, and the Mediterranean to the west. He was authorized to have under him twelve *da'i*s or missionaries and some other ministers of a lower rank. The writings of the Druzes also inform us that Sekkin was not content with his rank and wanted to assume a higher one in the hierarchy; that he committed many robberies that rendered the name of the Druzes odious; and finally, that he introduced novelties, idolatry and other abominations into the religion.[31] This Sekkin is probably the same of whom Abu'l-Fida reports the intrigues and the death in the year 434, in the following terms (*Annales Moslemici*, Vol 3, p 119):

In this same year, in the month of Rajab, there rose up in Misr a man called *Sekkin*, who resembled Hakim. He pretended to be Hakim; he was followed by a group of men who counted on Hakim's return. These people marched towards the palace, at a time when the caliph was alone and had withdrawn into his apartments, and shouted: *Here is Hakim.* Those who were guarding the gate at this moment were at first frightened; but then, suspecting some mistake, they arrested Sekkin, and he was crucified with his partisans.

Incidentally, I am only mentioning this as a conjecture, which can even be questioned by the fact that *Sekkin*, as the proper name of a man, does not ordinarily have an article. It is nevertheless useful to observe that in one of the writings directed against Sekkin, it is said that *he put his trust in the mountains where he resides*; which adds considerable strength to my conjecture (*Trad. manus. des livres religieux des Druzes*, Vol 2, p 1000).

Let us go on to another etymology, or rather to two different etymologies, proposed by a scholar whose authority has great weight in the field of Arabic literature. It is Reiske whom I have in mind (*Annales Moslemici*, Vol 3, p 714, annotation 251). This clever orientalist assumes that the word *assassins* is simply a corruption, and that the Isma'ilis or Batinis were called *Hassanini* or *Hassanici* after the head of their sect, Hasan bin Sabbah. 'Or perhaps,' he says, 'since this name is often written *chassassin*, which the Germans would render as *schassasin*, their name in Arabic was *jassas*: this word is pronounced in Arabic approximately like *chassas* in French or *schassas* in German, and means "spy".' There is no need for me to dwell on the discussion of these two etymologies, the first of which is based on a very far-fetched assumption, while the second is devoid of all verisimilitude. Suffice it to say that if Reiske had, as I have, come across the name *Assassins* written in Arabic letters, he would have ventured neither of these conjectures.

A very different and apparently better grounded etymology is that of abbot Simon Assemani, Professor of oriental languages at the seminary of Padua, recently proposed in the dissertation I already mentioned, which is included in the June 1808 [1806] issue of the *Literary Journal of Padua*. It is entitled *Ragguaglio storico-critico sopra la setta Assissana, detta volgarmente degli ASSASSINI.*

Mr Simon Assemani says:

While I was in Syrian Tripoli, a city where the nearby mountains still contain remnants of this sect, I often heard this rhymed jibe against those who came to do their errands in town: *Assissani (al-sisani) la muslim wa la nasrani*, the Assissani is neither a Muslim nor a Christian, meaning that these people have no religion, precisely because as followers of the doctrine of Hasan, they have no external cult.[32] Note that the historians of the Crusades here transposed the two vowels *i* and *a*, so that instead of *Assissani* they said *Assassini*; and this is how the name entered our language, to designate the villains who lay in ambush to commit homicide. The rulers of this sect were indeed well-known for sending their professional killers everywhere to massacre anyone they disliked.

　　Assissani [he adds] comes from *assissa* (*al-sisa*), meaning rock, fortress, a fortified place offering a safe retreat; hence *Assissani* (*al-sisani*), in Arabic, designates a man who lives among rocks and fortified places, as we would say a mountain-dweller, a man who lives in the mountains.

Despite the esteem I have for the talents of abbot Assemani, I cannot concur with his opinion on the origin of the name *Assassins*. Here are my reasons: first, *sisa*, or rather *sisiya*, does not really mean a rock, but anything that serves as a defence, the horn of a bull, the spur of a cock, the antler of an antelope, and by the same token, a citadel, a fortified place. Secondly, *sisani* is not regularly formed from *sisiya*, it should have been *sisi*; on the other hand, *sisani* is regularly formed from *sisan*, plural of *sus*, chicken, from which is also formed the verb *sawsa*, to cheep like a little chicken; from the plural *sisan*, the word *sisani*, chicken-seller, is formed, just as *dajajati*, poultry-seller, is formed from *dajajat*, the plural of *dajaja*; *kutubi*, bookseller, from *kutub*, plural of *kitab*, book; *lubudi*, felt-seller, from *lubud*, plural of *libd*, felt; *sanadiqi*, chest-seller, from *sanadiq*, plural of *sanduq*, chest; *hawayisi*, belt-seller, from *hawayis*, plural of *hiyasa*, belt. The proverb reported by Assemani may thus apply to mountain dwellers or villagers who come to town to sell their poultry, and what it means is that these people are dishonest and uncouth and that due to their great ignorance, they belong to no religion.

　　I must point out, moreover, that this proverb is also used in another sense, which might be closer to its origin. Instead of *al-sisani*, the word often used is *al-sasani*, as Michel Sabbagh of Acre informed me; which means *of the family of Sasan*. This term is used by the Arabs to indicate a vagrant, an adventurer, a man who roams around to make money without doing anything. It is in this sense that Hariri, in his forty-ninth assembly, has Abu Zayd Saruji, a person of this type, say:

　　I have not found easier gain, a more pleasant subsistence, a more lucrative profession, a brook with purer water, than the trade created by Sasan, of which he devised various modifications . . . It is a business that never flags, a reservoir that never dries out, a torch in whose light a great number of men assemble, and which enlightens the blind and the one-eyed. Those who practise this profession are the happiest people, the most fortunate race . . . They have no fixed dwelling, they fear no authority. There is no difference between them and the birds who rise with an empty stomach and by the evening, have eaten their fill . . . But the first condition for practising this profession is to move around a great deal; the first quality required is constant activity. A resourceful mind must be the torch of him who adopts it; impudence, the armour that he must be equipped with . . . So do not tire in your search, do not lose heart in exercising every kind of diligence; for it was written on the staff of our chief Sasan: He who will search will find; he who comes and goes will obtain.

It was in the same spirit that Hariri, in his second assembly, says of Abu Zayd: 'He made up all kinds of genealogies to show himself off, and he resorted to every possible way of making money. Sometimes he said that he belonged to the family of Sasan, and sometimes he claimed to be a descendant of the kings of Ghassan.'

Mutarrizi, the commentator of Hariri, explains the word Sasan as follows:

Sasan [he says,] is the chief of beggars and their patron. The Sasan in question is the ancient Sasan, son of Bahman, son of Isfandiyar, son of king Gushtasp. This is how his story is told by Ibn al-Muqanna.[33] When Bahman was about to die, he summoned his daughter Humay, who was pregnant. She surpassed all mortals in beauty, and no one, among the Persians of that time, equalled her in wisdom. Then the king asked for his crown, put it on his daughter's head, and declared that she was to be queen after him, ordering that, if she gave birth to a male child, she should continue ruling the kingdom until her son reached the age of 30, at which time she should hand the government to him. Sasan, the son of Bahman, was a very handsome man, well-bred and full of wisdom and all kinds of accomplishments; no one doubted that he would inherit the throne. When Bahman had thus bequeathed his kingdom to Humay, the sister of Sasan, the latter was greatly vexed, so he went away, bought some sheep, led them to the mountains himself and occupied himself with taking them to pasture, living among the Kurds, all this as a result of the anger he had felt because of the contempt his father had shown him by depriving him of the crown and giving it to his sister. From that time until today, the name Sasan has been adopted as a metaphorical term for a man who drives a flock of sheep, being referred to as *Sasan the Kurd* or *Sasan the shepherd*. Hence the name Sasani is applied to designate any man who begs or who does a low job, such as blind or one-eyed men, jugglers, people who train and show dogs or monkeys, and others of this type, although they do not descend from Sasan. Such men are very numerous, and they include many different classes and types. Abu Dulaf Khazraji mentions them in a poem in which he describes, by having them speak in their own words, all their trades, their juggleries, their tales, and the special language they use among themselves. This poem, known by the name of *Sasaniyya*, was commented on by Sahib bin Abbad; the reader will find in it a detailed account of what I have briefly described.

It is easily conceived, by reading the above, that the proverb *he is a Sasani, neither a Muslim nor a Christian* makes sense as such, but bears no relation to the *Assassins*.

After Assemani, another orientalist published an article in the first issue of the journal entitled *Les Mines de l'Orient*,[34] in which he rejects Hyde's etymology, which he attributes to de Volney, and proposes to derive the word *Assassins* from ʿ*asas*, night watch.

I also heard from Dominique Sestini that an Armenian scholar, asked about the etymology of this word, derived it from *habash habash*, a pack of people of all sorts.

The first of these two etymologies might have been acceptable, if we were reduced to conjectures on the subject; the second one cannot even be proposed.

Since I have already mentioned Mariti's *Historical Memoirs on the Assassins and the Old Man of the Mountain*, I must add here that this writer favours one of the least plausible etymologies proposed for the name *Assassins*. He thinks that their true name was *Arsasides* or *Arsacides*, and that they were thus called because the first founders of this tribe who, after arriving in Syria, were known there by the name of *Assassins*, had been Kurds who originally lived in the surroundings under the jurisdiction of the city of Arsacia. It is not even worth our while to disprove this theory.

It may surprise the reader that I have not yet mentioned another etymology reported by Ménage, whose author is Étienne Lemoine, a Protestant minister at Rouen. It is included in a letter written by

Lemoine to Ménage, which the latter published in his *Dictionnaire étymologique de la langue Françoise* (*Etymological Dictionary of the French Language*), under the word *Assassins*. I shall merely quote the part which concerns my subject.

> The word *Assassin* [says Lemoine,] was applied to the Old Man of the Mountain, king of the *Assassins*, who is thus called in the sense of *king of pastures, of meadows, of gardens.* Indeed, this king occupied, at the foot of the Lebanon, a very good land which may well have derived its name from its fertility. *Assessa,* or *Assissa,* means herb, pastures, gardens, things that existed in abundance in the countries ruled by this prince. You know how he deceived many of his subjects by means of these delightful gardens, and how he engaged them to take every risk by promising them that they would enjoy all these beautiful places after their death ... Benjamin calls him *sheikh el-chasisin,* and that is how he is called all over the Orient. This is why we came to call him *the king of the Assassins.* But these words, as I already said, mean king of the prairies, of cultivated lands, of gardens in which art and nature vie with one another to provide an infinite number of delightful things.

This etymology was disapproved of, according to Ménage's report, by Ferrari, the learned professor of Padua, who preferred to derive the word *assassin, ab assidendo*; and Ménage himself did not hesitate to embrace the opinion of de Caseneuve, who derived this word from the old Teutonic *sahs*, knife. Falconet also says, without much ado, that the etymology is as false as the conclusions drawn from it by Lemoine (*Mémoires de l'Académie des Inscriptions et Belles Lettres,* Vol XVII, p 155). Nevertheless this is the only correct etymology, as I hope to prove; but Lemoine did not know why the Isma'ilis bore the name *Hashishin,* and he gave a very bad reason for it which caused his etymology to be rejected. I hope to offer a much more satisfactory reason for this designation. I therefore have to show two things: first, that the Isma'ilis or Batinis also bore the name *Hashishin*; secondly, what the reason for this designation was.

The first proposition is easy to establish. We need only observe that in the word *Hashishin,* the ending *in* is the plural sign. In classical Arabic the ending of the masculine plural is *una* for the nominative and *ina* for the two other cases; in everyday language, the final vowel *a* is eliminated and the ending is pronounced *in* without any case distinctions. Example: *Muslimin,* the Muslims; *Mu'minin,* the faithful;

Kafirin, the infidels. *Hashishin*, or more grammatically *Hashishiyyin*, is hence the plural of *Hashishi*: the same word can also form the plural *Hashishiyya*, which is even more elegant. We must not lose sight of this trivial observation, which I had to make for people who have no idea of the Arabic language.

Abu'l-Fida in his *Annals* and Baha al-Din in his *Life of Saladin* report that in the year 571, while this prince was laying siege to the citadel of Izaz, some Isma'ilis tried to assassinate him. It was the second time that his life had been threatened by people of this sect; an unsuccessful attempt had already been made in 570. As Abu'l-Fida's account is more detailed, I shall quote from him (*Annales Moslemici*, Vol 4, pp 21, 25).

In the year 570, Sa'd al-Din Gumushtigin sent a large sum of money to Sinan, the chief of the Isma'ilis, so that they should kill Saladin. Sinan sent several men who suddenly attacked Saladin; but they were killed without being able to take his life.

In the year 571 ... sultan Saladin advanced towards Izaz; he laid siege to the place on the 3rd of Dhu'l-Qa'da and took it on the 11th of Dhu'l-Hijja. While he was besieging this town, an Isma'ili fell upon him, stabbed him in the head with a dagger and wounded him. Saladin caught hold of the Isma'ili, who continued attacking him, without managing to stab him. He was killed in this situation. A second one attacked the sultan and was also killed. Then a third one met with the same fate. Frightened, the sultan went into his tent, had his troops inspected and sent away the people he did not know.

We shall now see in what terms these two events are reported by Abu Shama, the author of the *Kitab al-rawdatayn*,[35] a very detailed history of Nur al-Din and Saladin (Arabic Manuscript of the Bibliothèque du Roi, no 707 A, under the year 570, fol 127v):

In the year 570, Saladin advanced towards Hamat and took it on the first day of Jumada II. From there he marched towards Aleppo and laid siege to this city on the 3rd of the same month. As the inhabitants found themselves in a desperate situation and in great need of help, they appealed to the Isma'ilis, promised them certain lands and made them all kinds of generous gifts. One day when it was very cold and the winter was severely making itself felt, a few of the most determined of these villains came. They were recognized by the emir Nasih al-Din Khumartekin, the master of Buqtish, whose properties bordered on those of the Isma'ilis. What are you doing, said the emir, and how could you dare come here without being deterred by fear? So they killed him; a man who came running to defend him was also wounded by them. One of them suddenly came forth to hurl himself on the sultan, but the emir Tughril Khazandar was resolutely waiting for him without moving and without saying a word; and the moment he arrived, he cut off his head with his sabre. The others were only killed after they themselves had killed a large number of men, and those who were confronting them ran great risks. So on this occasion, God saved the life (literally, *the last breath*) of the sultan from the daggers of *al-Hashishiyya*.

The author here makes a play on words with *hushasha*, the last breath, and *hashishiyya*, plural of *hashishi*; and it is perhaps for the sake of this play on words that he uses this designation instead of the word *Isma'ilis*.

We shall go on to the second event. This is how it is reported (Arabic Manuscript of the Bibliothèque du Roi, no 707 A, under the year 571, fol 137v):

Chapter containing the narrative of the second attempt of the *Hashishi*s on the life of the sultan: this one took place while he was besieging Izaz; the first one had happened in front of Aleppo.

On the 11th of Dhu'l-Qa'da, says Imad al-Din, during the night of the first day of the week, the *Hashishi*s attacked the sultan while he was camping in front of Izaz. The emir Jawali Asadi had his tent near the machines, and the sultan was going to this tent to inspect the machines, to give orders regarding the most important affairs, and to arouse the ardour of the warriors. While he was busy distributing gifts and making up for the evils caused by fortune's cruelty, some *Hashishi*s were standing there disguised as soldiers, and the troops forming several lines were near the sultan. Suddenly one of the *Hashishi*s fell upon the sultan and stabbed him in the head with his dagger. The metal plates inside his helmet prevented the dagger from injuring his head, and the weapon only slightly wounded his cheek. Without losing heart, the sultan seized the head of the *Hashishi* and pulled it towards him, then threw himself on the man and straddled him; thereupon Sayf al-Din Yazkuj appeared, took the *Hashishi*'s life, and cut him in pieces. Another one advanced; but the emir Da'ud, son of Minkilan, rushed at him and stopped him. The *Hashishi* dealt him a wound in his side, from which he died a few days later. A third one appeared; the emir Ali, son of Abu'l-Fawaris, caught him in his arms and held him tightly embraced under his armpits. The *Hashishi*'s hand was caught behind his back, so that he could not strike or disengage himself from his awkward position.[36] The emir shouted: 'Kill me with him; for he has dealt me a mortal blow, he has deprived me of my strength and made me incapable of fighting.' Then Nasir al-Din, son of Shirkuh, pierced this man with his sword. Another one came out of the tent and fled, ready to strike anyone who might stand in his way; but the servants of the army fell on him and killed him.

I leave out the rest of this account. The author adds an excerpt from a letter by the *qadi* Fadil containing an account of the same event, where he says that the *Hashishi* had merely given the sultan a scratch, from which he had lost only a few drops of blood.

Finally, as is the custom with Orientals, the author reports another account of the same event, by an author called Ibn Abi Tayy. I shall translate that as well, despite the repetitions it involves, because the expressions used in this account are worth considering (Arabic Manuscript of the Bibliothèque du Roi, no 707 A, under the year 571, fol 137 v):

Here is how Ibn Abi Tayy expresses himself, says the author of the *Rawdatayn*: When the sultan had captured Bazagha and Manbij, those who were the masters of Aleppo fully realized that they would inevitably find themselves deprived of one after the other of the fortified places and citadels they possessed. So they went back to their usual intrigues and started setting traps for the sultan again. They consequently wrote a second letter to Sinan, the *master of the hashisha* [I shall explain this expression below], won him over with money and persuaded him to send his men to kill the sultan. Sinan (may God curse him!) actually dispatched some of his men, who joined Saladin's army, disguised as soldiers. They mingled with the warriors, participated in military operations, and did so with great bravery. They took care to mix with the sultan's people, in the hope of finding an opportunity to carry out their project, and to seize the appropriate occasion.

So one day when the sultan was sitting in the tent of the emir Jawali, while the fight was going on and the sultan was watching it, one of the *Hashishi*s pounced on him and dealt him a blow on the head with his dagger. As the sultan always suspected some surprise on behalf of the *Hashishi*s, he never took off his armour and always had his head protected by metal plates. The blow dealt by the *Hashishi* did not cut through the metal plates covering the sultan's head; and having felt these metal plates, the *Hashishi* let his hand with the dagger slide down toward the sultan's cheek, wounding him so that the blood ran down his face. This made the sultan reel. The *Hashishi* took advantage of this moment, leapt on the sultan, and pulled his head toward himself so that he dragged him to the ground; and sitting astride him, he tried to slit his throat.[37] Those who were surrounding the sultan were in a state of stupor that seemed to deprive them of their reason. At this moment Sayf al-Din Yazkuj appeared. Some say that he had been present before. He drew his sabre, struck the *Hashishi* with it and killed him.

Another *Hashishi* ran up to throw himself on the sultan; but the emir Minkilan the Kurd stood in his way and struck him with his sword. The *Hashishi* had, however, forestalled Minkilan and wounded him in the forehead. Minkilan killed him, but he himself died a few days later from the blow the *Hashishi* had dealt him. Yet another of the Batinis appeared, and stood near the emir Ali, son of Abu'l-Fawaris. The emir swooped down on the Batini, but the Batini advanced under his impact to strike him. Ali seized him under the armpits, and the Batini's hand remained behind him, so that he could not strike him. The emir Ali then shouted: *Kill him and kill me with him*; and Nasir al-Din, son of Shirkuh, came forward and plunged his sword into the Batini's belly and moved it around in all directions until the man fell down dead. This was how Ali, the son of Abu'l-Fawaris, was saved. Then another one of the *Hashishi*s came out to escape; he was intercepted by the emir Shihab al-Din Mahmud, the sultan's maternal uncle. The Batini turned around to avoid the emir, but the emir's men ran towards him and cut him to pieces with their sabres. As for the sultan, he immediately mounted his horse and returned to his tent. Blood was running down his cheek.

A little further on, the author of the *Rawdatayn* adds:

In the year 572, peace having been made, the sultan remembered the revenge he had to take on the Isma'ilis, and the way they had come to attack him during this war. So he set out on Friday the 19th of Ramadan, laid siege to their fortress of Masyat, and put up great war machines against them. He killed many of their people, took a great number of prisoners, took the men with him, ravaged the homes, destroyed the buildings, had their houses pillaged, until his maternal uncle Shihab al-Din Mahmud bin Tekish, prince of Hamat, interceded in their favour. For they had sent him messages to ask him to do so, seeing that they were his neighbours. The sultan then withdrew from their country, having had his revenge.

After what we have just read, there is hardly any need to prove that the *Hashishi*s, the *Batinis* and the *Isma'ilis* are the same people, or if you like, the same sect. We have seen that Ibn Abi Tayy uses the first two names indiscriminately, and that the author of the *Rawdatayn* says *Isma'ilis* when referring to the people he had previously called *Hashishi*s (*al-Hashishiyya*).

There would be no use looking for other authorities to prove this identity. I shall only point out that Ibn al-Khatib, the Arab historian of Spain, when referring to the violent death of the caliph Amir bi-Ahkam Allah, said that he was killed by *Hashishi*s, while other historians, Abu'l-Fida, Mirkhwand, Maqrizi, say that this prince was assassinated by *Isma'ilis*, *Batinis*, or *Nazaris* [*Nizaris*]. I shall explain this last word below.

Nor should there be any doubt, in my opinion, that the word *hashishi*, plural *hashishin*, is the origin of the corruptions *heisessini*, *assassini*, and *assissini*. It should not surprise us that the Arabic *shin* was transcribed by all our writers who used the Latin language by an *s*, and in the Greek historians by a sigma. They had no choice. It should, moreover, be observed that the *shin* is pronounced less strongly than the *ch* in French. What can rightly be asked is the reason why the Isma'ilis or Batinis were called *Hashishi*s. This is the second thing I shall have to examine, and to which I shall merely reply by a conjecture, but by a conjecture that is, to my mind, of a highly plausible nature.

Lemoine perhaps knew of some passages by Arab authors in which the Isma'ilis were referred to by the name *Hashishi*s, and he had seen that this name was inevitably derived from *hashish*. *Hashish* means herb, forage. However, since this meaning bore no relation to what history teaches us about the Assassins, he assumed that *hashish*, which signifies herb, forage, could also be understood as meadows, prairies, delightful gardens. This false conclusion may have contributed to discrediting his proposed etymology in the minds of scholars, all the more so since he cited no Arab writer as evidence to prove that the Isma'ilis actually bore the name *Hashishi*s in the Arabic language.

Perhaps he really knew of no other source than this passage by Benjamin of Tudela, although he does add, after mentioning the testimony of this rabbi, who called the Old Man of the Mountain *Sheikh alchassisin*, that this is how the latter was called all over the Orient.

Lemoine did not know that among the simple or compound substances used by the Orientals to achieve a more or less advanced state of intoxication, there is one that is known by the name of *hashish* or *hashisha*. In my *Chrestomathie Arabe*, I published a very curious chapter of Maqrizi's *Historical Description of Egypt and Cairo*, a chapter dealing with this kind of electuary commonly known as *hashisha*, herb, but whose full name is *hashishat al-fuqara*, the *herb of fakirs*. According to Maqrizi, this is the name of the hemp leaf, and in fact, the same is also mentioned by Prosper Alpin, whom I find it necessary to quote verbatim (*De Medic. Aegypt.*, pp 258, 261):

I am not ignorant of the fact that the Egyptians, in order to provide themselves with these kinds of visions, use several compound drugs such as the electuary called *bernavi*, which is brought from the nearest regions of India, the *bers* and the *bosa*; but the one that is most commonly used among them is simply the hemp plant, which they call *assis*.[38] This word means nothing other than herb, so that it appears that they call hemp the herb *par excellence*. This proverbial way of expressing themselves, by saying *to take herb* instead of *to take an intoxicating drug* comes from the fact that hemp, as I have heard it said, is the first substance in which the property of arousing these fantastic visions has been recognized, or else it possesses this quality in a higher degree than all other drugs.

The *assis* is simply a powder prepared from hemp leaves mixed with lukewarm water and made into a paste. Five or more boluses of it, the size of a chestnut, are swallowed. After an hour, they have their effect, and those who have taken them fall into a kind of drunkenness and indulge in all sorts of follies. They remain for a long time in a state of ecstasy, enjoying those visions they had longed for. The common people are particularly fond of using this drug, because it costs less than the others. It will hardly surprise you that hemp produces this effect; for as you know, Galien, in his first book of *De alim. facult.*, states that it makes the vapours rise to the brain, and violently affects this organ. It is through this singular property that this plant has, as I said, earned itself the name *assis*, or as it were, *the herb par excellence* in this country.

Kaempfer described three of the substances the Persians prefer to use to attain this kind of drunkenness which they call *kayf*. These substances, coming from the vegetable kingdom, are tobacco, opium and hemp. He describes the latter as follows (*Amoenitatum exoticarum*, Lemgo, 1712, p 645):

> I shall now discuss hemp. Those who like to use a variety of intoxicating drugs, or who dislike the taste of opium, take hemp to achieve this kind of ecstatic intoxication. I shall not examine here whether this plant is really our hemp, or a particular variety called *bang*, described by the authors of the *Hortus Malabaricus* (Vol 10, p 119). As far as I am concerned, it seemed to resemble our common hemp like two peas in a pod, both the male and the female. I, therefore, tend to believe that this hemp owes its particular quality to the soil and the climate. The parts of the plant that produce this artificial gaiety are the seed, called *shadanech*; the pollen, called *jars*, and the leaves, which are known by the name of *bang* . . . The leaves are used by infusing them in cold water. Drinking this water produces a gaiety accompanied by a highly intoxicated state. I shall describe the methods used for its preparation, as I have seen it done by four dervishes I met at a hostelry on the Indian border . . . Some people knead the leaf powder with syrup and make it into pastilles or boluses which they swallow with that intention. It is after the hemp leaves, the most valued of all intoxicating drugs, that men who have acquired the habit of intoxicating preparations are called *banghi* in Persia and India.

Chardin informs us that in Persia, people who like to get intoxicated on tobacco, mix hemp seeds with it, which has the effect of making the vapour rise to the brain and quickly produce dizziness (*Voyage de Chardin*, Paris, 1811, Vol 3, p 302).

Hemp is also used as an intoxicating substance in Barbary and Morocco, as Hoest and Lamprière attest, and there, too, it is called *hashish*. Leo Africanus mentioned it by the name *l'hasis*, which is the same word with an article. In Aleppo, it serves the same purpose and has the same name, as Dr Russell confirms. It is smoked with the same intention in several countries, and even in Africa.

> Just like those in the cities [says Niebuhr (*Description de l'Arabie*, p 50),] the common Arabs also want to have their *kayf*, that is, their enjoyment, but as they cannot afford strong liquors, and

often are not even able to find any, they smoke *hashish*: it is a kind of herb that Forskal and some others who preceded us in the Orient took for hemp leaves. Those who are fond of it assert that it inspires courage. We saw an example of that in the person of one of our Arab servants. After smoking *hashish*, he met four soldiers in the street and took it into his head to chase them away. One of them gave him a good hiding and brought him home. Despite this little adversity, he would not calm down and was still quite convinced that four soldiers were unable to resist him.

On the hemp grown in Egypt, Forskal says (*Flor. Aeg. Ar.*, p 1v): *Cannabis. Arab.* sjadanek. *Colitur passim; floret fine april.; folia ad usus medicos; semina inebriantia. Usus textorum ignorantur.*[39]

Olivier also says (*Voyage dans l'empire Othoman*, Vol 2, p 169), talking of Egypt:

The people have replaced the use of opium with that of hemp leaves, because they are much cheaper. Ground to a powder and mixed with honey, and sometimes with aromatic substances, they are made into boluses which are taken in order to obtain pleasant sensations, but their most certain effect is delirium, stupor, consumption and death, for those who continue using them. This plant, moreover, does not thrive well in Egypt.

The same traveller, after referring to the use made of opium in coffee-houses in Persia, adds (*Voyage dans l'emp. Oth.*, Vol 3, p 156):

In these same coffee-houses, a much stronger, much more intoxicating beverage was often served: it was made of leaves and heads of ordinary hemp, to which a little nux vomica was added. The law, which allows or tolerates other beverages, has always prohibited this one. When we were in Persia, Mehemet Khan punished those who distributed it and those who took it, with the death sentence.

Sonnini seems to make a distinction between the European hemp and the plant grown in Egypt, of which *hashisha* is made. Although the passage in which he discusses it is a little long, I shall copy the whole of it (*Voyage dans la haute et basse Égypte*, Vol 3, p 103).

Hemp is grown in the plains of the same regions (of upper Egypt);

but they do not make thread out of it, as in Europe, although it could probably serve that purpose. It is nevertheless a plant which is widely used. In the absence of intoxicating liquors, the Arabs and Egyptians make various preparations out of it, which provide them with a kind of mild drunkenness, a dreamy state which gives them gaiety and pleasant illusions. This kind of annihilation of the faculty of thought, this sleep of the soul, is unlike the drunkenness caused by wine and strong liquors, and our language has no terms to express it. The Arabs use the word *kayf* to describe this voluptuous abandon, this kind of delicious stupor.

The most frequent way of preparing the hemp consists of crushing the fruits with their membraneous capsules (or rather *husks*); the resulting paste is then boiled with honey, pepper and nutmeg, and this concoction, which is as big as a nut, is swallowed. Poor people, who charm away their misery through the dizziness caused by hemp, content themselves with grinding the seed capsules mixed with water, and eating the paste. The Egyptians also eat these capsules without any preparation, and they even mix them with the tobacco they smoke. Sometimes they grind only the capsules and pistils into a fine powder, throwing away the seeds. They mix this powder with an equal amount of tobacco and smoke the mixture in a kind of pipe, a very simple and coarse imitation of the Persian pipe: just a hollow coconut filled with water, through which they inhale the acrid and inebriating smoke. This way of smoking is one of the most common pastimes of the women of southern Egypt.

All these preparations, as well as the parts of the plant that are used to make them, are known by the Arabic name *hashish*, which really means *herb*, as though this plant were the herb *par excellence*. *Hashish*, of which considerable amounts are consumed, can be found in all markets. When people want to refer to the plant itself, leaving aside its properties and its use, they call it *bast*.

Although Egyptian hemp is very similar to ours, it nevertheless differs from it through a few characteristics that seem to make it a particular species.[40] When carefully comparing this hemp with the European hemp, we notice that its stalk is much shorter, and that it makes up in thickness what it lacks in height; that the shape of the plant is more like that of a shrub, with its trunk often measuring more than two inches in circumference, and its numerous alternate branches starting from the bottom. Its leaves are also broader and more serrate. The entire plant has a stronger smell, and the fruits are smaller and at the same time more numerous than those of the European species.

After all that has been said, it is no doubt easy to believe that the Isma'ilis were called *Hashishi*s because of their using *hashish*, in the same way as those who use *bang* (whether *bang* is also an electuary made of hemp leaves, as Kaempfer says, or rather an extract of the narcotic plant called *datura*, as other authors maintain), opium, called *afyun*, and other drugs known by the general term *tariak*, are called *bangi, afyuni, tariaki*.

And what I am saying about the use of *hashish* among the Isma'ilis is confirmed by this passage of Maqrizi (Silvestre de Sacy, *Chrestomathie Arabe*, Paris, 1806, Vol 1, p 130; Vol 2, p 133):

> Around this time (the year 795) there came to Cairo a man of the sect of the *Mulhids* or Isma'ilis of Persia, who prepared the *hashisha* by mixing it with honey, and adding various dry substances to it, like mandrake root and other drugs of the same kind. He called this mixture *uqda* (that is, jelly, confection), and secretly sold it.

It is worth noting that the two adjectives or epithets *hashishi* and *hashshash* are also formed from the word *hashish* or *hashisha*. We have seen how the former [*hashishi*] was used in various passages I quoted, and that is certainly what Maqrizi had in mind when he said (*Chrestomathie Arabe*, Vol. 1, p 129; Vol 2, p 132): 'I know of a time when only people of the lowest class dared eat it; and even they were loath to hear themselves called by a name derived from this drug.'[41] The latter, *hashshash*, is found in the following passage by Shams al-Din Muhammad, son of Abu'l-Surur (*Notices et Extraits des Manuscrits*, Vol 1, p 274): 'The new bridge over the big canal is now known by the name *bridge of the hashshash* (*qantarat al-hashshashin*), because it is the place where the *mastuls* (the drunkards, as it were) among the inhabitants of Cairo took their *hashish*.'

The words *hashishin* and *hashshashin* produced the two denominations *assissini* and *assassini* mentioned by Joinville.

I will not deny, however, that two objections may be raised against what I just said: the first is that the drunkenness caused by *hashish* merely consists of a kind of quiet ecstasy, rather than a vehemence apt to fire the courage and the imagination to undertake and carry out daring and dangerous acts; the second is that, according to Maqrizi, the introduction of *hashish* into Syria and Egypt, and even the discovery of the intoxicating effect of hemp, came later than the period of the Assassins.

To reply to the first objection is not difficult. Reports about the obedience of the Assassins to their chief and the determination with which they risked their lives to kill the designated victims; the journeys they ventured upon to reach their destination; the cold-blooded way in which they watched for the right moment to carry out their plan, and knew how to take the appropriate action; all this does not point to furious men, like the Indian Amoks, capable of doing anything through a kind of artificially induced delirium,[42] but rather to fanatics convinced that by laying down their life to obey the commands of heaven manifested by those of their chiefs, they would secure themselves eternal happiness and all the enjoyments of the senses. And this is actually how the historians represent them. What, then, was the effect of *hashisha* on these men? It was to procure them, when it pleased their master to administer them a dose of this electuary, of which he alone possessed the secret, a state of ecstasy and sweet, profound illusions, during which they enjoyed or imagined they enjoyed all the sensual delights that embellish the paradise of Muhammad. Let us hear what Marco Polo, or rather the redactor of the Italian text of his account, tells us; this account is the best commentary on what I just said:

> I shall now discuss the Old Man of the Mountain. *Mulehet* is a region formerly inhabited by the man called the Old Man of the Mountain. For the name *Mulehet* means, in the language of the Saracens, the place where the heretics live; and from the name of this place, those who live there are called *Mulehetics*, that is, heretics of their religion,[43] as are the Patarins[44] among the Christians. This is what Marco Polo relates about the Old Man of the Mountain, having heard it told by several people. This prince was called *Alaodin*[45] and was Mahometan. He had created, in a lovely valley enclosed between two very high mountains, a very beautiful garden full of every variety of fruit and trees that could be obtained, and around these plantations, various palaces and pavilions decorated with golden ornaments, paintings and furniture all made of silk. There, in little canals corresponding to different parts of these palaces, one could see running streams of wine, of milk, of honey, and of the most limpid water. He had brought young girls of perfect beauty and full of charm to live here, and they were trained to sing, to play all sorts of instruments, to dance, and above all, to make the most seductive

advances to men that can be imagined. These young girls could be seen all the time, covered in gold and silk, walking along in these gardens and palaces. As for the women who served the prince, these were always kept indoors and were never seen outside. This is the reason why the Old Man had this palace built: Mahomet having said that those who obeyed his will would go to paradise, where they would find all the pleasures and delights of the world, beautiful women and rivers of milk and honey, this man wanted to pretend that he was a prophet and a companion of Mahomet, and that he could make anyone he wished enter this very paradise. No one could penetrate into the garden we described, for they had built, at the entrance to the valley, a very fortified and impregnable castle; it could only be entered by a secret road.

This Old Man had at his court young men aged from 12 to 20, chosen among those mountain dwellers who appeared to him to be capable of handling arms, daring and brave. He constantly talked to them every day about this paradise of Mahomet's, and of his own power to make them enter it. Whenever it pleased him, he ordered that 10 or 12 of these young men be given a *certain drink that put them to sleep*; and when they looked as though they were half dead, he had them transported to various rooms of these palaces. When they woke up in these places, they saw all the things we described; each one of them was surrounded by these young girls who sang, played instruments, and practised all the caresses and games they could imagine, and presented them with the most exquisite dishes and wines. In this way the young men, intoxicated with so many pleasures and the streams of milk and wine they saw, had no doubt whatever that they were in paradise, and never wanted to leave it.[46]

Four or five days later, the Old Man had them put to sleep again and carried out of the garden. He would then summon them and ask them where they had been. By your grace, Sire, they would say, we were in paradise. Then they would describe what they had seen in everybody's presence. Their story would arouse the admiration of all those who heard it, as well as the desire for a similar happiness. The Old Man would answer: this is the commandment of our prophet; he makes anyone who fights to defend his lord enter paradise. If you obey me, you will enjoy the same bliss. Through such speeches, he influenced their minds to such an extent that the person whom he ordered to die in his service would consider himself happy. All the sovereigns or other persons who were enemies of the Old Man of the Mountain were

killed by these assassins who were at his service. For none of them
feared death, as long as they carried out the orders and wishes of
their Sire, and they willingly exposed themselves to all the most
obvious dangers, completely disregarding the loss of their present
life. That is why the Old Man was feared in all these countries as
a tyrant. He had established two lieutenants, one in the surroundings of Damascus, the other in Kurdistan; and these behaved in
the same manner with regard to the young men he sent them. So
no matter how powerful a man was, if he was an enemy of the
Old Man, he was bound to be killed.

All the authors who have written about the Assassins, such as
Amalric, Hayton, William of Tyre, Jacques de Vitry, Jean de Joinville
and Arnold of Lübeck, knew of no other principle governing their
conduct than blind obedience to their chief, based on the hope of
boundless happiness in the future (*Gesta Dei per Francos*, Vol 1,
p 1062). It is quite remarkable that Marco Polo mentions an
intoxicating beverage, which their chief had them drink when he
wanted to have them transported to his enchanted gardens.[47] As we
have seen, all the intoxicating preparations made with hemp, such as
boluses, mixtures, liquors, fumigations, are equally called *hashisha*. In
fact, I do not know whether we should literally believe in the existence
of these enchanted gardens, or whether they were nothing but a vision
produced by the excited imagination of the young men who were
intoxicated by the *hashisha*, and who had long been deluded by the
image of such bliss. What we know for certain is that even today,
people who take opium or *hashish* can, even if covered in poverty's rags
and staying in a miserable tavern, derive happiness and pleasures that
are short of nothing but reality.

I have already mentioned that the constructions, the plantations, and
the running waters with which Hasan had adorned the fortress and
surroundings of Alamut, his residence, may have contributed to
spreading the legend of his enchanted gardens. Arnold of Lübeck also
mentions beautiful palaces situated in the mountains, where young men
destined to practise the profession of assassins were trained.[48]

Let us hear what Prosper Alpin has to say about the effects the
Egyptians attribute to the use of opium, *hashish* and other substances
they take to attain this desired state of delirium and reverie (*De Medic.
Aegypt.*, p 257):

Some of them maintain that, when they have taken a dose of
opium, assis, bousa or *bernavi*, or else a pinch of *bers*, they see, as

in a dream, a great number of magnificent orchards and beautiful girls, full of attractions and charms; others say that, when in this state, they only see the objects they like best: those who enjoy the sight of orchards see orchards; lovers see their mistresses; warriors see battles.

Russell, in his *Natural History of Aleppo*, says that he had witnessed the folly of one of these opium-eaters who, thinking he was a pasha, had without further ado occupied the place of honour on the sofa and was talking familiarly with the master of the house, entering into details about the affairs of his would-be government, condemning one person to be beaten, another to jail, dismissing some of his officers, appointing others, and thus enjoying his newly acquired fortune, which had cost him no more than a strong dose of opium, until a sudden noise made behind him on purpose drew him out of his dreams and put an end to his happiness.

It is true that the immoderate and habitual use of *hashish* destroys all the faculties and would have been inappropriate in serving the aims of the Isma'ilis. Here is what the physician Ibn Baytar says about it (*Chrestomathie Arabe*, Vol 1, p 127; Vol 2, p 131):

There is a third variety of hemp which is called *Indian hemp*. I have seen it nowhere else except in Egypt. They grow it in gardens and call it *hashisha*. It is highly intoxicating, if one or two drachmas of it are taken. If used in immoderate quantities, it produces a kind of insanity. People who have used it regularly have felt this pernicious effect. It weakens their minds and finally leads to lunacy; sometimes it even leads to death. I have seen fakirs use it in various ways: some of them boil the leaves of this plant, then knead it with their hands to form a kind of paste of which they make pastilles; others leave them to dry, then roast them, crush them with their hands, mix them with a few sesame seeds without the tegument, add some sugar, and then eat this dry drug, chewing on it for a long time. At the same time, they gesticulate and are in high spirits; and as it intoxicates them, they reach a state of madness or something very close to it.

Ala al-Din bin Nafis, another physician quoted by Maqrizi, also says that the use of this drug produces base inclinations and degrades the soul, and that, in those who have acquired the habit, all the natural faculties deteriorate, so that at the end they no longer have any of the attributes of humanity (*Chrestomathie Arabe*, Vol 1, p 127; Vol 2, p 131).

Maqrizi himself confirms all this through his own observations, and attributes the moral depravity and the apathy of his contemporaries to the immoderate use of *hashisha* (*Chrestomathie Arabe*, Vol 1, p 131; Vol 2, p 134).

We have seen that, according to Olivier, its most certain effect is delirium, stupor, consumption and death, if a person continues to use it.

Finally, in a decree issued by the French general in Egypt, on the 17th vendémiaire of the year IX, we read:

> The use of the strong liquor made by some Muslims with a certain potent herb called *hashish*, as well as the smoking of hemp seed, are prohibited throughout Egypt. Those who are accustomed to drinking liquor and smoking this seed, lose their senses and fall into a violent delirium which often causes them to commit all sorts of excesses.

This inconvenience attached to the excessive and daily use of *hashish*, which cannot be called into question, certainly did not apply to the Isma'ilis. It would have been diametrically opposed to the aim they were pursuing, and it may be supposed that an electuary, or, as Marco Polo mentioned, a beverage that was only administered by order of the chief, and of which only he had the secret, was used sparingly and within certain limits.

I say *of which only the chief had the secret*; for this is how I understand the words of a historian I quoted above, who maintains that when those who governed Aleppo wanted to rid themselves of Saladin, they wrote to Sinan, the *master* or *possessor* of the *hashisha*, *sahib al-hashisha*.[49]

What I just said also serves as an answer to the second objection I raised against my own assertion, an objection resulting from Maqrizi's account, according to which the use of *hashish* was not introduced among the Muslims until about the beginning of the seventh century of the Hegira, that is long after the period of the great Isma'ili power, and shortly before their destruction by Hulagu.

Maqrizi, in fact, following a great number of authorities, attributes the discovery of the intoxicating properties of the hemp leaf to Sheikh Haydar, who died in 618 of the Hegira. He adds that this secret remained for some time exclusively with the fakirs, the disciples of Sheikh Haydar; that the use of hemp was introduced into Iraq for the first time in 628, by two sovereign princes, one of Hurmuz, the other of Bahrayn, and that it only later reached Syria, Egypt and Asia Minor.

There is hardly any doubt that the use of *hashish*, at least in Egypt, started after the sixth century of the Hegira; for Abd al-Latif, who wrote in 605, does not mention it; and on the other hand, it must have been introduced there soon after this period, since Ibn Baytar, who died in 646, already found it commonly used among the fakirs in that country.

I am not far from believing, however, that Sheikh Haydar did not have the honour of making the discovery attributed to him. The name *qunnab Hindi* (Indian hemp) given, according to Ibn Baytar, to the kind of hemp used under the name of *hashish* in Egypt, makes me think that this electuary originally came from India, that Haydar may have known it through some Indian *yogi*, and that it was perhaps from the same source that the Isma'ilis had come to know it before him. This is all the more plausible because in the doctrine of the Isma'ilis, we can recognize certain characteristics resembling Indian doctrines, such as the transmigration of souls, the incarnations of the divinity or *avatars*, emanations, etc. The conjecture I advance here is supported by Maqrizi himself, who says (*Chrestomathie Arabe*, Vol 1, p 120; Vol 2, p 126):

> However, I have it from Sheikh Muhammad Shirazi Qalandari that Sheikh Haydar never used any *hashisha*, and that the people of Khurasan only attribute the origin of this drug to him because his disciples are known to make regular use of it. From what he told me, *hashisha* goes back to a considerably earlier period than that of Sheikh Haydar. A sheikh called Biraztan, who lived in India, taught the people of this country to eat *hashisha*; they did not know it before. The use of this drug became so widespread in India that it was even introduced in Yaman; from there it spread to the province of Fars, and finally the inhabitants of Iraq, of Asia Minor, of Egypt and of Syria heard it mentioned for the first time in the year I indicated above. Biraztan lived at the time of the Khosroeses; he lived up to the Islamic period and became a Muslim.

Whatever position we may take with regard to this question, it is obvious that *hashisha* could have been used by the Isma'ilis long before the sixth century of the Hegira, and that such an assumption does not contradict the historical facts that attribute its introduction among the fakirs to Sheikh Haydar, and its propagation to the disciples of this sheikh.

I must now discuss various other names by which the Assassins are sometimes designated by the oriental writers.

Neither Ibn Khaldun, in his historical *Prolegomena*, nor Shahrastani ever mentioned the *Hashishi*s. The former says that the Isma'ilis were also called *Batinis*, *Mazdakis* and *Qarmatis* in Iraq, and that in Khurasan they were called *Ta'limis* and *Mulhid*s, but as far as they were concerned, they called themselves *Isma'ilis*. We shall explain each one of these names.

The name *Batini*, that is, partisan of the inner meaning, is given to the *Isma'ilis*, as I have mentioned elsewhere, because they teach that everything external, such as the practices of worship, the precepts of the law, the profession of faith, etc., has an inner meaning, *batin*; that all revelation, *tanzil*, has an allegorical signification, *ta'wil*. This is what Shahrastani also says; and Ibn Khaldun is wrong in maintaining that they are called *Batini* because they recognize an internal imam, *batin*, meaning, as he adds, hidden, *mastur*. In the texts I have seen, the hidden imam is never called *batin*, but *mastur* or *maktum*. Every page of the books of the Druzes provides evidence in favour of the first explanation.

Mazdaki means member of the sect of *Mazdak*. This is an abusive term applied to the Isma'ilis because of the true or supposed conformity of their doctrine and their licentious behaviour with the morals and practices of Mazdak, an innovator who had caused great troubles in Persia under the reign of Qubad, and who was put to death under Khosroe Nushirvan.[50] The reader may refer, on this subject, to Mirkhwand's history of the Sasanid dynasty, which I published in my *Mémoires sur diverses antiquités de la Perse*.

That the Isma'ilis were called *Qarmatis* is a subject I need not dwell upon, since I already mentioned several times that the Qarmatis were the same as the Isma'ilis. The name *Qarmati* was applied to them because one of their chiefs was thus nicknamed, the reason being, apparently, that he had short legs and could only take small steps.

Malahida or *mulhidun* is the plural of *mulhid*, which means *impious*. According to Mirkhwand, this name was only given to the Isma'ilis of Persia after the fourth prince of their dynasty, Hasan son of Muhammad,[51] had publicly abjured the dogmas and practices of the Muslim religion; but the name continued to be applied to them since that time, and was even extended to the princes who had preceded the apostasy, although they were practising Muslims.

And finally, again according to Shahrastani, the Isma'ilis were also called *Ta'limi* in Khurasan. To explain this denomination, it must be pointed out that among the Muslim sects who agreed on the *dogmas* (*usul*), and only disagreed regarding the *moral laws and practices* (*furu*), there were three different schools. The first, called *ahl al-taʿlim, the partisans of teaching*, is based on these four authorities, the *Koran*, the *Sunna*, the *consent of the imams* on a point of doctrine (*ijma*), and *reasonings* based on induction (*qiyas*). The second only recognizes *positive written authorities*; it is therefore called *ahl al-nusus*. The third mainly follows *reason* or probabilities: as a result, it is called *ahl al-raʾy*. Hasan bin Sabbah professed to follow the first school. As this system is called *taʿlim*, Hasan and the members of his sect were called *Taʿlimi*. When explaining the four foundations of Hasan's doctrine, Shahrastani very positively maintains that the first one established the necessity of teaching (*taʿlim*) and was destined to refute those who accepted no other authority to decide about theological questions than *reason* and *judgement* (*al-raʾy waʾl-aql*).[52] The second foundation was meant to refute those who admitted no other authority but the *Traditions, al-hadith* (*Notices et Extraits des Manuscrits*, Vol IV, p 687; Maracci, *Prodr. ad ref. Alcor.*, Part 3, p 84).

The Assassins have sometimes been confused with the Druzes and the Nusayris. Mr Venture, in a *Memoir* about the Druzes,[53] says that to all appearances, the Old Man of the Mountain was none other than the chief of the Druze nation. On the other hand, de Volney is convinced that the Assassins mentioned by William of Tyre were the *Ansariyya*. De Volney ought to have followed all the Arab authors, as well as Venture, and called these sectarians *Nusayri* or *Nusayriyya* in the plural. Falconet also confused the *Nusayris* with the Assassins, and reproached Assemani for having substituted the name *Nazaris* for the *Nusayris* or *Nosroye* of the Syrian historians.

There is no doubt that the Nusayris are a branch of the Ismaʿilis which is very close to the Qarmatis, even if it differs from the latter sect as regards its origin.[54] As for the Druzes, although their origin goes back to the Ismaʿili sect itself, they differ from the Nusayris and other Ismaʿili sects in several important dogmas, above all in believing in the divinity of the Fatimid caliph Hakim, in awaiting his return, and in obeying the commands of Hamza, his first minister.[55] They anathematize the other Ismaʿili sects, and in their sacred books there is an express refutation of the Nusayri system. What is more, the Nusayris, and even the Druzes, preceded the *Hashishi*s; for I believe that this name was never applied to the Ismaʿilis of the second period, or, to use Shahrastani's term, the *second mission, al-daʿwa al-thaniya*. Hasan bin Sabbah, who initiated this *second mission*, did not appear until about the year 483. It is through him that the Ismaʿili power in the Jibal was established, a power that later extended to Syria, around the year 520;

and it was not until the establishment of this power in Alamut that the Batinis began to threaten the lives of kings and grandees. So it is an anachronism to confuse the Isma'ilis or Batinis, called *Assassins*, with the Druzes and Nusayris.[56] But I shall proceed to discuss a few other names given to the Assassins.

One of the reasons why Venture thought that the Druzes were the Assassins mentioned by the historians of the Crusades, and that the chief or emir of the Druzes was the *Old Man of the Mountain* was, as he says,

> that the emir of the Druzes always had at his service a select troop called the *Fidawiyya*, that is, people ready to sacrifice themselves for his sake. Previously they were all Druzes by religion; now they are almost all Christians. There are no dangers or perils to which this troop does not expose itself when it is a matter of carrying out the prince's orders, and a recent example can be mentioned to show the blind devotion they profess.
>
> About 17 or 18 years ago, the emir Mulhim ... violently quarrelled with a customs officer of Sidon, sent to him by the pasha of the province to expedite the payment of the tribute. The emir Mulhim swore to him in his wrath that he would have him killed whenever he could do so without violating the right of the people and of hospitality. One day when this customs officer was sitting in an open kiosk used as a warehouse for the Sidon customs, one of these Fidawiyya presented himself, armed with his gun and a pair of pistols. He examined everything coldbloodedly, recognized the customs officer among these people, took aim and killed him. When he had made quite sure that he had not missed him, he tried to reach the city gate, where he had a horse waiting for him; but before he could reach it, he was beaten to death by the rabble.

It must be admitted that these *Fidawiyya* or *Fidawi*s are closely connected with the ministers of vengeance of the chief of the Isma'ilis or Old Man of the Mountain. The difference is, however, that they are unlikely to be motivated by religious fanaticism, because, according to Venture, those who render this service to the emir of the Druzes are for the most part Christians.

It might be added, though this would appear at first glance to confirm the opinion I am arguing against, that the killers or assassins of the chief of the Isma'ilis are also quite often called *Fidawi* or, which comes to the same, *Fida'i*, by Arab and Persian authors. For the time

being, I shall only quote one passage where this word is applied to the
Assassins; but it will be sufficient to prove what I contend. The passage
is by Abu'l-Faraj. When the Mongol Hulagu decided to destroy the
Isma'ili power in Persia, this sect had as their chief Rukn al-Din
Khurshah, son of Ala al-Din. 'This prince', says Abu'l-Faraj (*Hist.
dyn.*, Arabic text, p 506; Latin translation, p 330),

first tried several ways to deceive Hulagu by feigning submission;
but the Tartar let him know that the only course he could follow
was to leave the fortress of Alamut where he was residing, and to
go personally to the Mongol camp, or, if he did not want to do so,
to prepare himself to sustain a siege. Rukn al-Din sent an
accomplice to tell Hulagu that he dare not leave the place for fear
that those who were confined there with him should try to kill
him; but that, as soon as he would find an opportunity, he would
come out. Convinced that Rukn al-Din was merely playing for
time, Hulagu laid siege to the fortress; when Rukn al-Din saw
this, he sent this message to Hulagu: I only delayed until now
because I was not sure of your arrival; today or tomorrow, I shall
come to you. When he tried to go out, the most fanatic of the
*Mulhid*s rose against him, and the *Fida'i*s rushed at him and
prevented him from leaving. He advised Hulagu about their
rebellion, and this prince sent word that he should treat them
gently and cajole them for the time being, in order to protect his
life from their attempts, but that he should somehow or other
devise a way to come out, even if he had to disguise himself. At
the same time, Hulagu ordered his emirs to surround the place
from all sides, to set up machines against it, and to fight, each one
on his part, those of the Isma'ilis who were to attack them. While
the *Mulhid*s were occupied in this engagement, Rukn al-Din went
out with his son and the members of his court and surrendered to
Hulagu.

The *Syriac Chronicle* of Abu'l-Faraj (Greg. Bar-Hebraeus [Ibn
al-'Ibri], *Chron. Syr.*, Syriac text, p 520, Latin translation, p 540)
reads: 'When Rukn al-Din wanted to go out, his men pointed their
daggers at him, saying: If you go out, we will kill you.'
It is certain that in this passage of Abu'l-Faraj, the *Fida'i*s are not
Isma'ilis or *Mulhid*s in general, but a particular class of men, the most
fanatic, the *devoted*, in short most probably those whom the Isma'ilis
employed to kill their enemies;[57] it does not follow, all the same, that

wherever there were *Fida'is*, these were Isma'ilis. Each sect, each prince, could have his own *Fida'is*.

For instance in India, according to friar Vincent-Marie of Saint Catherine of Sienna, every prince, and even every Christian church, have their Amoks, who vow to risk their lives in order to protect the rights, privileges and properties of their patrons against everyone, even against another sovereign (*Viaggi all'Ind. Orient.*, pp 145, 237).

Muradjea d'Ohsson hence did not express himself accurately when saying that the sectarians of Hasan bin Sabbah, called *Humayri* after his name, were also called *Fida'is* because of the fervour with which they exposed their lives by marching under his banners (*Tabl. gén. de l'empire Othoman*, Vol 1, p 37).

We can, therefore, assert that all the Isma'ilis were not *Fida'is*, although the professional assassins devoted to the sect were known by this name. Further proofs of this fact will be provided below, when I shall deal with this name as applied to the Isma'ilis.

The confusion of the Assassins with the *Nusayris*, whom Assemani calls *Nazarei*, would no doubt have been generally admitted, albeit with no good reason, if it had been known that the Isma'ilis of Persia and Syria were also called *Nizaris*. I shall prove this fact, and at the same time explain the origin and meaning of this denomination.

In the year 524 of the Hegira, the Fatimid caliph Amir bi-Ahkam Allah was killed by the Batinis, as is reported by Abu'l-Faraj, Abu'l-Fida, Renaudot, etc. (*Hist. dyn.*, Arabic text, p 380; Latin translation, p 250; *Annales Moslemici*, Vol 3, p 439; *Hist. patr. Alex.* p 496); however, Maqrizi attributes this assassination to the *Nizaris*, and Mirkhwand to the Batinis and the *Nizaris*. But this apparent contradiction can easily be explained. For the Nizaris are none other than a faction of the Batinis founded on the death of the Fatimid caliph Mustansir billah. This caliph had as his successor his son Abu'l-Qasim Ahmad Musta'li billah; but as I indicated at the beginning of this *Memoir*, Musta'li did not succeed his father by general consent, since his brother Nizar had been a contestant for the throne. 'On this occasion', says Maqrizi (Arabic Manuscript of the Bibliothèque du Roi, no 682, fol 199v), 'the Isma'ilis split into two parties, the *Nizaris* who considered Musta'li as an illegitimate caliph, and another party, who acknowledged him as the legitimate caliph.' Renaudot mentioned Nizar's revolt against Musta'li; but he did not mention the schism that this caused among the Isma'ilis (*Hist. patr. Alex.*, p 475), a schism continuing under several reigns. Here I cannot dispense with quoting an excerpt from Mirkhwand, which will perfectly clarify these facts. This is what he reports while briefly outlining the history of the Fatimid caliphs of Egypt (Arabic Manuscript of the Bibliothèque de L'Arsenal, no 20):

Mustansir had first named his eldest son, Mustafa li-Din Allah Nizar, as his successor; but later, being dissatisfied with him, he ordered in his testament that Nizar was to renounce all pretension to becoming the sovereign, and that the crown should be conferred on his other son Musta'li billah. When Mustansir died, the Isma'ilis split into two parties: some swore allegiance to Musta'li and made him accede to the throne; others, following the dogmas of their sect, believed that the earlier provision ought to be maintained, and embraced Nizar's party. Hasan bin Sabbah Humayri adopted the second party. Indeed, the Nizari of Kuhistan was one of the partisans of Mustafa li-Din Allah, and his very name, Nizari, proves this assertion. These people argue, in support of their opinion, that the imam Ja'far Sadiq had first chosen his son Isma'il as his successor to the imamate; and that later, having found out that Isma'il indulged in drinking wine, he disowned him and ordered that after his death the imamate should be transmitted to Musa Kazim. But as the Isma'ilis think that the first designation should retain all its force, they consider Isma'il, rather than Musa, as the successor of Ja'far Sadiq to the dignity of imam. Once Musta'li saw himself in possession of the caliphate, he decided to rid himself of his brother Nizar; but to protect his life, Nizar retired to Alexandria and stayed with a servant of his father's who was governor there. The latter declared Musta'li as deposed from the caliphate, and proclaimed Nizar as caliph. Musta'li, however, had a great army march against Alexandria. The governor of the city, who had embraced Nizar's party, was captured and put to death. Nizar was arrested with his two sons and sent to Musta'li, who imprisoned him in Cairo; he remained a prisoner there until his death. Musta'li had been reigning for seven years when he was stabbed to death, it is said, at the age of 28, by some of Nizar's partisans.

His son Amir bi-Ahkam Allah succeeded him . . . While he was reigning, he was killed by some *Nizaris*, enemies of the *amir al-juyush* (or generalissimo of the armies) who was Amir's father-in-law . . . Aqsunqur, one of the principal lords of the caliph's court, was also stabbed to death in the *jami* of Mosul, by some of the *Fida'is* among the *Nizaris*. Under Amir's reign, the *Nizari* faction started to appear in Syria, and some fortified places of this province fell into their hands. On the 4th of Dhu'l-Qa'da 524, a troop of Batinis and fanatics of the *Nizari* faction assassinated Amir as a reprisal for the death of Nizar. Hafiz li-Din Allah, who succeeded him, had conferred the office of vizier to Abu Ali Ahmad, son of Afdal *amir al-juyush*, who, having been promoted to this dignity, was killed by some *Fida'is* among the *Nizaris* within the first days of his administration. A few days later, they also killed the person who had been appointed to replace him, again to avenge the same blood.[58]

This explains in what way and for what reason Hasan bin Sabbah, who had merely established himself in Kuhistan[59] as a *da'i* of the Fatimid caliphs, and who acknowledged their sovereignty, having allegedly received the patents of investiture from Mustansir, went so far as not only to make himself independent in this province, but also to take possession of some places in Syria that belonged to the Fatimids. For since the schism that had occurred among the Isma'ilis after Mustansir's death, Hasan had embraced Nizar's party and considered Musta'li and his successors as usurpers of the caliphate.

So at his death, he ordered that Kiya Buzurg-Ummid and the *Dihdar* Abu Ali should administer, one of them the affairs of the sect, the other those of the *divan*, in agreement with the generalissimo Hasan Qasrani, *until such time as the imam himself came to assume the head of the government*. Mirkhwand informs us that since one of the princes of the Isma'ili dynasty of Persia, Hasan son of Muhammad, son of Buzurg-Ummid, had exempted his subjects from all legal observances, he was the cause, through this conduct, of their being attributed the name of *Mulhids*, which was extended to include even his predecessors, even though this latter had observed the laws of Islam. Although this prince was publicly acknowledged to be the son of Muhammad bin Buzurg-Ummid, he nevertheless sometimes ambiguously, sometimes openly declared, in a great number of writings he sent to various places, that he was a descendant of Nizar, son of the caliph Mustansir, and that he was the true caliph and the imam.[60] 'The *Nizaris*', adds Mirkhwand,

have invented all sorts of legends and ridiculous tales to justify this pretension of Hasan's. Even during his father's lifetime, he wanted to pass himself off as the imam promised by Hasan bin Sabbah; but Muhammad had stopped this folly by publicly declaring that Hasan was his son, that for him he was not the imam, but only one of the *da'is* of the imam, and by putting to death a great number of those who had accepted Hasan's eccentricities.

Here we must observe, as we already announced above, that Mirkhwand always uses the word *Fida'i* when referring to the men the Isma'ilis employed to assassinate their enemies. Thus he says that the illustrious Nizam al-Mulk, the vizier of Malikshah, was assassinated by a *Fida'i* by order of Hasan bin Sabbah; that under the reign of Hasan bin Sabbah, many Muslim princes who had quarrels with the Isma'ilis were assassinated by *Fida'i*s; that under the reign of his successor, Kiya Buzurg-Ummid, the *Fida'i*s killed a considerable number of Muslim princes or great dignitaries, such as the great Qadi Abu Sa'id of Herat; a son of Musta'li, the caliph of Egypt, who was assassinated by seven of the *Rafiqs*; Dawlatshah, *ra'is* of Ispahan; Aqsunqur, the governor of Maragha; Mustansir,[61] the caliph of Baghdad; the *ra'is* of Tabriz, Hasan son of Abu'l-Qasim, the *mufti* of Qazwin, etc.; he repeats the same thing at the end of the reign of Muhammad, son of Kiya Buzurg-Ummid, etc. The word *Fidawi* is also used in his narrative of the undertakings of sultan Malik al-Nasir Muhammad, son of Qala'un, against Qarasunqur, of which I provided an excerpt above. This observation confirms what I said about the meaning of the word *fida'i*, and at the same time provides me with the opportunity to explain another expression which I often encountered in Mirkhwand; I mean the word *rafiq*, plural *rafiqan*.

Rafiq in Arabic literally means *companion, assistant, fellow-traveller*; but several passages in Mirkhwand that I quoted in this *Memoir*, and a great number of others that I could mention, prove that this word had a special and, as it were, technical connotation among the Isma'ilis.

Hasan bin Ali bin Sabbah says the following about himself:

> I had always, like my fathers, professed the doctrine of the Shi'ites, who accept the succession of the twelve imams. It happened by chance that I met a man among the *Rafiqs*, whose name was *Amira Darrab*, and a close relationship developed between us ... Each time Amira spoke in support of the Isma'ili doctrine, I would have an argument with him on this subject ... Later, I came into contact with another Isma'ili, called *Abu Najm Sarraj*, and I asked him to instruct me fully in the doctrine of the Isma'ilis ... Finally I met a *da'i* of this religion, called *Mu'min*, who had received from Sheikh Abd al-Malik bin Atrush, *da'i* of the province of Iraq, the permission to exercise the ministry of *da'i*.[62]

This passage proves that *Rafiq* and *Isma'ili* are two synonymous words, or at least that those who were known by the name of *Rafiq* were Isma'ilis. It also proves that this denomination preceded Hasan bin Sabbah; but it gives rise to the suspicion that there was a difference between the *da'i*s and the *Rafiq*s. The following passage confirms this opinion:

> Hasan [to quote Mirkhwand again,] having consolidated himself in the possession of Alamut and neighbouring places, left nothing to chance in his efforts to make himself master, either by force or by mildness, of the entire government of Rudbar; after which he sent the *da'i* Husayn Qa'ini with a troop of *Rafiq*s to preach his doctrine to the peoples of Kuhistan. Malikshah had one of his generals, Qizil Sariq, march into Kuhistan to oppose the progress of Husayn Qa'ini. As a result, Qizil Sariq made his utmost efforts to drive off the *Mulhid*s from Kuhistan. Husayn Qa'ini withdrew with his *Rafiq*s into a fortress in the territory of Mu'minabad. While Qizil Sariq was laying siege to it, news of Malikshah's death arrived, forcing him to raise the siege.

When relating the siege of Alamut by the troops of Malikshah, the same historian says that Hasan had no more than 70 *Rafiq*s with him.

Speaking about the princes and illustrious personalities who were assassinated under the reign and by order of Kiya Buzurg-Ummid, he says: 'During the government of Buzurg-Ummid, the *Fida'i*s killed several princes and illustrious personalities. Among those who were killed were the *qadi* of the East and West, Abu Sa'id of Herat; a son of Musta'li, who was assassinated in Egypt by seven of the *Rafiq*s, etc.'

And finally, when reporting the events that took place under the reign of Kiya Buzurg-Ummid, Mirkhwand uses the word *Rafiq* a great many times. I shall quote an excerpt from the report, retaining this word each time it occurs.

> When Sultan Mahmud the Saljuqid wanted to make peace with Kiya Buzurg-Ummid, one of his officers was put in charge of making the initial overtures to the Isma'ili prince, who sent a deputy to Ispahan to negotiate the affair. This deputy, called Khwaja Muhammad Nasihi Shahrastani, was leaving the audience of sultan Mahmud when he was killed together with a *Rafiq* by the rabble, in a bazaar. The sultan immediately sent someone to apologize to Buzurg-Ummid, and to protest that he had had no hand in this assassination. Buzurg-Ummid sent word to the sultan that he must punish the murderers, otherwise he was to expect the vengeance he would not fail to wreak on this act of perfidy. As

Mahmud paid no attention to the demands of Buzurg-Ummid, the *Rafiqs* came to the gate of Qazwin at the beginning of the year 523, killed four people and took away many animals. The inhabitants of Qazwin started to pursue them; but one of the principals of the city was killed, and they saw themselves obliged to flee. When in the year 525, 1000 men of the troops of Iraq approached the fortress of Lankir, the *Rafiqs*, having been informed of their advance, put them to flight without there being any bloodshed. Sultan Mahmud having died about that time, the *Rafiqs* again raided the territory of Qazwin, took away some animals, and killed a 100 Turkomans and 20 inhabitants of Qazwin.

In the year 526, the army of Alamut advanced into Gilan to make war against Abu Hashim Alawi, because the latter had assumed the title of imam, and was sending letters everywhere to have himself acknowledged as such. Kiya Buzurg-Ummid had first written him a letter full of advice and representations, to make him retract, or to have a proof of his crime. Abu Hashim's only reply was that the Isma'ili sect professed a doctrine containing incredulity, heresy and *Zindaqa* (or Magism). So the *Rafiqs* entered Daylam and fought against Abu Hashim, who was put to flight and hid in a forest. But the *Rafiqs* pursued him and gained control over him; and having sharply reprimanded him, they burnt him.

It can be seen, from these excerpts, that Mirkhwand distinguishes the *Rafiqs* or *Rafiqis* from the *Da'i*s as well as from the *Fida'i*s. I think that the *Rafiqs* are all members of the sect, with the exception of the *Da'i*s, who formed the clergy, and *Fida'i*s, who were specifically destined to act as assassins.[63]

I do not know whether this distinction also applies to the name *Hashishi*s. I have not come across a sufficient number of passages containing this word to have a definite opinion in this respect; but I tend to believe that, among the Isma'ilis, the names *Hashishi* or *Hashshash* were applied only to people specially trained to function as assassins and induced, through the use of *hashish*, to display this absolute resignation to the wishes of their chief. This would not have prevented other peoples, and above all Westerners, from extending this denomination to include all the Isma'ilis.

The Isma'ili sect was probably known by other names as well; for Shahrastani says that it has a different denomination in each nation. Abraham *Ecchellensis* says that they are called *Ta'tili*, which is plausible, because this name refers to a partisan of the dogma of *ta'til*, which consists of divesting God of all attributes, a dogma amounting to pure deism and almost approaching atheism. According to Muradjea, they are also called *Humayri* after their chief Hasan bin Sabbah who was surnamed *Humayri* (*Tabl. gén. de l'empire Othoman*, Vol 1, p 36). However, I have found no trace of this denomination.

I shall end this *Memoir* by pointing out a passage in the *Voyage* of Niebuhr, (*Voyage en Arabie*, Vol 2, p 361), who informs us that there still exist Isma'ilis in Syria, and by quoting an excerpt of a letter Rousseau's son wrote to me from Teheran, dated 1 June 1808.

I have collected some fairly exact notions about the Batinis or Isma'ilis commonly called *Mélahédèhs*, a sect which still survives and is widespread and tolerated, like many others, in the provinces of Persia and in the Sind. As I have very little free time, please excuse my putting off the task of going into a detailed discussion until some other time. Meanwhile, it may be useful to tell you that the *Mélahédèhs* even today have their imam or pontiff, descending, as they claim, from Ja'far Sadiq, the chief of their sect, and residing at Kehek, a village in the district of Qom. He is called Sheikh Khalil Allah and succeeded in the imamate to his uncle, Mirza Abu'l-Hasan, who played a great part under the reign of the Zends. The Persian government does not worry him, for he receives annual revenues from it. This person, whom his people grace with the pompous title of caliph, enjoys a great reputation and is considered to have the gift of performing miracles. They assure me that the Muslim Indians regularly come from the banks of the Indus to receive his blessings in exchange for the rich and pious offerings they bring him. He is more specifically known to the Persians by the name of *Seid Keheki*.[64]

Notes and References

1. The introduction to my *History of the Druze Religion*, read on 19 May 1809 to the Class of History and Ancient Literature of the Royal Institute.
2. The Nusayris, known today in Syria also as Alawis, represent one of the most famous extremist Shi'i sects. They were never a branch of the Qarmatis or the Isma'ilis. See H. Halm, *Die islamische Gnosis: Die extreme Schia und die Alawiten* (Zurich-Munich, 1982), pp 284–355; and W. Kadi, 'Alawi', EIR, Vol 1, pp 804–6. (F.D.)
3. These practices were observed only by the Isma'ilis, especially in Cairo, during the Fatimid period. No information is available on the contemporary practices of the Qarmatis, who at the time had their own state in Bahrayn and were

hostile towards the Fatimids. There were also fundamental differences between the doctrines of the Qarmatis and the Isma'ilis. See F. Daftary, 'Carmatians', EIR, Vol 4, pp. 823–32. (F.D.)

4. Abu Mansur Ahmad died in 359/970. (F.D.)

5. Al-Hasan al-A'sam (d. 366/977) was the commander of the Qarmati forces and led the Qarmatis only in their military campaigns outside Bahrayn. See M. Canard, 'al-Hasan al-A'sam', EI2, Vol 3, p 246. (F.D.)

6. Al-Mu'izz, the fourth Fatimid caliph (341–365/953–975), actually entered Cairo in 362/973. (F.D.)

7. The Qarmati state of Bahrayn was eventually uprooted in 470/1077 by the local tribesmen under the leadership of the Uyunids. See M.J de Goeje, 'La fin de l'empire des Carmathes du Bahrain', *Journal Asiatique*, 9 série, 5 (1895), pp 5–30. (F.D.)

8. J. Mariti, known from various books, has published in Livorno, in 1807, a history of the Assassins, under the title *Memorie istoriche del popolo degli Assassini e del vecchio della montagna, loro capo-signore.* This history was written without any critical sense. The author has the Assassins descend from the Kurds and ill-advisedly confuses them with the *Shamsis* or worshippers of the Sun and the *Yazidis.* His erudition may be judged by the etymology he provides for the name of the *Yazidis*: he pretends that this name means *Jesuits, disciples of Jesus* (p. 41). He is no more accurate in what he says about the *Metoualis* and the *Nasiris* or rather the *Nusayris* (pp 47 ff.). In short, his book is a web of mistakes and of haphazard assertions.

9. Since this *Memoir* was written, this piece of history was published in Persian and French by Am. Jourdain in Volume IX of the *Notices et Extraits des Manuscrits.*

10. The complete Persian text of this account of the Persian Nizari Isma'ilis, utilized so extensively by de Sacy here, may now be found in Mirkhwand, *Rawdat al-safa* (Tehran, 1338–39/1960), Vol 4, pp 199–235. (F.D.)

11. The succession of the twelve imams, starting with Ali and ending with Muhammad al-Mahdi, who has been in occultation since 260/873, is accepted only by the Shi'i sect of the Ithna'ashariyya, or the Twelvers. See E. Kohlberg, 'From Imamiyya to Ithna-'ashariyya', BSOAS, 39 (1976), pp 521–34; and S.H. Nasr, 'Ithna'ashariyya', EI2, Vol 4, pp 277–9. (F.D.)

12. I am somewhat abridging Mirkhwand's account.

13. At the time, the *amir al-juyush* was Badr al-Jamali (d. 487/1094), who also headed the civil, judicial and religious administrations in the Fatimid state. Hasan arrived in Egypt in 471/1078 and stayed there for three years. The reasons for Badr's hostility towards Hasan remain obscure, but it is almost certain that they did not relate to the issue of al-Mustansir's succession. (F.D.)

14. There is no historical evidence suggesting this revocation, and the dispute over al-Mustansir's succession belongs to a later period. It occurred on the death of al-Mustansir in 487/1094, when Nizar was deprived of his succession rights by Badr's son and successor al-Afdal, the new effective ruler of the Fatimid state. (F.D.)

15. To be pronounced Alamoot; for, according to Mirkhwand and the author of the *Burhan qati*, this name consists of the words *aluh* (eagle) and *amut* (nest) in

the local language; and the place was thus named because it was placed, like an *eagle's nest*, on a steep rock.

16. Hasan died in 518/1124. (F.D.)
17. The defeat in question, the loss of the Isma'ili fortress of Shahdiz to the Saljuqs, occurred in 500/1107 during the reign of the sultan Muhammad Tapar (498–511/1105–18). (F.D.)
18. See note 16 above. (F.D.)
19. This event occurred in 520/1126. (F.D.)
20. This name has been written in several ways, and it is doubtful whether it should be spelt Masyat or Masyaf. Schultens, in the geographical index which he annexed to the *Life of Saladin* by Baha al-Din, reads Masyat; Koehler, on the other hand (*Tab. Syr.*, p 20, n 82), maintains that it should be read Masyaf. Reiske (*Annal. Mosl.*, Vol 3, p 485) cannot decide between the two, but prefers the second. Renaudot (*Hist. patr. Alex.*, p 541) writes Mosiab. This place name can be found neither in the *Qamus*, nor in the *Dictionary* of geographical homonyms by Yaqut; but in the *Marasid al-ittila* it is spelt Masyath.

I am convinced that the true name of this place is Masyat. In the apocryphal Latin letter reported in the *Chronicle* of Nicolas de Treveth, it is written Messiat. Here is the passage: *Leopoldo, duci Austriae, vetus de monte, salutem ... Et sciatis quod litteras fecimus istas in domo nostra ad castellum nostrum* MESSIAT, *in dimidio septembris, anno ab Alexandro 1505* (*Voy. Veter. aliq. scriptor. Spicil.* op. D.L. Achery, Vol 3, p 175). In Rousseau's *Memoir* on the Isma'ilis and the Nusayris of Syria, published in the *Annales des Voyages*, Vol XIV, pp 271 ff., this place is called Mesiade.

21. The Syrian Isma'ilis captured the fortress of Masyat, or Masyaf, in 535/1140. (F.D.)
22. On this enigmatic event, the declaration of the *qiyama* or Resurrection, and its implications for the Nizari Isma'ili community, see F. Daftary, *The Isma'ilis: Their History and Doctrines* (Cambridge, 1990), pp 386–402; and C. Jambet, *La grande résurrection d'Alamût* (Lagrasse, 1990), especially Part One. (F.D.)
23. This Hasan was murdered in 561/1166 and his son, Muhammad, died in 607/1210. (F.D.)
24. The Old Man of the Mountain here refers to Rashid al-Din Sinan, the original holder of this European epithet and the most famous of the Nizari Isma'ili leaders in Syria. Sinan dispatched the embassy in question in 569/1173. See J. Hauziński, 'On the Alleged Attempts at Converting the Assassins to Christianity in the Light of William of Tyre's Account', *Folia Orientalia*, 15 (1974) pp 229–46. (F.D.)
25. Mirkhwand reports that Rukn al-Din, after submitting to Hulagu, issued orders to the governors of the places he held in Syria to surrender these places to Hulagu's officers.
26. The fall of Alamut into Mongol hands, marking the collapse of the Nizari Isma'ili state of Persia, occurred in 654/1256. See Daftary, *The Isma'ilis*, pp 421–30. (F.D.)
27. If it is spelt *xasioi* in Anna Comnena and Nicetas, this is certainly a copyist's error. Abbot S. Assemani thought that *xasioi* might be the Arabic word *qāsī* –

hard – (he meant *qāsī*); but this etymology is unacceptable, and we do not know of any oriental writer referring to the Isma'ilis by that name.

28. *Illa Bateniorum secta, qui postea Hassissin ab Arabibus, a nostris Assassini appellati sunt.*

29. Constantin Lempereur and Baratier thought that *Molhat*, in Benjamin's writings, was the name of a country where the Assassins lived. The first translated *in regionem Molhath, ubi populi degunt qui*, etc.; the second said *au pays de Molhat, ou sont des peuples* (*Voy. de Rabbi Benjamin*, Vol 1, p 176): this is a mistake. Benjamin was well aware that *Molhat* was not the name of a country, but that of a people; for he said: 'From there it is a four-day's walk to the territory of the *Molhats*: they are the people who', etc. (*Mém. de l'Acad. des Inscript.*, Vol XVII, p 159). Falconet failed to avoid this error.

30. Hasasa, says the author of the *Qamus*, is a small town near Qasr bin Hubayra.

31. See what I said about Sekkin and his doctrine in my *Memoir* on the Druzes' worship of the figure of a calf, inserted in Vol. III of this collection, pp 111 ff.

32. What Mr Assemani says here is not true of the Isma'ilis in general, and only applies, as regards the *Mulhids* or Isma'ilis of Persia, to the reign of Hasan bin Muhammad and that of his son, a period of about fifty years.

33. Read Ibn al-Muqaffa. He was the author of the Arabic translation of Bidpai's fables known under the title *The Book of Kalila and Dimna*.

34. This periodical, published in Vienna from 1809 to 1818, also carried a German title, *Fundgruben des Orients*. (F.D.).

35. For the three excerpts in Arabic, quoted here by de Sacy from a manuscript of Abu Shama, now see Abu Shama, *Kitab al-rawdatayn fi akhbar al-dawlatayn* (Cairo, 1287–88/1870–71), Vol 1, pp 240 and 258. (F.D.)

36. It may seem uncertain whether the words *he could not* refer to the assassin or to the emir. According to Ibn Abi'l-Tayyi's account, it appears certain that the assassin is meant.

37. In the first account, it was Saladin who pulled the assassin's head toward himself, threw him on the ground and straddled him; here it is the assassin who seizes the sultan's head. Perhaps the passage should read *wa jadhaba ra'sahu al-sultan, but the sultan pulled his head toward himself.*

38. I have found in the Turkish tales of the *Forty Viziers* (*Les Quarante Vizirs*) the Turkish word *ut*, herb, used in the same sense as the Arabic word *hashish*. A woman who wanted to enjoy herself with an admirer under the very eyes of her husband, organized an outing with the latter in a wood where she had made a tryst with her lover, who was hiding there. When husband and wife had sat down under a tree, she took a small dose of a cordial, *mufarrah*, and made her husband take a large dose of it. Having eaten and rested afterwards, they were intoxicated with the effect of this drug. The wife climbed a tree, and pretending that she saw her husband with another woman under the tree, she chided him for it. The husband protested that it was not true. The wife then said: Is it the effect of the herb we have eaten, or is there some extraordinary quality in this tree? I leave out the rest of this indecent and incidentally quite well-known story. See *Forty Viziers*, 31st morning.

In writing *assis* for *hashish*, Prosper Alpin did what our historians did when they wrote *Assissini* without an *h*.

39. What Herodotus says about the way the hemp seed was used by the Scythians is well known. Larcher's translation, Vol 3, p 177.

40. Mongez, who mentioned this use of hemp in his *Recherches sur l'emploi du chanvre chez les anciens*, published in the *Memoirs* of the Institute, Class of Literature and Fine Arts, Vol V, p 457, quotes the opinion of Lamark, who calls this variety of hemp *cannabis Indica*, and differentiates it from that which is grown in Europe. This is also the opinion of Ibn Baytar, who considers Egyptian hemp as a particular variety which he calls *qunnab Hindi, Indian hemp*.

41. This is the literal meaning of the words *ya'nafun min intisabihum laha*, which I failed to render with the necessary precision in my *Chrestomathie*.

42. I nevertheless have no doubt that the hemp leaf mixed with some other drugs can produce a violent mania, a fury resembling that of the Amoks, who threw themselves fearlessly amidst swords and lances. And it is in fact opium, a substance whose effects are similar to those of *hashish*, which produces this furious delirium in the Amoks; but to do this, it has to be mixed with lemon juice several days in advance. Some people think that other ingredients are added to it (*Voyage au Bengale*, by Cossigny, Vol 3, pp 103 and 163). The following references can be looked up regarding the Amoks: Kaempfer, *Amoenit. exot.*, p 649; Anquetil-Duperron, *Zend-Av.*, Vol 1, p clviii; de Grandpré, *Voyage dans l'Inde et au Beng.*, Vol 1, p 71; Father Vincent Marie of Saint Catherine of Sienna, *Viaggi all'Ind. Orient.*, pp 145, 150, 237 and 238; Legoux de Flaix, *Tableau de l'Indoustan*, Vol 2, p 394; Percival, *Voyage à Ceylan*, Vol 1, p 222. According to the latter, it was not with opium as such that the Ceylanese went amok, but with the sap or leaves of *bang*, a small shrub whose leaf resembles the tobacco leaf in its texture and shape, but is not longer than the sage leaf. The same author says that these furious men, when running after their victim, shout *amok, amok*, meaning, *kill, kill*; Legoux de Flaix maintains that the Malayans call this state of drunkenness *amok* in their language; Anquetil says that the word *amoque* comes from the Portuguese, and that the Amoks are called Narangols by the Malabars. But I think that Narangol is the name of a tribe which is surnamed Amok because these people are professional assassins. I find in the *Malay Dictionary* of Howison the word *amuq* translated as *desperado, murderer, one who kills all he can*; the verb *amaq* means to kill, to massacre. (See the *Dictionnaire Malai* of W. Marsden.) In the excerpt of the voyage of a young Englishman to Batavia and China, published in the *European Magazine* and included in the *Journal de littérature étrangère* (March 1807, p 135), we also read that the Amoks work themselves into a state of frenzy by taking strong doses of opium, and that the murders they then commit are called *mocks* because, in these expeditions, they cry *amok, amok*, meaning *kill, kill*. Be that as it may, there is no fact, to my mind, that justifies a comparison between the *Assassins* and the *Amoks*.

43. I have already corrected Marco Polo's mistake regarding the word *mulehet*. This author was the cause of Baratier's and Falconet's mistakes.

44. The Albigensians.

45. Ala al-Din was the penultimate emir of the Isma'ilis of Persia. The gardens Marco Polo mentions here were made by Hasan bin Sabbah.

46. In the book entitled *Les Quarante Vizirs*, there is a romance which seems modelled on the story I related here after Marco Polo. It occurs on the nineteenth morning of this book of episodes. The nineteenth vizier wants to prove to the king that women are capable of all sorts of stratagems and ruses to satisfy their passions, so he tells him the story of a princess who had fallen madly in love with one of the pages of her father, the king. Having for a long time concealed her passion, she confides it to the woman who serves her. The latter soon finds a way to satisfy her. Disguised as a man, she enters the room where the young page spends the night, and having made him drink a soporific beverage, she transports him, without his being aware of it, into the apartment of the princess, and puts him, fast asleep, on some rich cushions. The princess then approaches him and gently wakes him up by pouring a few drops of strong vinegar on his forehead. He gradually wakes up and, seeing himself surrounded by the most seductive luxury and beauty, says: Surely I must be dead and they have transported me to paradise. Needless to add that the same method that had been employed to bring him, without his knowledge, into the apartment of the princess was used again to take him back to his own room.

47. Boccaccio seems to have followed a slightly different tradition when attributing the effect in question to a certain powder used by the Old Man of the Mountain to put to sleep those whom he wanted to take into his paradise or out of it (3rd journ., 8th tale). This diversity of traditions confirms rather than weakens my conjecture, since *hashish* was taken equally as a powder, an electuary and a beverage.

48. I am not quoting the chapter of Pepin's *Chronicle*, which includes (Book III, Ch XXXIX) details quite similar to those given by Marco Polo (see *Script. rer. Ital.* by Muratori, Vol IX, col 705 ff.) This monk, who translated Marco Polo's *Travels* into Latin, must have borrowed from him what he says about the Assassins.

49. I first thought that there was a mistake in the manuscript, and that it should read *sahib al-Hashishiyya, master of the Hashishi*s, but I believe that this correction would have truly altered the text, the more so since *sahib* more usually has as its complement the name of a country or a thing, rather than the name of a man or of a nation.

50. See the *History of the Sasanids*, translated from Mirkhwand's Persian in the *Mémoires sur diverses antiquités de la Perse*, pp 273 ff. [Now, see the helpful survey by E. Yarshater, 'Mazdakism', in *The Cambridge History of Iran*, Vol 3 (II), ed. E. Yarshater (Cambridge, 1983), pp 991–1024; and P. Crone, 'Kavad's Heresy and Mazdak's Revolt', *Iran, Journal of the British Institute of Persian Studies*, 29 (1991), pp 21–42. (F.D.)]

51. See the Note on the universal history of Mirkhwand, in Vol IX of the *Notices et Extraits des Manuscrits*, pp 117 ff. [Hasan is regarded by the Nizaris as a descendant of Nizar b. al-Mustansir, and not as Muhammad's son. It was with this Hasan that the line of the Nizari Isma'ili imams re-emerged openly during the Alamut period. (F.D.)]

52. For the relevant quotations now see al-Shahrastani, *Kitab al-milal wa'l-nihal*, ed. W. Cureton (London, 1842), pp 150–2; English trans. *Muslim Sects and Divisions*, tr. A.K. Kazi and J.G. Flynn (London, 1984), pp. 167–70. For a

summary exposition of this Nizari Isma'ili doctrine of *ta'lim*, see Hodgson, *The Order of Assassins*, (The Hague, 1955), pp 51–61.(F.D.)

53. The French original of this *Memoir* was not printed during Venture's lifetime, and was only recently included in the *Annales des Voyages*; but an English translation of it has been published.

54. See note 2 above. (F.D.)

55. On the origins of the Druzes and their doctrines, now see Nejla M. Abu-Izzeddin, *The Druzes: A New Study of their History, Faith and Society* (Leiden, 1984); D.R.W. Bryer, 'The Origins of the Druze Religion', *Der Islam*, 52 (1975), pp 47–84, 239–62, and 53 (1976), pp 5–27; and M.G.S. Hodgson, 'Duruz', EI2, Vol 2, pp 631–4. Silvestre de Sacy's own *Exposé de la religion des Druzes* remains a classic in the field. (F.D.)

56. Mr de Volney committed even a greater anachronism in saying that the caliph Ali was killed by a Batini or Assassin. *Voyage en Syrie et en Égypte*, Vol 1, p 429.

57. Ét. Quatremère, in his *Mémoires géographiques et historiques sur l'Égypte*, Vol 2, p 504, also attributes the denomination of *Fidawi*s among the Isma'ilis exclusively to professional assassins.

58. Mirkhwand's account, quoted here, is full of errors and inaccuracies. (F.D.)

59. De Sacy often confuses Persia with Kuhistan (Arabic, Quhistan), one of the main Persian Isma'ili territories in southern Khurasan. (F.D.)

60. The ancestry of this Hasan, called *ala dhikrihi'l-salam* by the Nizaris, and his successors at Alamut was traced to Nizar, and their Nizarid Fatimid genealogy and imamates were acknowledged by the contemporary Nizari Isma'ili community. (F.D.)

61. The Abbasid caliph in question was al-Mustarshid (512–529/1118–35). (F.D.)

62. The *da'i* in question was Abd al-Malik ibn Attash who, at the time, headed the Isma'ili movement throughout the central and western regions of Persia, and possibly also in Khurasan and Iraq. (F.D.)

63. It appears that the word *laziq, attaché, follower*, was also used in the same sense as *rafiq*. This seems to follow from two passages of Arab authors, quoted by Ét. Quatremère in his *Mémoires géographiques et historiques sur l'Égypte*, Vol 2, pp 111 and 502.

64. Shah Khalil Allah, the 45th imam of the Nizari Isma'ilis, succeeded his father, Abu'l-Hasan Ali, also known as Sayyid Kahaki, in 1206/1792. Shah Khalil Allah spent the final years of his life at Yazd, and was murdered there in 1232/1817. See Daftary, *The Isma'ilis*, pp 503–4. (F.D.)

Select Bibliography

The Bibliography includes some basic works of reference and the works cited in the Notes and References. For abbreviations see page vi.

Abd al-Jalil Qazwini Razi, *Kitab al-naqd*, ed. Mir Jalal al-Din Muhaddith (2nd edn, Tehran, 1980).

Abu'l-Fida, Isma'il b. Ali, *Abulfedae Annales Moslemici*, tr. J.J. Reiske (Leipzig, 1754–78).

Abu Firas, Shihab al-Din al-Maynaqi, *Fasl min al-lafz al-sharif*, ed. and tr. S. Guyard in his 'Un grand Maître des Assassins', pp 387–489.

Abu-Izzeddin, Nejla M., *The Druzes: A New Study of their History, Faith and Society* (Leiden, 1984).

Abu Shama, Shihab al-Din Abd al-Rahman b. Isma'il, *Kitab al-rawdatayn fi akhbar al-dawlatayn* (Cairo, 1287–88/1870–71).

Académie des Inscriptions et Belles Lettres, *Centenaire de Silvestre de Sacy (1758–1838)* (Paris, 1938).

Alexandri historia fabulosa, ed. C. Mueller (Paris, 1867).

d'Alverny, Marie Thérèse, 'Deux traductions latines du Coran au Moyen Age', *Archives d'histoire doctrinale et littéraire du Moyen Age*, 22–23 (1947–48), pp 69–131.

——, 'Notes sur les traductions médiévales d'Avicenne', *Archives d'histoire doctrinale et littéraire du Moyen Age*, 27 (1952), pp 337–58.

——, 'La Connaissance de l'Islam en Occident du IXe siècle au milieu du XIIe siècle', in *L'Occident e l'Islam nell' alto medioevo* (Spoleto, 1965), pp 577–602, 791–803.

Ambroise, *L'Estoire de la Guerre Sainte*, ed. and tr. G. Paris (Paris, 1897).

al-Amir bi-Ahkam Allah, Abu Ali al-Mansur, *al-Hidaya al-Amiriyya*, ed. Asaf A.A. Fyzee (Bombay, etc., 1938).

——, *Iqa' sawa'iq al-irgham*, ed. Asaf A.A. Fyzee, in al-Amir, *al-Hidaya al-Amiriyya*, pp 27–39.

Anon, 'Assassins', in *The Encyclopaedia of Islam*, ed. M. Th. Houtsma et al. (Leiden-London, 1913–38), Vol 1, pp 491–2.

189

Arnold of Lübeck, *Chronica Slavorum*, in G.H. Pertz et al. (eds), *Monumenta Germaniae Historica: Scriptores* (Hanover, 1826–1913), Vol 21, pp 100–250.

Assemani, Simone, 'Ragguaglio storico-critico sopra la setta Assissana, detta volgarmente degli Assassini', *Giornale dell' Italiana Letteratura*, 13 (1806), pp 241–62.

Atiya, Aziz S., *The Crusade: Historiography and Bibliography* (Bloomington, 1962).

al-Baghdadi, Abu Mansur Abd al-Qadir b. Tahir, *al-Farq bayn al-firaq*; English trans. *Moslem Schisms and Sects*, Part II, tr. A.S. Halkin (Tel Aviv, 1935).

Baldwin, Marshall W., 'The Latin States under Baldwin III and Amalric I, 1143–1174', in *A History of the Crusades*, Vol 1, pp 528–61.

Barthold, V.V., *La découverte de l'Asie*, tr. B. Nikitine (Paris, 1947).

Benjamin of Tudela, *The Itinerary of Benjamin of Tudela*, ed. and tr. Marcus N. Adler (London, 1907).

Berchem, Max van, 'Épigraphie des Assassins de Syrie', *Journal Asiatique*, 9 série, 9 (1897), pp 453–501, reprinted in his *Opera Minora* (Geneva, 1978), Vol 1, pp 453–501.

Bianquis, Thierry, *Damas et la Syrie sous la domination Fatimide, 359–468/969–1076*, (Damascus, 1986–89).

Bosworth, C. Edmund, *The Islamic Dynasties* (Edinburgh, 1980).

Bouthoul, Betty, *Le Vieux de la Montagne* (Paris, 1958).

Bowen, Harold, 'The Sargudhasht-i Sayyidna, the Tale of the Three Schoolfellows and the Wasaya of the Nizam al-Mulk', JRAS (1931), pp 771–82.

—— and C.E. Bosworth, 'Nizam al-Mulk', EI2, Vol 8, pp 69–73.

Browne, Edward G., *A Literary History of Persia* (Cambridge, 1928).

Bruijn, J.T.P. de, 'al-Kirmani', EI2, Vol 5, pp 166–7.

Bryer, David R.W., 'The Origins of the Druze Religion', *Der Islam*, 52 (1975), pp 47–84, 239–62, and 53 (1976), pp 5–27.

al-Bundari, al-Fath b. Ali, *Zubdat al-nusra*, ed. M. Th. Houtsma, in his *Recueil de textes relatifs à l'histoire des Seldjoucides* II (Leiden, 1889).

Burchard of Mount Sion, *Descriptio Terrae Sanctae*, in J.C.M. Laurent (ed.), *Peregrinatores medii aevi quatuor* (Leipzig, 1864), pp 1–100; English trans. *A Description of the Holy Land*, tr. A. Stewart (London, 1897), pp 1–136.

Burchard of Strassburg, *De statu Egypti vel Babylonie*, in Arnold of Lübeck, *Chronica Slavorum*, pp 235–41.

Burman, Edward, *The Assassins* (London, 1987).

Bustan al-jami, ed. Claude Cahen, in his 'Une chronique Syrienne du VIIe/XIIe siècle: Le *Bustan al-Jami*', *Bulletin d'Études Orientales*, 7–8 (1937–38), pp 113–58.

Cahen, Claude, *La Syrie du Nord à l'époque des Croisades* (Paris, 1940).

——, 'Points du vue sur la Révolution Abbaside', *Revue Historique*, 230 (1960), pp 295–338, reprinted in his *Les peuples Musulmans dans l'histoire médiévale* (Damascus, 1977), pp 105–60.

——, *Introduction à l'histoire du monde Musulman médiéval* (Paris, 1982).

Canard, Marius, 'L'impérialisme des Fatimides et leur propagande', *Annales de l'Institut d'Études Orientales*, 6 (1942–47), pp 156–93, reprinted in his *Miscellanea Orientalia* (London, 1973), article II.

——, 'Fatimids', EI2, Vol 2, pp 850–62.

——, 'al-Hasan al-A'sam', EI2, Vol 3, p 246.

Casanova, Paul, 'Monnaie des Assassins de Perse', *Revue Numismatique*, 3 série, 11 (1893), pp 343–52.

——, 'La doctrine secrète des Fatimides d'Égypte', *Bulletin de l'Institut Français d'Archéologie Orientale*, 18 (1921), pp 121–65.

Cathay and the Way Thither: Being a Collection of Medieval Notices of China, ed. and tr. H. Yule, revised by H. Cordier (London, 1911–14).

Cento novelle antiche (Florence, 1572).

Chambers, Frank W., 'The Troubadours and the Assassins', *Modern Language Notes*, 64 (1949), pp 245–51.

Chronicles of the Crusades; being Contemporary Narratives of the Crusade of Richard Coeur de Lion and the Crusade of Saint Louis (London, 1848).

Chronique d'Ernoul et de Bernard le Trésorier, ed. L. de Mas Latrie (Paris, 1887).

Chroniques gréco-romanes inédits ou peu connues, ed. C. Hopf (Berlin, 1873).

Continuation de Guillaume de Tyr, dite Manuscrit de Rothelin, in *Recueil des Historiens des Croisades: Historiens Occidentaux*, Vol 2, pp 483–639.

Corbin, Henry, *Temps cyclique et gnose Ismaélienne* (Paris, 1982); English trans. *Cyclical Time and Ismaili Gnosis*, tr. R.M. Manheim and James W. Morris (London, 1983).

——, *History of Islamic Philosophy*, tr. L. Sherrard (London, 1993).

Crone, Patricia, 'Kavad's Heresy and Mazdak's Revolt', *Iran, Journal of the British Institute of Persian Studies*, 29 (1991), pp 21–42.

—— and M. Cook, *Hagarism: The Making of the Islamic World* (Cambridge, 1977).

—— and M. Hinds, *God's Caliph: Religious Authority in the First Centuries of Islam* (Cambridge, 1986).

Dabashi, Hamid, *Authority in Islam: From the Rise of Muhammad to the Establishment of the Umayyads* (New Brunswick, NJ, 1989).

Dachraoui, Farhat, *Le califat Fatimide au Maghreb, 296–365 H./909–975 Jc* (Tunis, 1981).

Daftary, Farhad, *The Isma'ilis: Their History and Doctrines* (Cambridge, 1990).

——, 'The Earliest Isma'ilis', *Arabica*, 38 (1991), pp 214–45.

——, 'Persian Historiography of the Early Nizari Isma'ilis', *Iran, Journal of the British Institute of Persian Studies*, 30 (1992), pp 91–7.

——, 'A Major Schism in the Early Isma'ili Movement', *Studia Islamica*, 77 (1993), pp 123–39.

——, 'Carmatians', EIR, Vol 4, pp 823–32.

——, 'Rashid al-Din Sinan', EI2, Vol 8, pp 442–3.

—— (ed.), *Essays in Mediaeval Isma'ili History and Thought* (Cambridge, forthcoming).

Daniel, Norman, *Islam and the West: The Making of an Image* (Edinburgh, 1966).

Defrémery, Charles F., 'Nouvelles recherches sur les Ismaéliens ou Bathiniens de Syrie', *Journal Asiatique*, 5 série, 3 (1854), pp 373–421, and 5 (1855), pp 5–76.

——, 'Essai sur l'histoire des Ismaéliens ou Batiniens de la Perse, plus connus sous le nom d'Assassins', *Journal Asiatique*, 5 série, 8 (1856), pp 353–87, and 15 (1860), pp 130–210.

Dehérain, Henri, *Silvestre de Sacy, 1758–1838: Ses contemporains et ses disciples* (Paris, 1838).

Derenbourg, Hartwig, *Silvestre de Sacy (1758–1838)* (Paris, 1895).

Dussaud, René, 'Influence de la religion Nosairi sur la doctrine de Rachid ad-Din Sinan', *Journal Asiatique*, 9 série, 16 (1900), pp 61–9.

——, *Topographie historique de la Syrie antique et médiévale* (Paris, 1927).

Edbury, Peter W., and John G. Rowe, *William of Tyre: Historian of the Latin East* (Cambridge, 1988).

Elisséeff, Nikita, *Nur ad-Din, un grand prince Musulman de Syrie au temps des Croisades (511–569H./1118–1174)* (Damascus, 1967).

Elmacin, Georgius, *Historia Saracenica*, ed. and tr. Th. Erpenius (Leiden, 1625).

Encyclopaedia Iranica, ed. E. Yarshater (London, 1982–   ).

The Encyclopaedia of Islam, ed. H.A.R. Gibb et al. (new edn, Leiden-London, 1960–   ).

Esmail, Aziz and A. Nanji, 'The Ismaʻilis in History', in S.H. Nasr (ed.), *Ismaʻili Contributions to Islamic Culture* (Tehran, 1977), pp 227–65.

L'Estoire de Eracles Empereur, in *Recueil des Historiens des Croisades: Historiens Occidentaux*, Vol 2, pp 1–481.

Fabri, Felix, *Evagatorium in Terrae Sanctae*, ed. C.D. Hassler (Stuttgart, 1843–49); English trans. *The Book of the Wanderings of Brother Felix Fabri*, tr. A. Stewart (London, 1897).

Fakhry, Majid, *A History of Islamic Philosophy* (2nd edn, London, 1983).

Falconet, Camille, 'Dissertation sur les Assassins, peuples d'Asie', *Mémoires de Littérature, tirés des registres de l'Académie Royale des Inscriptions et Belles Lettres*, 17 (1751), pp 127–70; English trans. 'A Dissertation on the Assassins, a People of Asia', tr. Thomas Johnes, in Joinville, *Memoirs of John Lord de Joinville*, Vol 2, pp 287–328.

Filippani-Ronconi, Pio, *Ismaeliti ed 'Assassini'* (Milan, 1973).

Fyzee, Asaf A.A., 'The Ismaʻilis', in A.J. Arberry (ed.), *Religion in the Middle East* (Cambridge, 1969), Vol 2, pp 318–29, 684–5.

Gabrieli, Francesco, *Arab Historians of the Crusades*, tr. E.J. Costello (Berkeley, 1969).

Gesta Dei per Francos, ed. J. Bongars (Hanover, 1611).

Gesta Francorum et aliorum Hierosolimitanorum, ed. and tr. R. Hill (London, 1962).

al-Ghazali, Abu Hamid Muhammad, *Fadaʼih al-Batiniyya*, ed. Abd al-Rahman Badawi (Cairo, 1964).

Goeje, Michael J. de, *Mémoire sur les Carmathes du Bahrain et les Fatimides* (2nd edn, Leiden, 1886).

——, 'La fin de l'empire des Carmathes du Bahrain', *Journal Asiatique*, 9 série, 5 (1895), pp 5–30.

Goldziher, Ignaz, *Streitschrift des Gazali gegen die Batinijja-Sekte* (Leiden, 1916).

The Great Ismaili Heroes (Karachi, 1973).

Grousset, René, *Histoire des Croisades* (Paris, 1934–36).

Guignes, Joseph de, *Histoire des Huns* (Paris, 1760).

Guyard, Stanislas, *Fragments relatifs à la doctrine des Ismaélîs* (Paris, 1874).

——, 'Un grand Maître des Assassins au temps de Saladin', *Journal Asiatique*, 7 série, 9 (1877), pp 324–489.

Halm, Heinz, *Kosmologie und Heilslehre der frühen Isma'iliya* (Wiesbaden, 1978).

——, *Die islamische Gnosis: Die extreme Schia und die Alawiten* (Zurich-Munich, 1982).

——, 'Die Fatimiden', in U. Haarmann (ed.), *Geschichte der arabischen Welt* (Munich, 1987), pp 166–99, 605–6.

——, *Das Reich des Mahdi, 875–973: Der Aufstieg der Fatimiden* (Munich, 1991).

——, *Shiism*, tr. J. Watson (Edinburgh, 1991).

——, 'The Cosmology of Pre-Fatimid Isma'iliyya', in Daftary (ed.) *Essays in Mediaeval Isma'ili History and Thought*.

——, 'Abdallah b. Maymun al-Qaddah', EIR, Vol 1, pp 182–3.

——, 'Bateniya', EIR, Vol 3, pp 861–3.

Hamawi, Abu'l-Fada'il Muhammad, *al-Ta'rikh al-Mansuri*, ed. P.A. Gryaznevich (Moscow, 1963).

Hamdani, Abbas, 'Evolution of the Organisational Structure of the Fatimi Da'wa', *Arabian Studies*, 3 (1976), pp 85–114.

——, 'Fatimid History and Historians', in M.J.L. Young et al. (eds), *The Cambridge History of Arabic Literature: Religion, Learning and Science in the Abbasid Period* (Cambridge, 1990), pp 234–47, 535–6.

—— and F. de Blois, 'A Re-examination of al-Mahdi's Letter to the Yemenites on the Genealogy of the Fatimid Caliphs', JRAS (1983), pp 173–207.

al-Hamdani, Husayn F., *On the Genealogy of Fatimid Caliphs* (Cairo, 1958).

Hammer-Purgstall, Joseph von, *Die Geschichte der Assassinen* (Stuttgart-Tübingen, 1818); English trans. *The History of the Assassins*, tr. O.C. Wood (London, 1835).

——, 'Sur le paradis du Vieux de la Montagne', *Fundgruben des Orients*, 3 (1813), pp 201–6.

Hauziński, Jerzy, 'On the Alleged Attempts at Converting the Assassins to Christianity in the Light of William of Tyre's Account', *Folia Orientalia*, 15 (1974), pp 229–46.

——, *Muzułmańska sekta asasynów w europejskim piśmiennictwie wieków średnich* (Poznan, 1978).

Hellmuth, Leopold, *Die Assassinenlegende in der österreichischen Geschichtsdichtung des Mittelalters* (Vienna, 1988).

d'Herbelot de Molainville, Barthélemy, *Bibliothèque orientale* (Paris, 1697).

A History of the Crusades, ed. K.M. Setton: Vol I, *The First Hundred Years*, ed. M.W. Baldwin (2nd edn, Madison, WI, 1969).

Hodgson, Marshall G.S., *The Order of Assassins: The Struggle of the Early Nizari Isma'ilis against the Islamic World* (The Hague, 1955).

——, 'The Isma'ili State', in *The Cambridge History of Iran*: Vol 5, *The Saljuq and Mongol Periods*, ed. John A. Boyle (Cambridge, 1968), pp 422–82.

——, 'Alamut: The Dynasty', EI2, Vol 1, pp 353–4.

——, 'Duruz', EI2, Vol 2, pp 631–4.

——, 'Fida'i', EI2, Vol 2, p 882.

——, 'Hasan-i Sabbah', EI2, Vol 3, pp 253–4.

Holmes, Urban T., 'Life among the Europeans in Palestine and Syria in the Twelfth and Thirteenth Centuries', in *A History of the Crusades*, ed. K.M. Setton: Vol IV,

The Art and Architecture of the Crusader States, ed. H.W. Hazard (Madison, WI, 1977), pp 3–35.

Holt, Peter M., *The Age of the Crusades* (London, 1986).

Hourani, Albert, *Europe and the Middle East* (London, 1980).

——, *Islam in European Thought* (Cambridge, 1991).

Hourcade, Bernard, 'Alamut', EIR, Vol 1, pp 797–801.

Houtsma, Martijn Th., 'The Death of Nizam al-Mulk and its Consequences', *Journal of Indian History*, 3 (1924), pp 147–60.

Ibn al-Athir, Izz al-Din Ali b. Muhammad, *Kitab al-kamil fi'l-ta'rikh*, ed. Carl J. Tornberg (Leiden, 1851–76).

Ibn al-Dawadari, Abu Bakr b. Abd Allah, *Kanz al-durar*, Vol 7, ed. S.A. Ashur (Cairo, 1972).

Ibn Jubayr, Abu'l-Husayn Muhammad b. Ahmad, *Rihla*, ed. W. Wright, 2nd revised edn by M.J. de Goeje (Leiden-London, 1907); English trans. *The Travels*, tr. Ronald J.C. Broadhurst (London, 1952).

Ibn Khaldun, Abd al-Rahman b. Muhammad, *Muqaddima* (3rd edn, Beirut, 1900); English trans. *The Muqaddimah: An Introduction to History*, tr. F. Rosenthal (2nd edn, Princeton, 1967).

Ibn Muyassar, Taj al-Din Muhammad b. Ali, *Akhbar Misr*, ed. A.F. Sayyid (Cairo, 1981).

Ibn al-Qalanisi, Abu Ya'la Hamza b. Asad, *Dhayl ta'rikh Dimashq*, ed. H.F. Amedroz (Leiden, 1908); partial English trans. *The Damascus Chronicle of the Crusades*, tr. H.A.R. Gibb (London, 1932).

al-Imad, Leila S., *The Fatimid Vizierate, 969–1172* (Berlin, 1990).

Itinéraire de Londres à Jérusalem, in H. Michelant and G. Raynaud (eds), *Itinéraires à Jérusalem et descriptions de la Terre Sainte* (Geneva, 1882), pp 123–39.

Itinerarium peregrinorum et gesta regis Ricardi, ed. W. Stubbs, in *Chronicles and Memorials of the Reign of Richard I* (London, 1864), Vol 1, pp 1–450.

Ivanow, Wladimir, 'An Ismaili Poem in Praise of Fidawis', *Journal of the Bombay Branch of the Royal Asiatic Society*, New Series, 14 (1938), pp 63–72.

——, *Ismaili Tradition Concerning the Rise of the Fatimids* (Bombay, etc., 1942).

——, *The Alleged Founder of Ismailism* (Bombay, 1946).

——, *Ibn al-Qaddah* (2nd edn, Bombay, 1957).

——, *Alamut and Lamasar: Two Mediaeval Ismaili Strongholds in Iran* (Tehran, 1960).

——, *Ismaili Literature: A Bibliographical Survey* (Tehran, 1963).

——, 'Isma'iliya', in *Shorter Encyclopaedia of Islam*, ed. H.A.R. Gibb and J.H. Kramers (Leiden, 1953), pp 179–83.

Jafri, S. Husain M., *Origins and Early Development of Shi'a Islam* (London, 1979).

Jambet, Christian, *La grande résurrection d'Alamût* (Lagrasse, 1990).

James of Vitry, *Historia Orientalis*, in *Gesta Dei per Francos*, Vol 1, pp 1047–149.

——, *Lettres de Jacques de Vitry, évêque de Saint-Jean d'Acre*, ed. R.B.C. Huygens (Leiden, 1960).

Joinville, Jean de, *Histoire de Saint Louis*, ed. Natalis de Wailly (Paris, 1868; reprinted, Lille, n.d.).

——, *Memoirs of John Lord de Joinville*, tr. T. Johnes (Hafod, 1807).

Juwayni, Ala al-Din Ata-Malik, *Ta'rikh-i jahan-gushay*, ed. M. Qazwini (Leiden-London, 1912–37); English trans. *The History of the World-Conqueror*, tr. John A. Boyle (Manchester, 1958).

Kadi, W., 'Alawi', EIR, Vol 1, pp 804–6.

Kaempfer, Engelbert, *Amoenitatum exoticarum politico-physico medicarum* (Lemgo, 1712).

Kashani, Abu'l-Qasim Abd Allah b. Ali, *Zubdat al-tawarikh; bakhsh-i Fatimiyan va Nizariyan*, ed. M.T. Danishpazhuh (2nd edn, Tehran, 1366/1987).

Kedar, Benjamin Z., *Crusade and Mission: European Approaches toward the Muslims* (Princeton, 1988).

King, Edwin J., *The Knights Hospitallers in the Holy Land* (London, 1931).

al-Kirmani, Hamid al-Din Ahmad b. Abd Allah, *al-Risala al-kafiya*, in M. Ghalib (ed.), *Majmu'at rasa'il al-Kirmani* (Beirut, 1983), pp 148–82.

Kohlberg, Etan, 'From Imamiyya to Ithna-'ashariyya', BSOAS, 39 (1976), pp 521–34.

——, 'Western Studies of Shi'a Islam', in M. Kramer (ed.), *Shi'ism, Resistance, and Revolution* (London, 1987), pp 31–44.

——, *Belief and Law in Imami Shi'ism* (London, 1991).

Kraus, Paul, 'Hebräische und syrische Zitate in isma'ilitischen Schriften', *Der Islam*, 19 (1931), pp 243–63.

Kritzeck, James, *Peter the Venerable and Islam* (Princeton, 1964).

Lebey de Batilly, Denis, *Traicté de l'origine des anciens Assasins porte-couteaux* (Lyon, 1603), reprinted in C. Leber (ed.), *Collection des meilleurs dissertations, notices et traités particuliers relatifs à l'histoire de France* (Paris, 1838), Vol 20, pp 453–501.

Lev, Yaacov, *State and Society in Fatimid Egypt* (Leiden, 1991).

Lévesque de la Ravalière, Pierre Alexandre, 'Éclaircissemens sur quelques circonstances de l'histoire du Vieux de la Montagne, Prince des Assassins', *Histoire de l'Académie Royale des Inscriptions et Belles Lettres*, 16 (1751), pp 155–64; English trans. 'Explanations Relative to Some Circumstances of the History of the Old Man of the Mountain, Prince of the Assassins', tr. Thomas Johnes, in Joinville, *Memoirs of John Lord de Joinville*, Vol 2, pp 275–85.

Levey, M., 'Hashish', EI2, Vol 3, pp 266–7.

Lewis, Bernard, 'The Sources for the History of the Syrian Assassins', *Speculum*, 27 (1952), pp 475–89.

——, 'The Isma'ilites and the Assassins', in *A History of the Crusades*, Vol I, pp 99–132.

——, 'Kamal al-Din's Biography of Rašid al-Din Sinan', *Arabica*, 13 (1966), pp 225–67.

——, *The Assassins: A Radical Sect in Islam* (London, 1967); French trans. *Les Assassins: Terrorisme et politique dans l'Islam Médiéval*, tr. A. Pélissier (Paris, 1982); German trans. *Die Assassinen: Zur Tradition des religiösen Mordes in radikalen Islam*, tr. K. Jürgen Huch (Frankfurt, 1989).

——, 'Assassins of Syria and Isma'ilis of Persia', in Accademia Nazionale dei Lincei, *Atti del convegno internazionale sul tema: Persia nel medioevo* (Rome, 1971), pp 573–80.

——, Studies in Classical and Ottoman Islam (7th–16th Centuries) (London, 1976).

——, 'Assassins', in Dictionary of the Middle Ages (New York, 1981), Vol 1, pp 589–93.

——, 'Hashishiyya', EI2, Vol 3, pp 267–8.

Lockhart, Laurence, 'Hasan-i-Sabbah and the Assassins', BSOS, 5 (1928–30), pp 675–96.

——, 'Alamut: The Fortress', EI, Vol 1, pp 352–3.

Madelung, Wilferd, 'Fatimiden und Bahrainqarmaten', Der Islam, 34 (1959), pp 34–88; English version in Daftary (ed.), Essays in Mediaeval Isma'ili History and Thought.

——, 'Das Imamat in der frühen ismailitischen Lehre', Der Islam, 37 (1961), pp 43–135.

——, (ed.), Arabic Texts Concerning the History of the Zaydi Imams of Tabaristan, Daylaman and Gilan (Beirut, 1987).

——, Religious Trends in Early Islamic Iran (Albany, NY, 1988).

——, 'Hamdan Karmat', EI2, Vol 3, pp 123–4.

——, 'Isma'iliyya', EI2, Vol 4, pp 198–206.

——, 'Karmati', EI2, Vol 4, pp 660–5.

——, 'Maymun al-Kaddah', EI2, Vol 6, p 917.

——, 'Shiism: Isma'iliyah', in The Encyclopaedia of Religion, ed. M. Eliade (New York, 1987), Vol 13, pp 247–60.

al-Maqrizi, Taqi al-Din Ahmad b. Ali, Kitab al-mawa'iz wa'l-i'tibar bi-dhikr al-khitat wa'l-athar (Bulaq, 1270/1853).

Margoliouth, David S., 'Assassins', in Encyclopaedia of Religion and Ethics, ed. J. Hastings (Edinburgh–New York, 1908–26), Vol 2, pp 138–41.

Marino Sanudo Torsello, Liber Secretorum Fidelium Crucis, in Gesta Dei per Francos, Vol 2, pp 1–316.

Mariti, Giovanni F., Memorie istoriche del popolo degli Assassini e del Vecchio della Montagna, loro capo-signore (Livorno, 1807).

Massignon, Louis, 'Esquisse d'une bibliographie Qarmate', in T.W. Arnold and R.A. Nicholson (eds), A Volume of Oriental Studies Presented to Edward G. Browne (Cambridge, 1922), pp 329–38.

Melville, Marion, La vie des Templiers (2nd edn, Paris, 1974).

Michaud, Joseph F., Michaud's History of the Crusades, tr. W. Robson (London, 1852).

Miles, George C., 'Coins of the Assassins of Alamut', Orientalia Lovaniensia Periodica, 3 (1972), pp 155–62.

Mirkhwand, Muhammad b. Khwandshah, Rawdat al-safa (Tehran, 1338–39/ 1960).

Momen, Moojan, An Introduction to Shi'i Islam (New Haven, 1985).

al-Mufid, Abu Abd Allah Muhammad b. Muhammad, Kitab al-Irshad: The Book of Guidance, tr. I.K.A. Howard (London, 1981).

Nagel, Tilman, Untersuchungen zur Entstehung des abbasidischen Kalifates (Bonn, 1972).

Nanji, Azim A., 'Isma'ilism', in S.H. Nasr (ed.), Islamic Spirituality: Foundations (London, 1987), pp 179–98, 432–3.

Nasr, S.H., 'Ithna'ashariyya', EI2, Vol 4, pp 277–9.

al-Nawbakhti, al-Hasan b. Musa, *Kitab firaq al-Shi'a*, ed. H. Ritter (Istanbul, 1931).

Nizam al-Mulk, Abu Ali al-Hasan b. Ali, *Siyasat-nama*, English trans. *The Book of Government or Rules for Kings*, tr. H. Darke (2nd edn, London, 1978).

Il Novellino, ed. G. Favati (Genoa, 1970).

Nowell, Charles E., 'The Old Man of the Mountain', *Speculum*, 22 (1947), pp 497–519.

al-Nuwayri, Shihab al-Din Ahmad b. Abd al-Wahhab, *Nihayat al-arab*, Vol 25, ed. M.J. Abd al-Al al-Hini et al. (Cairo, 1984).

Odoric of Pordenone, *The Journal of Friar Odoric*, in *The Travels of Sir John Mandeville*, ed. A.W. Pollard (London, 1915), pp 326–62.

——, *The Journal of Friar Odoric, 1318–1330*, in *Contemporaries of Marco Polo: Consisting of the Travel Records of the Eastern Parts of the World of William of Rubruck . . .*, ed. Manuel Komroff (New York, 1928), pp 211–50.

Olschki, Leonardo, *Storia letteraria delle scoperte geografiche* (Florence, 1937).

Paris, Matthew, *Chronica Majora*, ed. Henry R. Luard (London, 1872–83); English trans. *Matthew Paris's English History*, tr. John A. Giles (London, 1852–54).

Pedro de Alfonso, *Dialogi in quibus impiae Judaeorum confutantur*, in J.P. Migne (ed.), *Patrologia Latina* (Paris, 1844–64), Vol 157, pp 527–672.

Polo, Marco, *The Book of Ser Marco Polo, the Venetian, concerning the Kingdoms and Marvels of the East*, ed. and tr. H. Yule, 3rd revised edn by H. Cordier (London, 1929).

——, *Marco Polo: The Description of the World*, ed. and tr. A.C. Moule and P. Pelliot (London, 1938).

Poonawala, Ismail K., *Biobibliography of Isma'ili Literature* (Malibu, CA, 1977).

Prawer, Joshua, *Crusader Institutions* (Oxford, 1980).

Quatremère, Étienne M., *Mémoires géographiques et historiques sur l'Égypte* (Paris, 1811).

——, 'Notice Historique sur les Ismaéliens', *Fundgruben des Orients*, 4 (1814), pp 339–76.

al-Qummi, Sa'd b. Abd Allah al-Ash'ari, *Kitab al-maqalat wa'l-firaq*, ed. M.J. Mashkur (Tehran, 1963).

Rashid al-Din Fadl Allah Tabib, *Jami al-tawarikh; qismat-i Isma'iliyan va Fatimiyan va Nizariyan va da'iyan va rafiqan*, ed. M.T. Danishpazhuh and M. Mudarrisi Zanjani (Tehran, 1959).

Recueil des Historiens des Croisades: Historiens Occidentaux, Académie des Inscriptions et Belles Lettres (Paris, 1844–95).

Reinaud, Joseph, 'Notice historique et littéraire sur M. le baron Silvestre de Sacy', *Journal Asiatique*, 3 série, 6 (1838), pp 113–95.

Ricoldo da Monte Croce, *Il Libro della Peregrinazione nelle parti d'Oriente*, ed. Ugo Monneret de Villard (Rome, 1948).

——, *Itinerarium*, in J.C.M. Laurent (ed.), *Peregrinatores medii aevi quatuor* (2nd edn, Leipzig, 1873).

Rodinson, Maxime, 'The Western Image and Western Studies of Islam', in J. Schacht and C.E. Bosworth (eds), *The Legacy of Islam* (2nd edn, Oxford, 1974), pp 9–62.

Röhricht, Reinhold, *Geschichte des Königreichs Jerusalem* (Innsbruck, 1880).

Rosenthal, Franz, *The Herb: Hashish versus Medieval Muslim Society* (Leiden, 1971).

Rousseau, Jean Baptiste L.J., 'Mémoire sur l'Ismaélis et les Nosairis de Syrie adressé à M. Silvestre de Sacy', *Annales des Voyages*, 14 (1811), pp 271–303.

Runciman, Steven, *A History of the Crusades*, (Cambridge, 1951–54).

Said, Edward W., *Orientalism* (London, 1978).

Sauvaget, Jean, *Introduction to the History of the Muslim East: A Bibliographical Guide*; English trans. based on the 2nd edn as recast by Claude Cahen (Berkeley, 1965).

——, 'The Arabic Historiography of the Crusades', in B. Lewis and P.M. Holt (eds), *Historians of the Middle East* (London, 1964), pp 98–107.

Sayyid, Ayman F., 'Lumières nouvelles sur quelques sources de l'histoire Fatimide en Égypte', *Annales Islamologiques*, 13 (1977), pp 1–41.

Scheffer-Boichorst, Paul, 'Der kaiserliche Notar und der Strassburger Vitztum Burchard', *Zeitschrift für die Geschichte des Oberrheins*, 43 (1889), pp 456–77.

Secret Societies of the Middle Ages (London, 1846).

al-Shahrastani, Abu'l-Fath Muhammad b. Abd al-Karim, *Kitab al-milal wa'l-nihal*, ed. W. Cureton (London, 1842); partial English trans. *Muslim Sects and Divisions*, tr. A.K. Kazi and J.G. Flynn (London, 1984).

Sharon, Moshe, *Black Banners from the East: The Establishment of the Abbasid State – Incubation of a Revolt* (Jerusalem-Leiden, 1983).

al-Shayyal, Jamal al-Din (ed.), *Majmu'at al-watha'iq al-Fatimiyya* (Cairo, 1958).

Silvestre de Sacy, Antoine I., *Chrestomathie Arabe* (Paris, 1806).

——, 'Mémoire sur la dynastie des Assassins, et sur l'origine de leur Nom', *Annales des Voyages*, 8 (1809), pp 325–43.

——, *Mémoire sur la dynastie des Assassins, et sur l'étymologie de leur Nom*, in *Mémoires de l'Institut Royal de France*, 4 (1818), pp 1–84; English trans. *Memoir on the Dynasty of the Assassins, and on the Etymology of their Name*, in Appendix to this book.

——, 'Recherches sur l'initiation à la secte des Ismaéliens', *Journal Asiatique*, 1 série, 4 (1824), pp 298–311, 321–31, reprinted in Jean Claude Frère, *L'Ordre des Assassins* (Paris, 1973), pp 261–74.

——, *Exposé de la religion des Druzes* (Paris, 1838).

Southern, Richard W., *Western Views of Islam in the Middle Ages* (Cambridge, MA, 1962).

Stark, Freya, 'The Assassins' Valley and the Salambar Pass', *Geographical Journal*, 77 (1931), pp 48–60.

——, *The Valleys of the Assassins and other Persian Travels* (London, 1934); French trans. *La Vallée des Assassins*, tr. M. Metzger (Paris, 1946).

Stern, Samuel M., 'The Epistle of the Fatimid Caliph al-Amir (al-Hidaya al-Amiriyya) – its Date and Purpose', JRAS (1950), pp 20–31, reprinted in his *History and Culture in the Medieval Muslim World* (London, 1984), article X.

——, 'Heterodox Isma'ilism at the Time of al-Mu'izz', BSOAS, 17 (1955), pp 10–33.

——, 'The Early Isma'ili Missionaries in North-West Persia and in Khurasan and Transoxania', BSOAS, 23 (1960), pp 56–90.

——, 'Abu'l-Qasim al-Busti and his Refutation of Isma'ilism', JRAS (1961), pp 14–35.

——, 'Isma'ilis and Qarmatians', in *L'Élaboration de l'Islam*, Colloque de Strasbourg (Paris, 1961), pp 99–108.

——, 'Cairo as the Centre of the Isma'ili Movement', in *Colloque international sur l'histoire du Caire* (Cairo, 1972), pp 437–50.

——, 'The Book of the Highest Initiation and other anti-Isma'ili Travesties', in his *Studies in Early Isma'ilism*, pp 56–83.

——, 'Fatimid Propaganda among Jews according to the Testimony of Yefet b. Ali the Karaite', in his *Studies in Early Isma'ilism*, pp 84–95.

——, *Studies in Early Isma'ilism* (Jerusalem-Leiden, 1983).

——, 'Abd Allah b. Maymun', EI2, Vol 1, p 48.

Stroeva, Ludmila V., *Gosudarstvo ismailitov v Irane v XI-XIII vv* (Moscow, 1978); Persian trans. *Ta'rikh-i Isma'iliyan dar Iran*, tr. P. Munzavi (Tehran, 1371/1992).

Sutuda, Manuchihr, *Qila'-i Isma'iliyya* (Tehran, 1345/1966).

al-Tabari, Abu Ja'far Muhammad b. Jarir., *Ta'rikh al-rusul wa'l-muluk*, ed. M.J. de Goeje et al. (Leiden, 1879–1901); English trans. *The History of al-Tabari*, tr. by various scholars (Albany, NY, 1985–).

Tabataba'i, Sayyid Muhammad Husayn, *Shi'ite Islam*, ed. and tr. S.H. Nasr (London, 1975).

Thietmar, *Magistri Thietmari Peregrinatio*, ed. J.C.M. Laurent (Hamburg, 1857).

Victor, A.C.L., 'Éloge de Silvestre de Sacy', in A.I. Silvestre de Sacy, *Mélanges de littérature orientale* (Paris, n.d.), pp iii–xxxii.

Walter of Compiègne, *Otia de Machomete*, ed. R.B.C. Huygens, in *Sacris Erudiri*, 8 (1956), pp 286–328.

Watt, W. Montgomery, *The Influence of Islam on Medieval Europe* (Edinburgh, 1972).

——, *Muslim–Christian Encounters* (London, 1991).

Wellhausen, Julius, *The Religio-Political Factions in Early Islam*, tr. R.C. Ostle and S.M. Walzer (Amsterdam, 1975).

Willey, Peter R.E., *The Castles of the Assassins* (London, 1963).

——, 'Further Expeditions to the Valleys of the Assassins', *Royal Central Asian Journal*, 54 (1967), pp 156–62.

——, 'The Assassins of Quhistan', *Royal Central Asian Journal*, 55 (1968), pp 180–3.

William of Newburgh, *Historia rerum Anglicarum*, ed. H.C. Hamilton (London, 1870).

William of Rubruck, *The Mission of Friar William of Rubruck: His Journey to the Court of the Great Khan Möngke 1253–1255*, tr. P. Jackson (London, 1990).

William of Tyre, *Willelmi Tyrensis Archiepiscopi Chronicon*, ed. R.B.C. Huygens (Turnhout, 1986); English trans., *A History of Deeds Done Beyond the Sea*, tr. Emily A. Babcock and A.C. Krey (New York, 1943).

Yarshater, Ehsan, 'Mazdakism', in *The Cambridge History of Iran*, Vol 3 (II), *The Seleucid, Parthian and Sasanian Periods*, ed. E. Yarshater (Cambridge, 1983), pp 991–1024.

Index

The index contains all the proper names of persons, places, and sectarian and dynastic groups, as well as most transliterated technical terms that appear in the book. Main entries are arranged alphabetically; their sub-headings are arranged thematically. The Arabic definite article 'al-' is ignored for the purposes of alphabetization. In the alphabetization, no distinction is made between different Arabic letters which are represented by the same letter in transliteration. The abbreviation 'b.' for *ibn* ('son of') is alphabetized as written. The letter 'n.' ('note') immediately following a page reference indicates the number of an endnote on that page, and *'passim'* indicates scattered references to the subject, not necessarily on consecutive pages.

al-Qummi, Sa'd b. Abd Allah al-
Ash'ari, Imami scholar, 15
Quran (Koran), 9, 10, 14, 24, 27, 57,
138, 140, 173
Paradise described in, 98, 99–100,
113, 116
translated into Latin, 58, 99
Quraysh, tribe, 8

rafiq, rafiqan (comrades), 144, 145,
179–81
Ralph of Merle, 67
Raqqada, in North Africa, 20
Rashid al-Din Fadl Allah, historian,
37, 39, 41, 90, 114–15
Rashid al-Din Sinan, Nizari leader in
Syria, 41, 42, 54, 67–70, 71,
73–4, 79, 94–9 *passim*, 100, 103,
106, 146, 156, 158, 170
Rawdat al-safa, of Mirkhwand, 141
Raymond, son of Bohemond IV, 75,
76
Raymond II, count of Tripoli, 67
Raymond of Aguilers, historian, 55
Raymond of Antioch, 67, 76
Raymond of St Gilles, 53, 54
Rayy (Rey), in Persia, 18, 31, 143,
145
Reconquista, 51
Red Sea, 20
Reformation, 62
Reginald of Vichier, Grand Master of
the Knights Templar, 79
Reiske, J.J., 138, 151
Renaissance, 120
Resurrection *see* qiyama
Rey *see* Rayy
Richard I, the Lionheart, king of
England, 72, 73, 74
Ricoldo da Monte Croce, 61, 63
Ridwan, Saljuq ruler of Aleppo, 64,
65
Robert of Ketton, 58
Roman Church, 57, 61
Rosenthal, Franz, 91
Rukn al-Din Khurshah, Nizari imam,
43, 44, 114, 146, 175
Rustichello (Rusticiano) of Pisa, scribe
of Marco Polo, 109, 115, 117

Sabbah, Hasan *see* Hasan Sabbah
Sab'iyya (Seveners), 16

al-Sadiq, Shi'i imam *see* Ja'far al-
Sadiq
Safavids, of Persia, 63, 64
St Louis, king of France *see* Louis IX,
St Peter, 81
Saladin (Salah al-Din), founder of the
Ayyubid dynasty, 30, 41, 42, 53,
54, 68, 69–70, 72, 74–5
and Nizaris, 42, 73, 95, 96, 156,
170
Salamiyya, in Syria, 19
Saljuqs, Saljuqids, 1, 3, 24, 31, 32–7
passim, 40, 52, 65, 88, 143, 180
Samanids, 18
Sanudo, Marino, historian, 106
Saracens, 3, 51, 56, 57, 70, 71, 77,
82, 95, 101, 110–11, 115, 148;
see also Islam
Sarah, wife of Abraham, 51
Sargudhasht-i Sayyidna, of Hasan
Sabbah, 39
Sasan, Banu, 152–4
Sasanid empire, 49
Sefardi, Moses *see* Pedro de Alfonso
segnors, segnors de montana, 70, 116
Seid Keheki *see* Abu'l-Hasan Ali
Senem, 70, 78
Senex, Senex de Monte, 101, 116,
117; *see also* Old Man of the
Mountain; Shaykh al-Jabal; *etc*
Shah Karim al-Husayni, Nizari imam
see Aga Khan IV
Shah Khalil Allah III, Nizari imam,
182
shahdanaj, 90, 162; *see also banj*;
hashish; *jars*; opium
al-Shahrastani, Muhammad b. Abd al-
Karim, theologian and
heresiographer, 142, 172, 173,
181
Sham *see* Syria
shari'a, sacred law of Islam, 24, 41,
88
Shaykh al-Hashishin, 69, 116, 155,
161
Shaykh al-Jabal, 116; *see also* Old
Man of the Mountain; *pir-i
kuhistan*; Vetus; *etc.*
Shi'a, *see* Shi'is
Shi'is, Shi'ism, 1, 2, 5, 8, 15, 33, 88,
122, 132, 137, 143
early development, 9–13

212